IMAGES
of America

MINDEN

IMAGES
of America

MINDEN

John A. Agan

ARCADIA
PUBLISHING

ISBN 978-0-7385-0580-0

Published by Arcadia Publishing
Charleston, South Carolina

Printed in the United States of America

Library of Congress Catalog Card Number: 00-104663

For all general information contact Arcadia Publishing at:
Telephone 843-853-2070
Fax 843-853-0044
E-Mail sales@arcadiapublishing.com
For customer service and orders:
Toll-Free 1-888-313-2556

Visit us on the Internet at www.arcadiapublishing.com

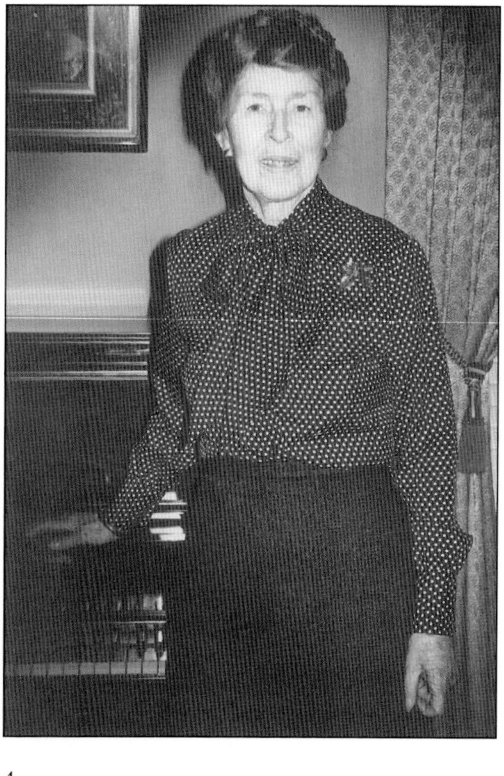

Mrs. Paul (Thomas Lorraine) Campbell was the first official historian of Webster Parish. She devoted the last 60 years of her life to preserving and researching the history of Minden and Webster Parish. Without her loving efforts and inspiration, this book would not have been possible. (Courtesy of *Minden Press Herald.*)

Contents

ACKNOWLEDGMENTS

Publication of this book would not have been possible without the hard work of my mother, Juanita Murphy Agan, who—through her many friends of more than 60 years—was able to obtain almost all of the pictures included in this volume. Special thanks are also extended to those that provided the images; you will find their names listed below each picture they provided. In addition, other individuals provided help in locating, documenting, and preserving the pictures. Among these are Jimmy and Grace Rogers; Jimmy and Jo Rogers; and Dr. Carter and Sue Norman. Although their newspaper is cited as a source for pictures, invaluable assistance was provided by Tracy Campbell and Sandra Brown of the *Minden Press Herald*; special thanks go to them. Final thanks go to all the wonderful people of Minden I have known throughout my life that helped inspire this "labor of love."

INTRODUCTION

Charles Veeder founded Minden, LA, in 1835. He hoped to establish his town as the economic and governmental center of Claiborne Parish. Although Veeder left Minden for California in 1849, his community did attract new settlers who made Minden the economic center of Claiborne Parish. However, Minden never became the parish seat of Claiborne. No known image of Charles Veeder has survived, but this volume contains images of pioneer families such as the Drakes, Chaffes, Rathbuns, Drews, and Lifes, who have been among the leaders of Minden for over 150 years. Pictures in this book will portray many members of these families, as well as other significant people, places, and events that allowed Minden to thrive in the years since Veeder left the city.

Among the pioneer settlers were the Drake brothers, William and Hervey, and the Chaffe brothers, John and Christopher. Rarely seen images of both the Drakes and the Chaffes are in the book, along with pictures of their descendants and the business enterprises operated by these families through the years.

One of Veeder's achievements was obtaining a charter for the Minden Academy from the state in 1838. No pictures are known to exist of the original academy, but there are several images in this book of the two schools that replaced the Minden Academy during the1850s: the Minden Male Academy and the Minden Female College.

Few, if any, images survive from the years of the Civil War and Reconstruction in Minden. Although removed from the scene of actual conflict, Minden was the site of a large Confederate winter quarters from 1864 to 1865 and was occupied by U.S. troops from June until December 1865. During the turbulent years of Reconstruction, Minden became the parish seat of the new Webster Parish. Pictures of pioneer officials of the new parish, including assessor J.W. Berry and Representative John Sidney Killen, Minden's delegate to the legislature when Webster Parish was created, are in this volume. Richard C. Drew, one of five generations of Drews who have served as judges in Minden, is shown being admitted to the bar in 1872. Also displayed is the first Webster Parish Courthouse, built in 1872 for a cost of $2,400.

During the late 19th and the early 20th century, Minden enjoyed an economic boom sparked by the railroad industry and the construction of the Minden Lumber Mill. Parks were landscaped; a new jail, courthouse, and post office were built. Images in this book will show these developments, as well as some of the leading citizens of that era.

Despite the mysterious fire that destroyed the Minden Lumber Mill in 1918, the nearby oil boom in the Cotton Valley field and the construction of the Louisiana & Arkansas (L&A)

Railroad shops revived Minden's economy. A new building boom began downtown, and the railroad workers sparked a growth in population. The buildings built by the L&A and the employees of the railroad are prominently displayed in these pages.

The economic strength that had emerged during the 1920s helped Minden survive a single disastrous year, 1933, that could have caused many communities to be irreparably damaged. That year, a fire destroyed nearly a quarter of downtown, the larger of the two banks in town failed, a powerful tornado claimed dozens of lives and destroyed over $1 million in property, a one-day 17-inch rainfall in July destroyed the cotton crop, and a financial shortfall forced early closure of the schools. In Minden, 1933 is remembered as the year the "north part burned, the middle went busted, and the south part blew away—but the town survived."

As World War II drew near, two significant events occurred in the Minden area. The first was the Louisiana Maneuvers of 1941, which brought thousands of troops and commanders such as Dwight Eisenhower and George Patton to the Minden area. The second event had a lasting impact—in June 1941, construction began on a shell-loading plant in rural Webster Parish. The Louisiana Ordnance Plant would become the driving force in Minden's economy for most of the next 40 years. The development of the plant will be covered in a subsequent volume in this series dealing with all of Webster Parish. Pictures of the maneuvers and the growth that occurred in Minden after the Ordnance Plant opened are in these pages.

Missing from this book are many images that need documentation and hopefully will be obtained and preserved very soon. Pictures of Minden's physical structures in the years prior to 1880 are very difficult to locate and, sadly, are not included in this volume. Also, photos portraying the history of the black residents of Minden are underrepresented in these pages. Hopefully, the publication of this work will help bring more of these pictures that are lying around in scrapbooks and attics to the public.

Beyond the wonderful images already mentioned, the most important and most interesting pictures in this book are the images of the people of Minden, living their day-to-day lives. Ranging from the upper-class young people of the 1880s, who went to a Dallas photo studio to pose for a picture as the "Minden Tennis Club," to a black shoeshine boy on the streets in the 1930s; from the aristocratic pose of the Minden German Club in 1890, to the children playing at the Hunter's Playground swimming pool in the 1940s; from the Minden High baseball team of 1905, to an All-American football player who played for Minden High in the 1970s; from a dance around the maypole in City Park in 1909, to a parade in downtown in the late 1940s, these are the people and events that are the heart and soul of small-town life. It is people and experiences such as these that have made the little town of Minden one of the best places to call home in our country. Enjoy these *Images of Minden*.

One

People

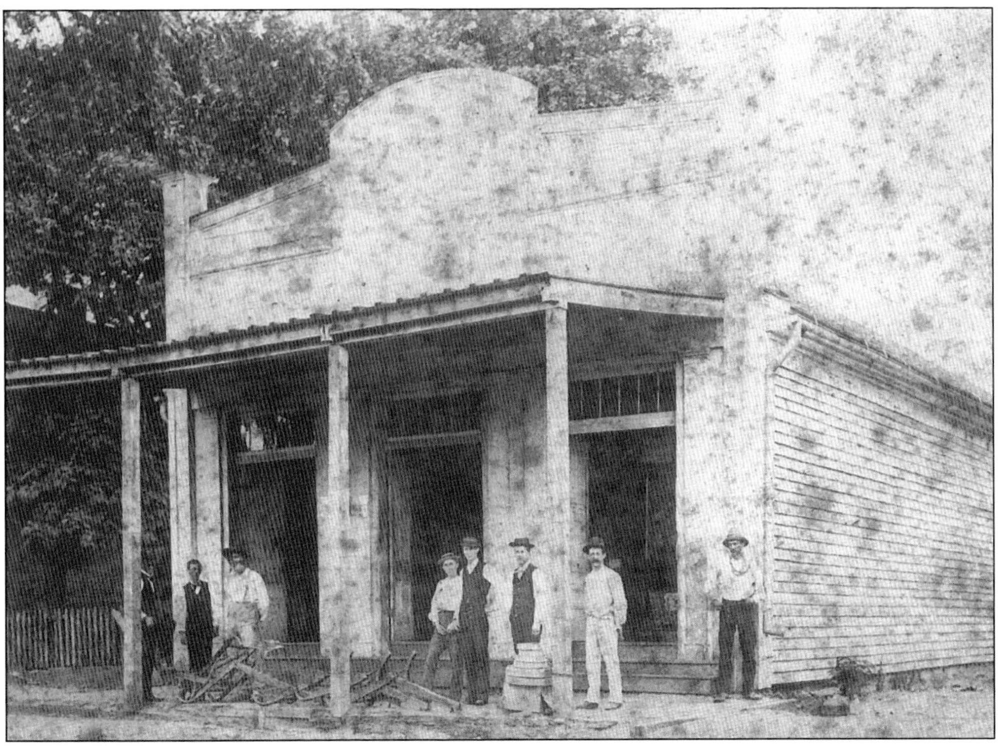

Drake's Store was used as the center point of the original corporate limits of Minden in 1854. The Drake family has owned the business buildings that have been built on the site from the 1840s until the present. Pictured above in front of the store in the 1880s are, from left to right, an unidentified man, Hervey Drake, Lodinrik Terry, "Old Man" McIntyre, C.S. Watson, F.H. Drake Sr., Walton Fort, and Jake Friedmare. (Courtesy of Luther & Claire Drake Moore and Charles Alden & Mary Rathbun.)

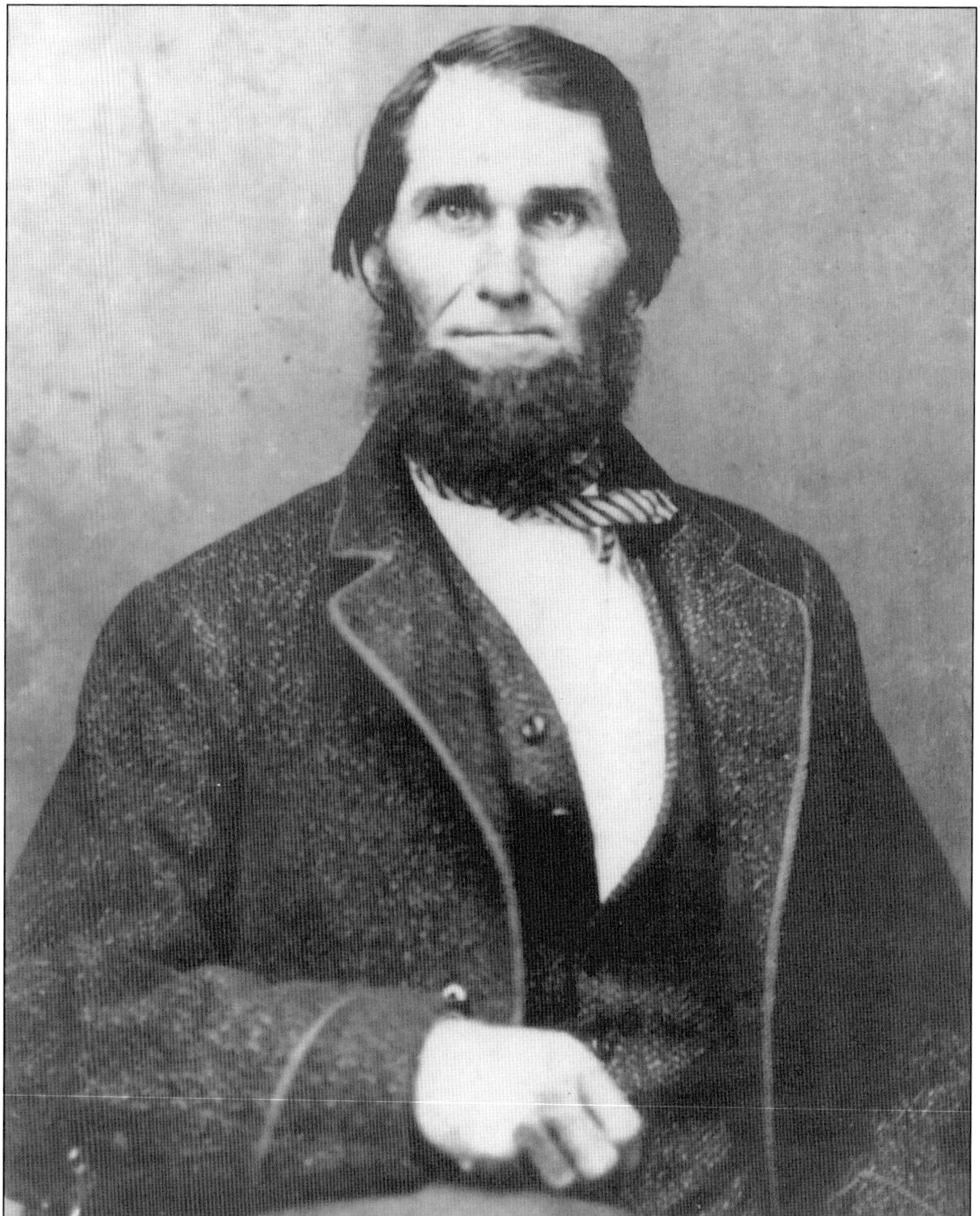

Colonel J.W. Berry (1818–1893), although a native of Indiana, was one of the leading citizens of Minden for more than 50 years. He moved with his family to Louisiana in 1835 and was living in Minden when the town was laid out in lots in 1837. Berry began working as a teenager—first on a farm, and later at a sawmill for three years—before gaining employment as a store clerk. Beginning in 1841, he operated a dry-goods business in Minden for 32 years. He became one of the leading cotton planters in the Minden area. Politically active, Berry served in the state legislature representing Minden under four different governors, including service in the Confederate Legislature of Louisiana. He also served in the Confederate Army. After the war, he was appointed tax assessor of Webster Parish and served in that post from 1880 to 1890. (Courtesy of Frank Griffith.)

Another pioneer settler of Minden was William Abner Drake (1825–1887). Drake came to Louisiana with a large group of settlers from the Edgefield District of South Carolina. He settled in Minden as a young man and became a community leader. He donated the land for the First Methodist Church and the Minden Male Academy. The church still uses that property today, while the latter plot is Academy Park today. Drake, along with his brother Hervey, operated several different businesses in Minden. (Courtesy of Luther and Claire Drake Moore.)

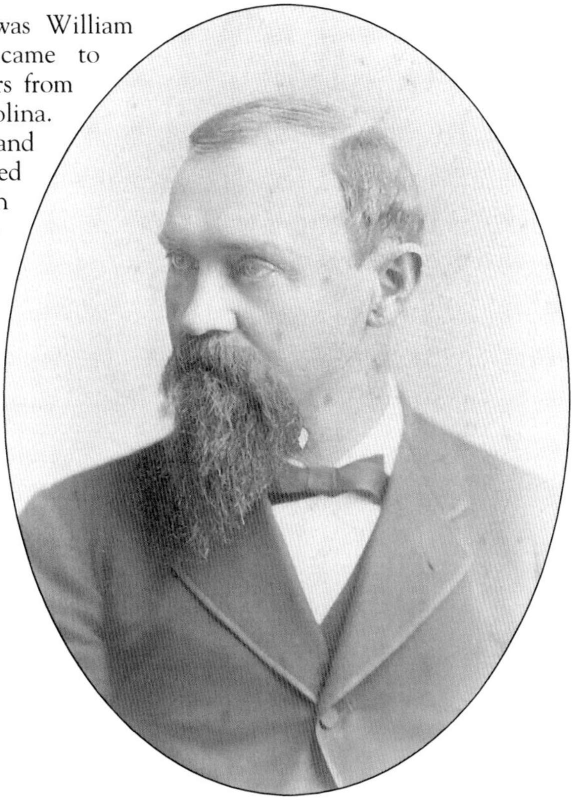

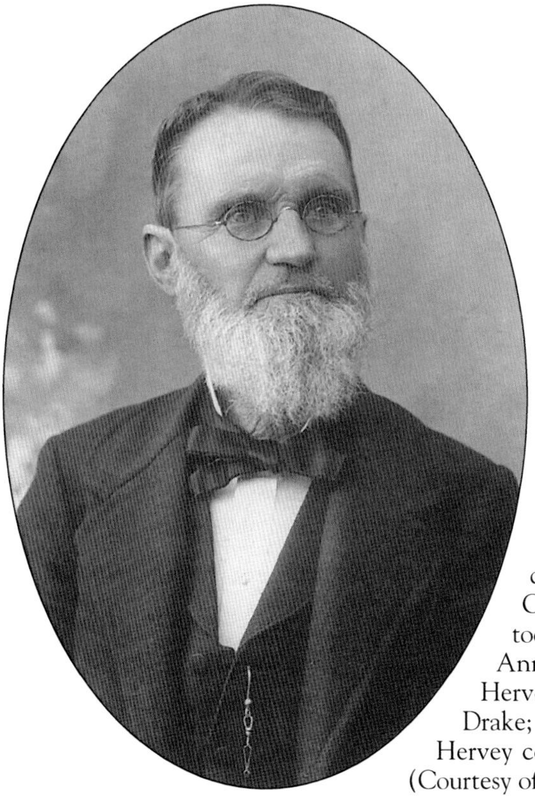

Hervey Drake (1823–1900), brother of William Abner Drake, was an early merchant of Minden. He served as deputy postmaster of Minden in 1846. Hervey donated land for the Minden Presbyterian Church, where the church is still located today. He had four children: F.H. Drake Sr., Annie Drake, Sallie Drake, and Mary Drake. Hervey and William were sons of Harvey Drake; however, a handwritten note survives from Hervey confirming the unique spelling of his name. (Courtesy of Luther and Claire Drake Moore.)

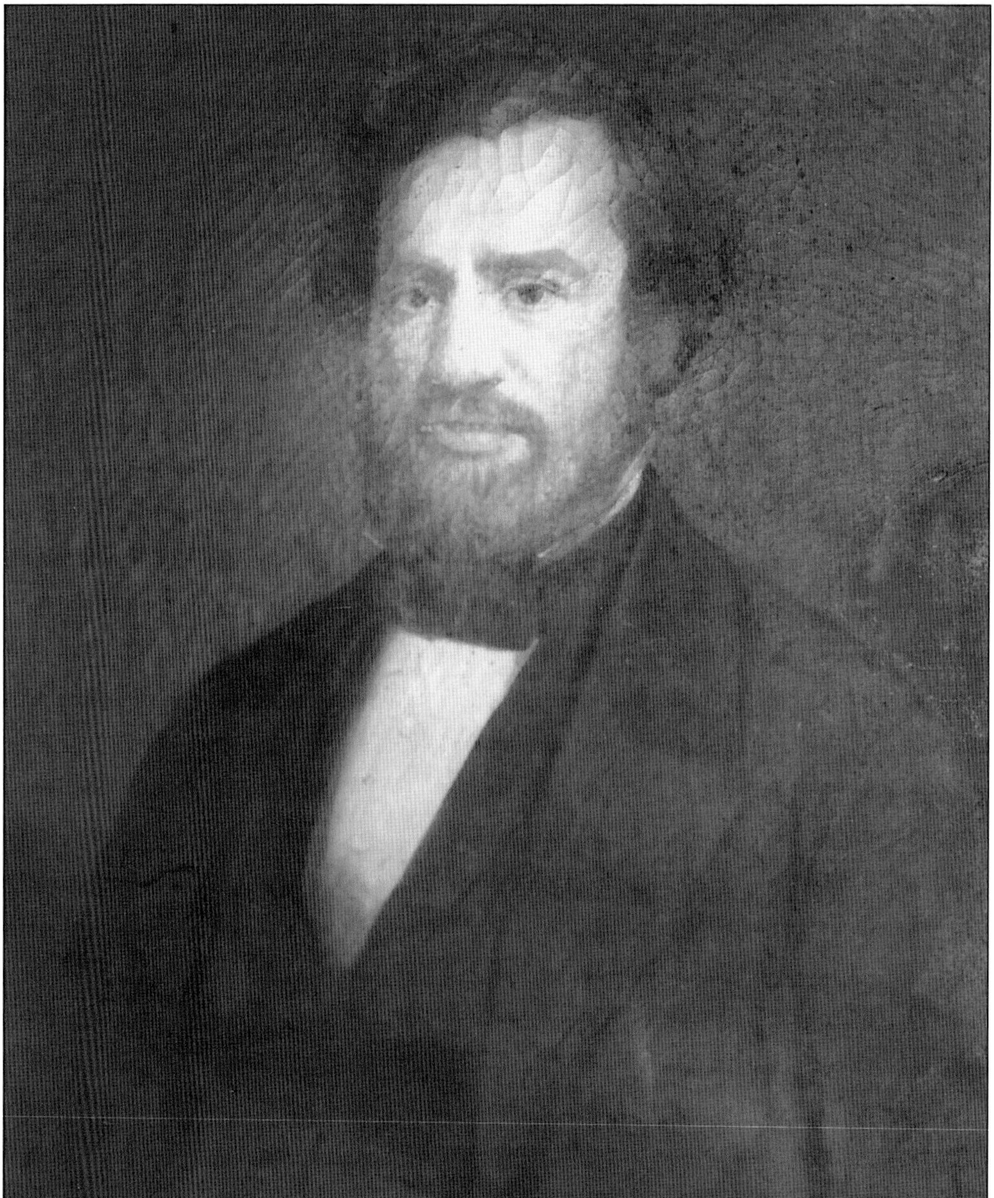

Christopher Chaffe (1818–1894) emigrated from England to Minden in 1851, following his brother John to the area. Born in Devonshire, England, as a youth, he learned his father's trade as a blacksmith. He began his first business in 1851 in Minden, but it was later destroyed by fire. Fires would also destroy his homes or businesses on four other occasions. Chaffe overcame these misfortunes and became one of the most successful and influential businessmen in Minden. He moved from a blacksmith shop operator to ownership of a foundry, then expanded to add a livery stable. He obtained the contract to deliver the mail first from Monroe to Minden, and later from Shreveport to Vicksburg. This led to his ownership of a stage line and conversion of his original home into a inn. A devout member of the Episcopal Church, he served as the first senior warden of Minden's St. John's Episcopal Church. His descendants are still active members of the Minden community today. (Courtesy of Thad Andress.)

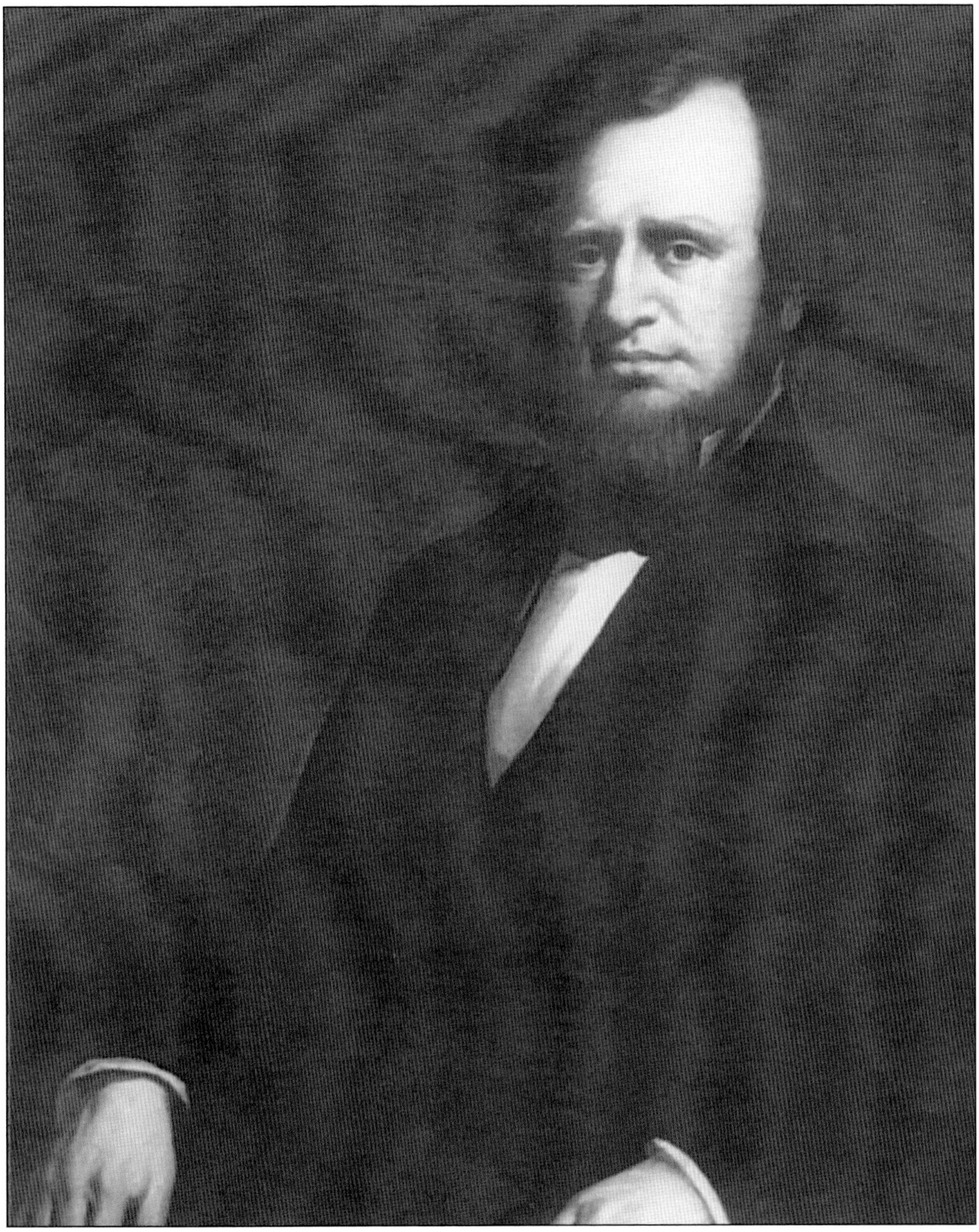

John Chaffe was an early Minden merchant, arriving in the area in the late 1830s shortly after the town was founded. The son of John and Johanna Skelton Chaffe, his presence in Minden caused his younger brother, Christopher, to come to Minden some years later. John landed in New York and eventually arrived in Louisiana after working in various occupations to support himself. He became a major merchant and cotton planter in the area of Minden and enjoyed great success in the years before the Civil War. After the war, although he still maintained his Minden ties and some business interests, he moved to New Orleans. In the Crescent City, he established a major cotton factorage house. His financial success in this endeavor led to many civic honors, including being named King of the Rex Ball, New Orleans' most prestigious Mardi Gras ball. (Courtesy of Thad Andress.)

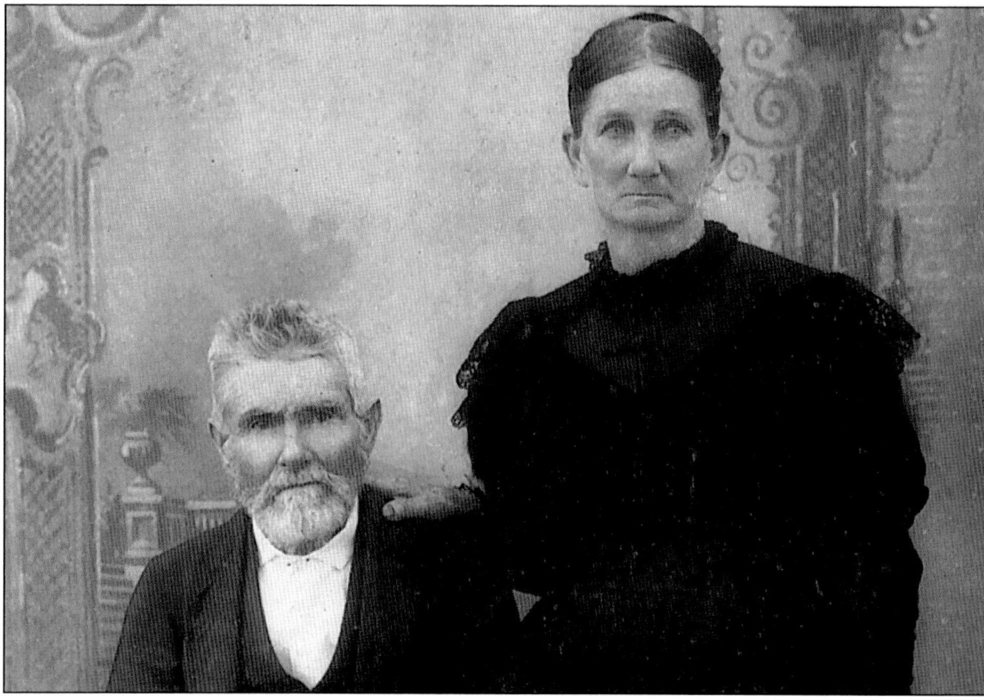

John Sidney Killen came to Minden in 1849. He married Sarah Monzingo, who is shown with him here. Killen was a leading Baptist layman in Minden. He served with the Minden Rangers during the Civil War. After the war, he became a successful farmer and served in the Louisiana Legislature. It was during his term of service that Webster Parish was created, with Minden as the parish seat. (Courtesy of George Turner.)

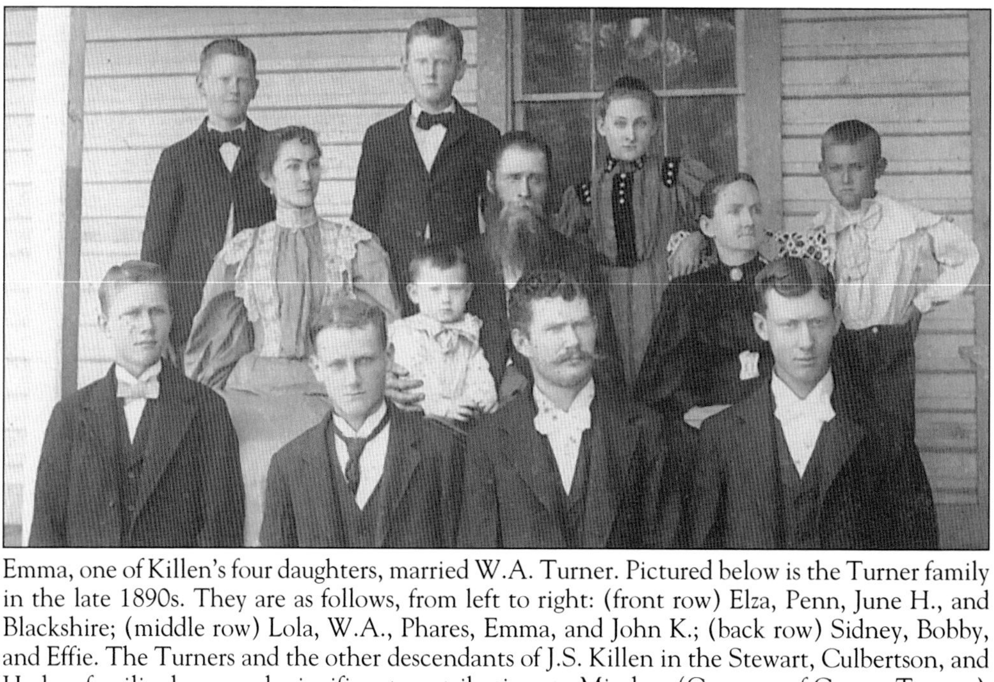

Emma, one of Killen's four daughters, married W.A. Turner. Pictured below is the Turner family in the late 1890s. They are as follows, from left to right: (front row) Elza, Penn, June H., and Blackshire; (middle row) Lola, W.A., Phares, Emma, and John K.; (back row) Sidney, Bobby, and Effie. The Turners and the other descendants of J.S. Killen in the Stewart, Culbertson, and Hodges families have made significant contributions to Minden. (Courtesy of George Turner.)

Richard Cleveland Drew is shown on the left, as he is admitted to the Louisiana Bar in 1872. The Drew family's legal tradition includes having had a family member on the bench in Minden almost continuously since 1850, covering five generations. R.C. Drew served as district attorney, parish judge, district judge, and, eventually, judge of the court of appeals. (Courtesy of R. Harmon Drew Jr.)

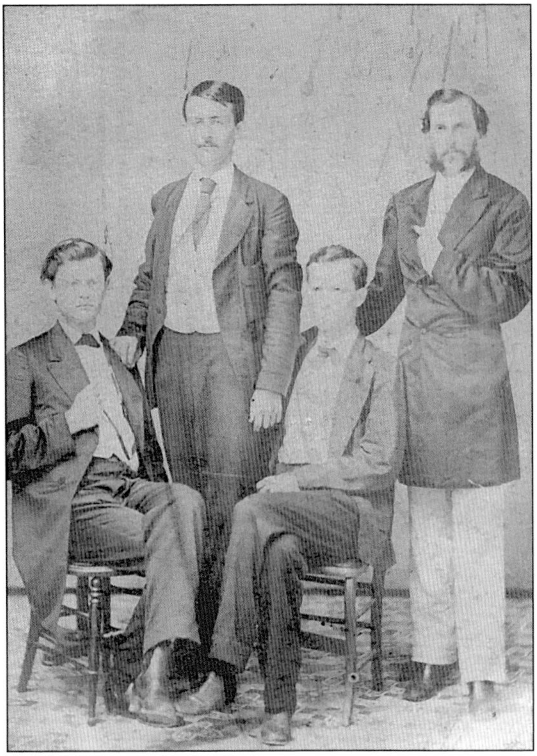

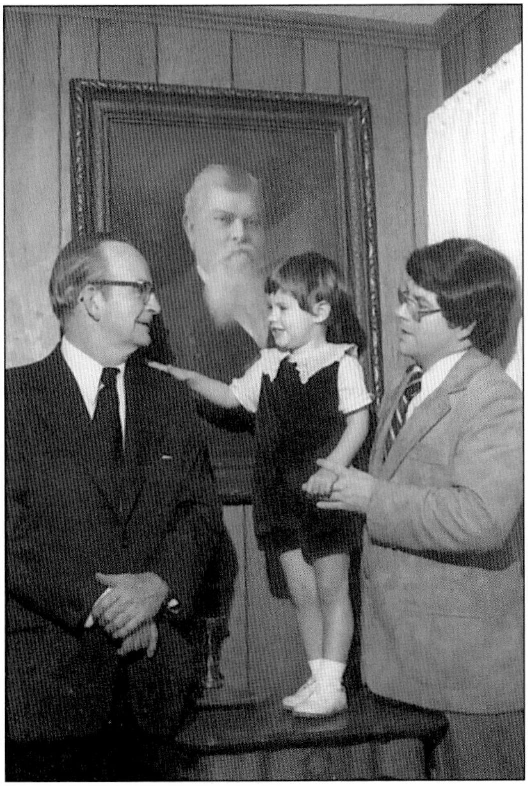

Shown in 1976, with a picture of Richard Cleveland Drew during his years on the court of appeals, are the following, from left to right: his grandson, the late Judge Richard Harmon Drew Jr.; R. Harmon Drew III, today a graduate student at the University of Virginia; and Judge R. Harmon Drew Jr., who today is also serving as a judge on the Louisiana Court of Appeals. (Courtesy of R. Harmon Drew Jr.)

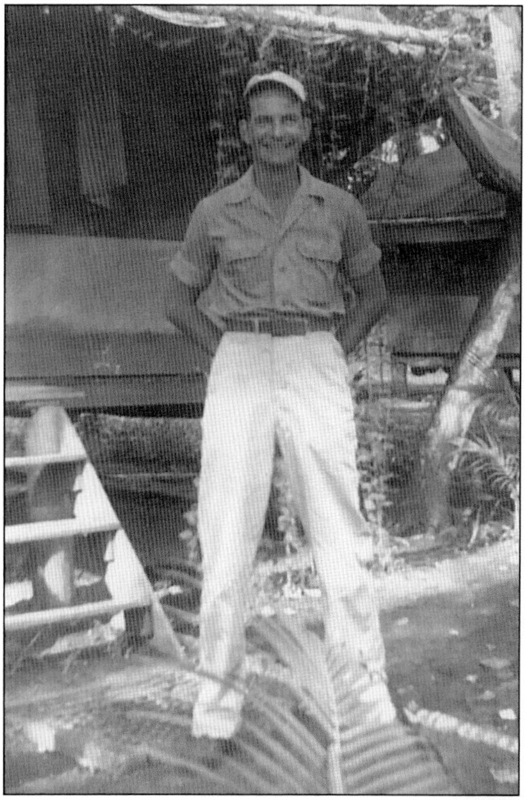

Judge Richard Harmon Drew Jr. is shown during his military service on Guadalcanal during World War II. After returning home to Minden after the war, he carried on the family tradition, serving as assistant district attorney, Minden city attorney, Minden city judge, and state representative. (Courtesy of R. Harmon Drew Jr.)

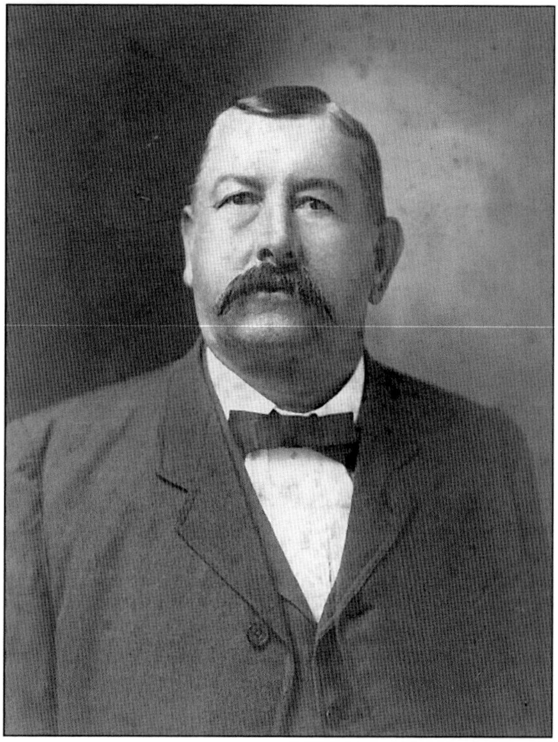

Serving as Webster Parish clerk of court for 27 years, longer than any other clerk, John H. Tillman came to Minden from Florida at age 21 in 1870. He first worked as a farmer before entering public service. Elected clerk in 1888, he served until 1892. He lost a bid for reelection in 1892, but was reelected in 1896, and served until his death in 1919. (Courtesy of John Tillman.)

Benjamin F. Griffith, seated, is pictured in the 1890s with his brothers, John and Tom. Mr. Griffith served as Webster Parish sheriff from 1900 to 1908 and then embarked on a long and successful career in the real estate business in Minden. He was also one of the founders of the Webster Parish Fair. (Courtesy of Frank Griffith.)

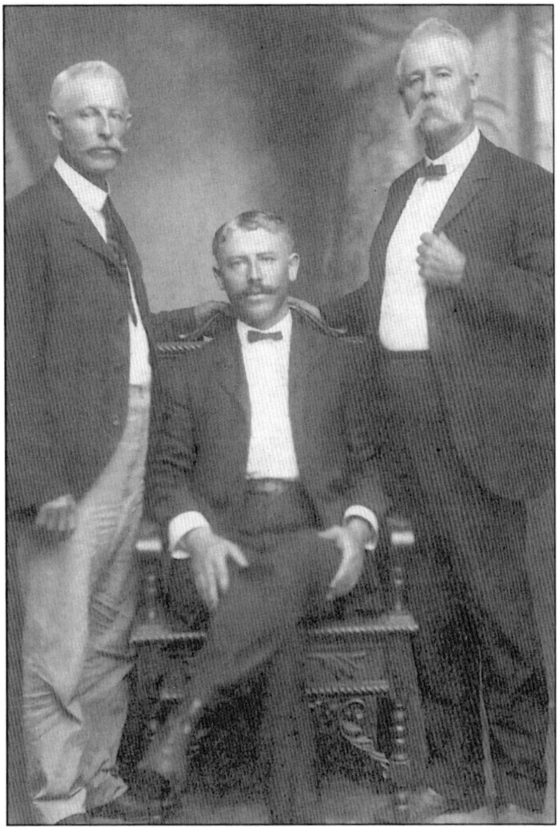

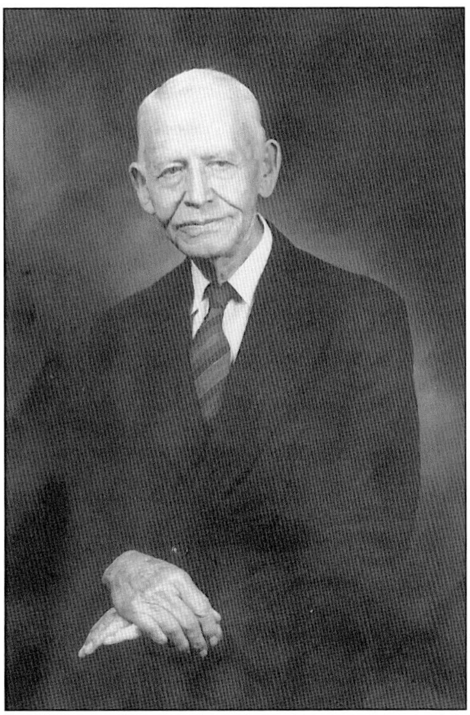

Mr. Griffith is pictured again as he neared 80 years of age in the late 1940s. He lived more than a decade after this picture was taken, before dying at more than 90 years of age in the early 1960s. The city of Minden honored Mr. Griffith's contribution to the city by naming the municipal baseball stadium, Griffith Stadium. The baseball field stands on the site where Mr. Griffith had constructed a horse racing track on the fairgrounds in the early years of the 20th century. (Courtesy of Frank Griffith.)

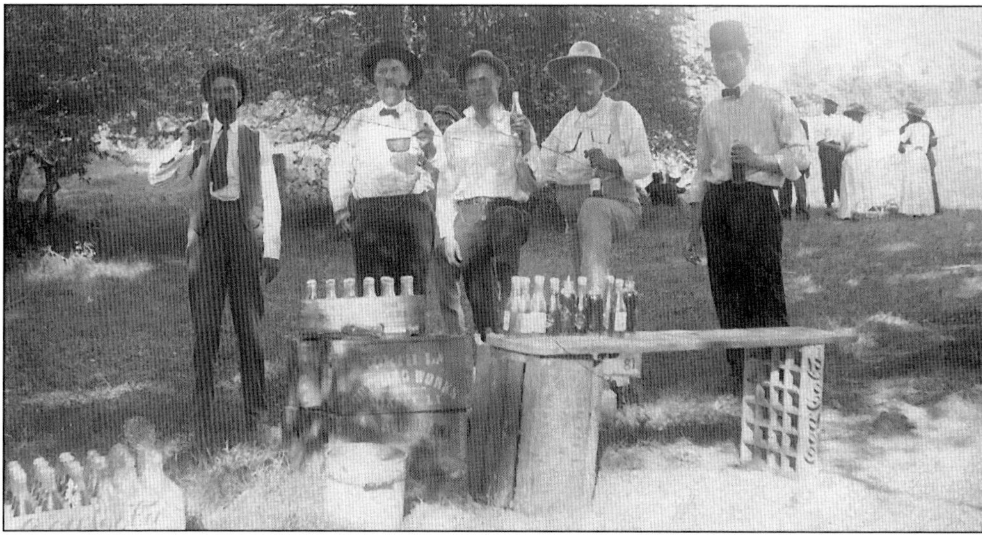

Here, the North Louisiana Bottle Works supplies Coca Cola for a Juneteenth Celebration on Bayou Dorcheat in the early 20th century. Pictured preparing the drinks are Connell Fort, Captain John J. Cahill, Ike Dyer, W.S. Hunter, and Pep Longino. (Courtesy of Ben Hunter.)

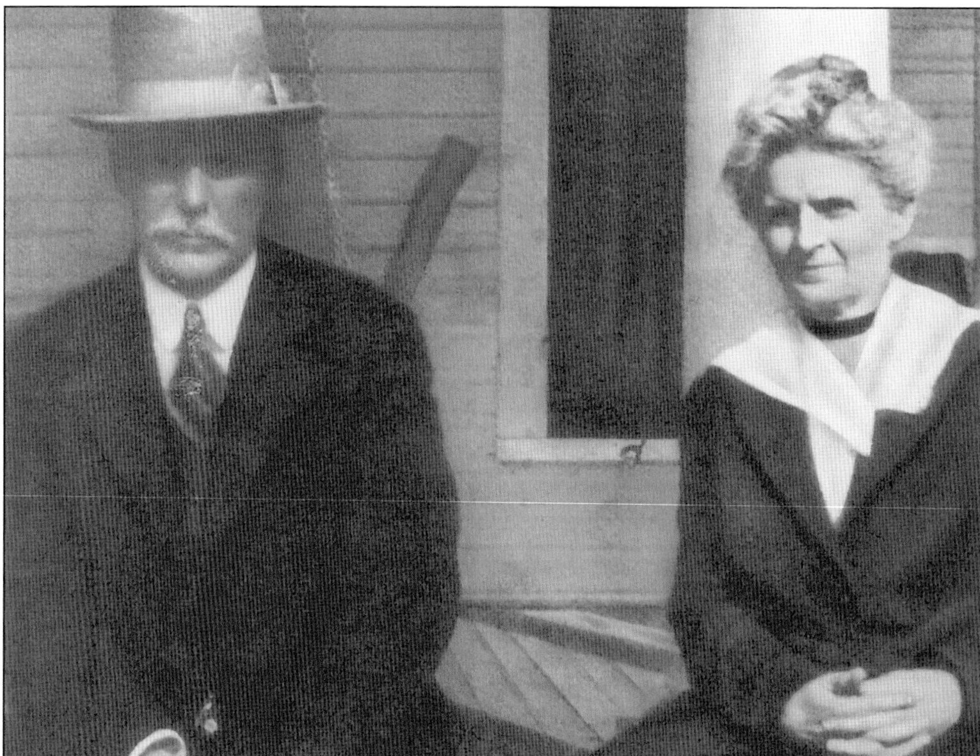

Felix H. Drake and Lizzie Eames Drake are pictured on the side porch of the home they built on Broadway. Today it is the home of Dr. Carl Hines. Mr. Drake was largely responsible for the construction of the Minden Tap Railroad, connecting Minden with the main east-west railroad line at Sibley. For many years, Mrs. Drake was one of the outstanding leaders in the First Baptist Church of Minden. (Courtesy of Luther and Claire Moore Drake.)

Joan Chaffe Miller, Minden's Mardi Gras queen for 1915, is shown in the regalia of her title. In the 1960s, Louisiana State University named a woman's dormitory Joan Chaffe Miller Hall in honor of her distinguished career as an LSU English professor, prior to her death in 1957. (Courtesy of Thad Andress.)

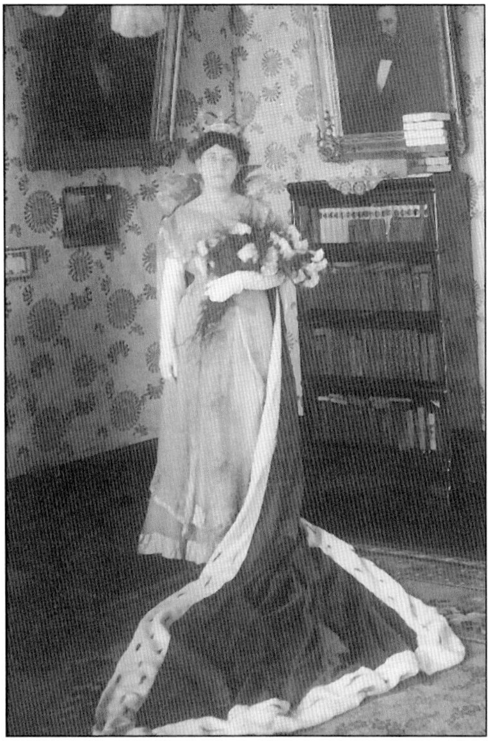

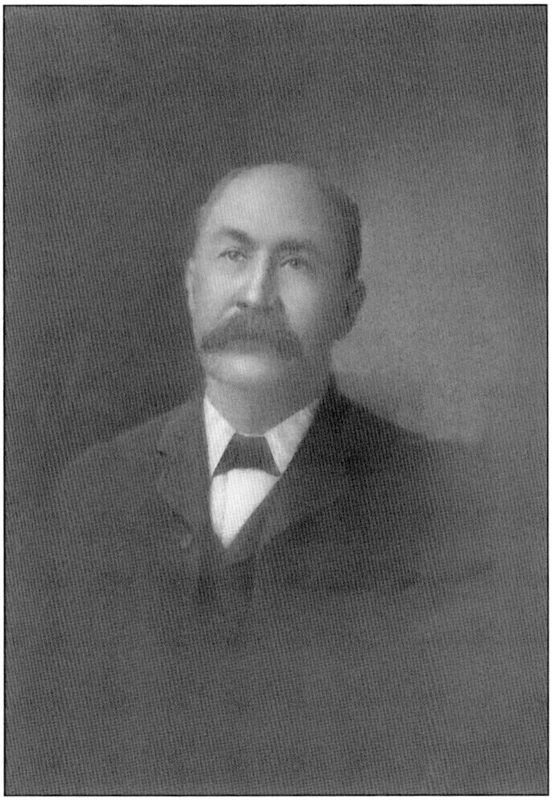

Mr. W.S. Hunter founded the North Louisiana Bottling Works in 1905. Later, the business became known as Coca Cola Bottling of Minden. The business passed to his son, Larry Hunter, who did so much to provide recreation for the children of Minden. Today, the company is still operating and being run by the third and fourth generations of the Hunter family. (Courtesy of Ben Hunter.)

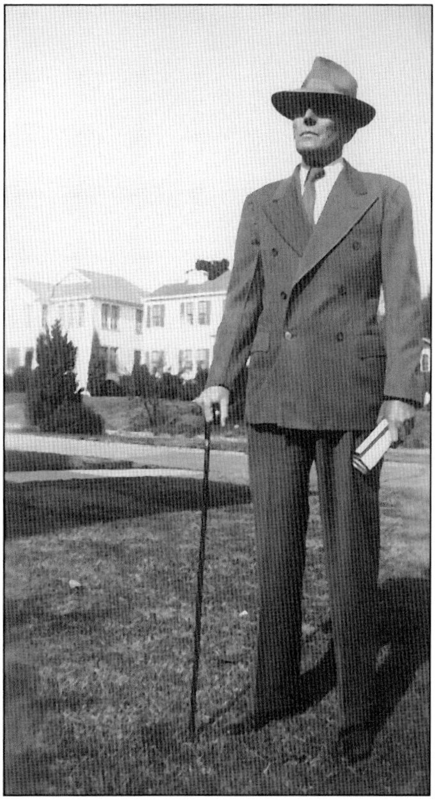

Mr. G. Alden Rathbun, was clerk of court of Webster Parish from 1924 until 1932. He was a tenth generation descendant of John Alden and Priscilla Mullins. (Courtesy of Charles Alden and Mary Rathbun.)

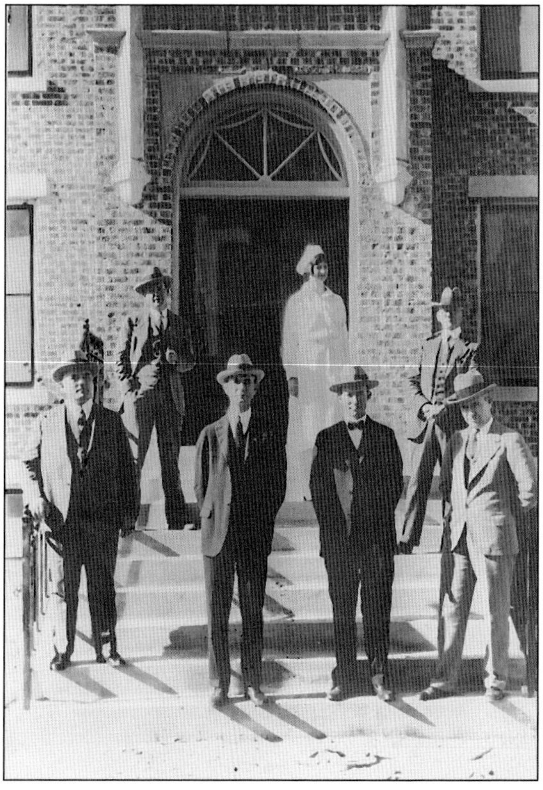

Pictured above are the founders of the Minden Sanitarium as shown in the centennial edition of the *Webster Signal-Tribune* of December 31, 1934. Pictured are the following, from left to right: (front row) Dr. J.D. Kilgore, Dr. Wilkins McDade, Dr. C.M. Baker, and the Rev. Frank Tripp, pastor of the First Baptist Church; (back row) Dr. J.B. Benton, Nurse Ola Sawyer, and Dr. S.F. Martin.

At the right end of the front row seated on the hose is John David, in this 1926 picture of the Minden Fire Department. Mr. David served as Minden's fire chief for many years, was elected to two terms as Minden's mayor, and also served on the Webster Parish Police Jury. (Courtesy of John S. and Lillian Life Willis.)

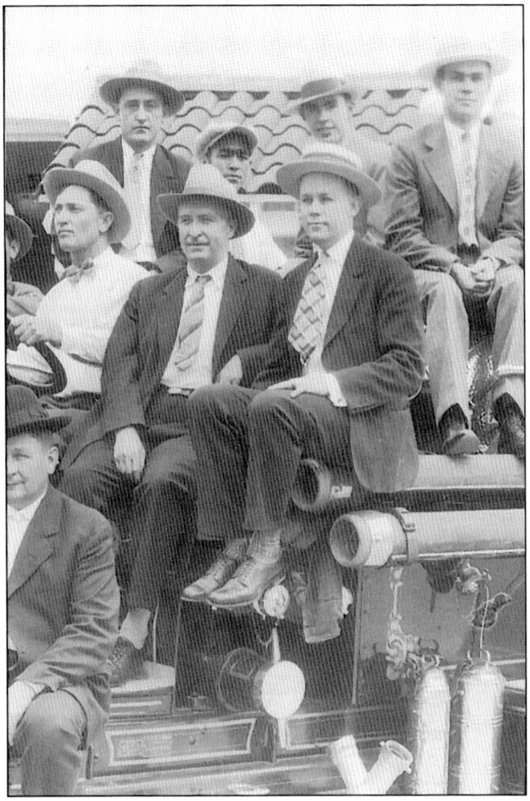

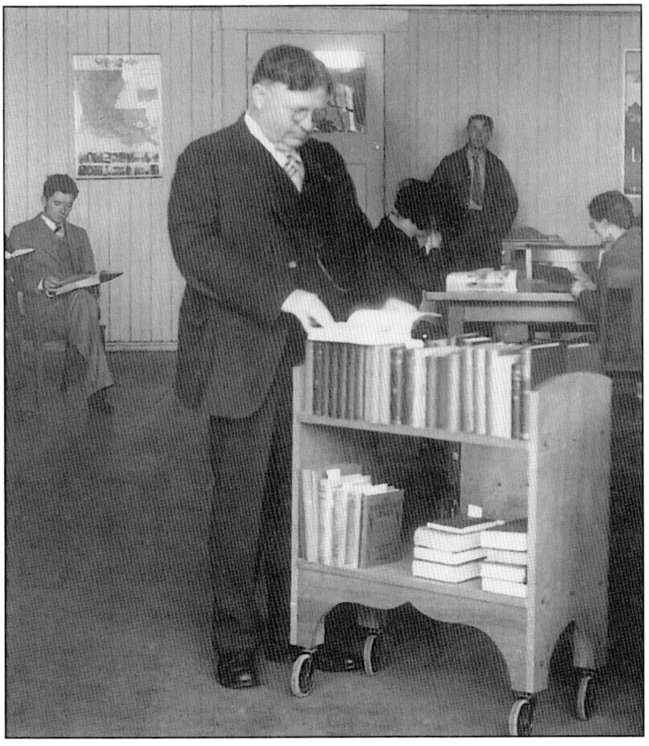

E.S. Richardson, superintendent of Webster Parish schools from 1920 to 1936, examines a cart of library books. Mr. Richardson, who left Webster Parish to become president of Louisiana Tech, streamlined and modernized the Webster Parish school system and made it a model system copied across the country.

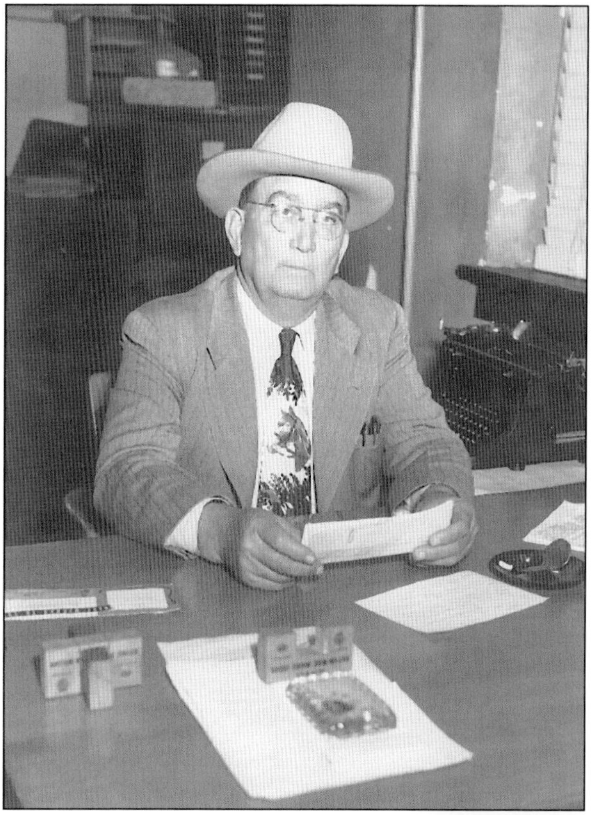

Sheriff Oscar H. Haynes Sr. was elected sheriff in a special election in 1933. He continued to serve in this office for 19 years, longer than any other man held the office. He started a family tradition as in the years since, O.H. Haynes Jr., O.H. Haynes III, and O.H. Haynes IV have all been law enforcement officers in Minden and Webster Parish. (Courtesy of Mrs. O. H. Haynes Jr.)

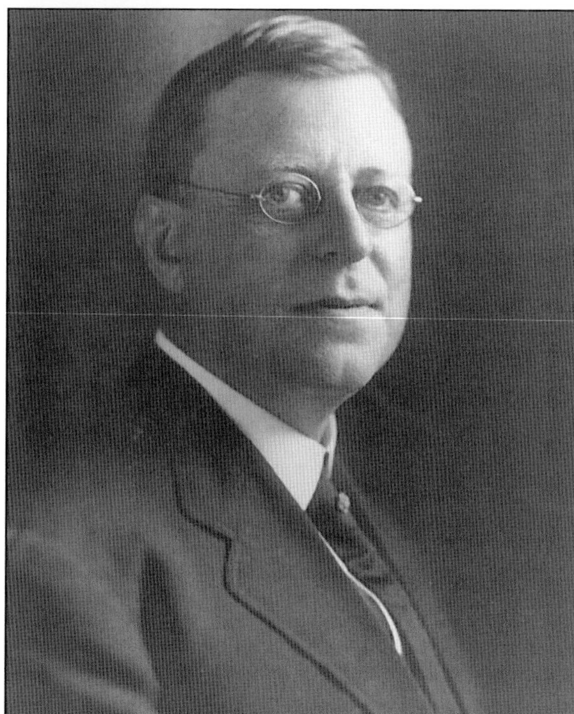

Establishing R.H. Miller Insurance in 1890, Robert Hyneman Miller was born in Alabama in 1863. He married Treeby Chaffe, daughter of pioneer merchant Christopher Chaffe. Mr. Miller later served as cashier, then president of the Bank of Minden, from its founding in 1890 until 1933. He operated the insurance agency until his death in 1941. (Courtesy of Thad Andress.)

Harry Andress and Treeby Miller Andress are shown here. Harry Andress was manager and president of Andress Motors Company, Inc., the Ford dealership in Minden, from 1929 until 1965. He was also an active civic leader, serving on the city council and in numerous volunteer positions. Treeby Andress was the daughter of R.H. Miller and worked as a teacher at Minden High School, was a founding member of the Minden Junior Service League, and was an active civic and church leader. (Courtesy of Thad Andress.)

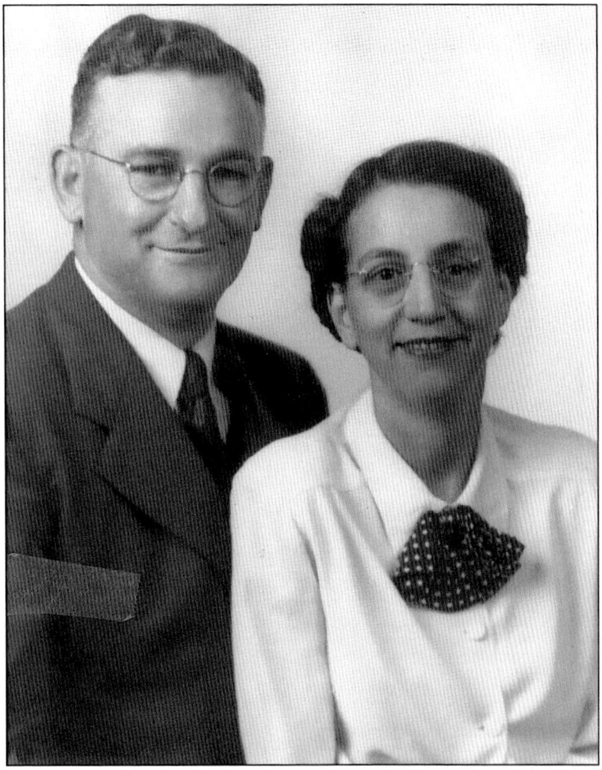

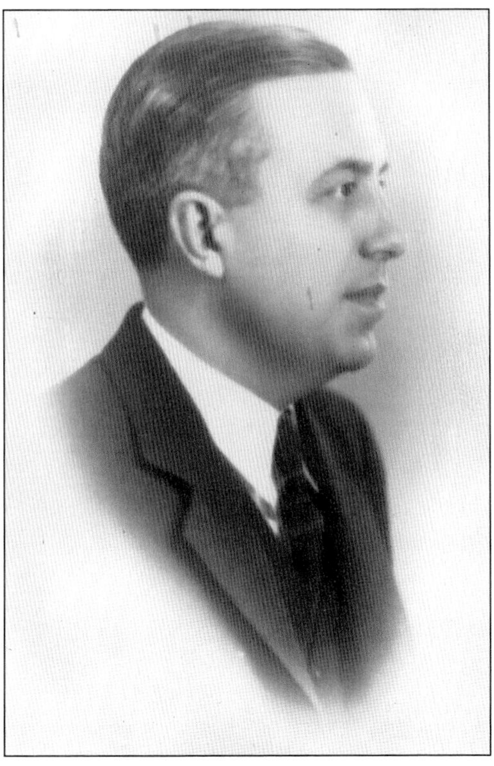

The oldest son of R.H. Miller was James Weston Miller. He was owner of R.H. Miller Insurance from 1941 to 1965. In addition, he served as president of the Minden Building and Loan Association from 1958 to 1977. (Courtesy of Thad Andress.)

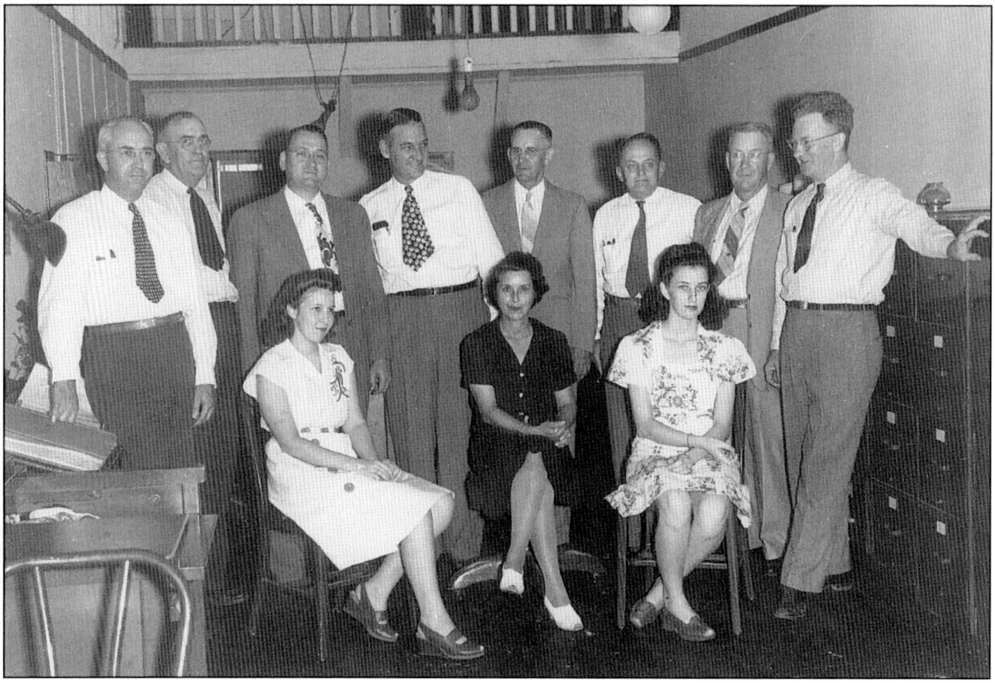

The Webster Parish Draft Board is shown in 1940. Mrs. Marie Agan Colclasure, front row center, was chief clerk of the Webster Parish Selective Service. With her in the front row are her assistants: her daughter, Dorothy Colclasure Calvit (left), and Carolyn Garland Hortman (right). The local representatives of the board are pictured in the back row. (Courtesy of George Calvit.)

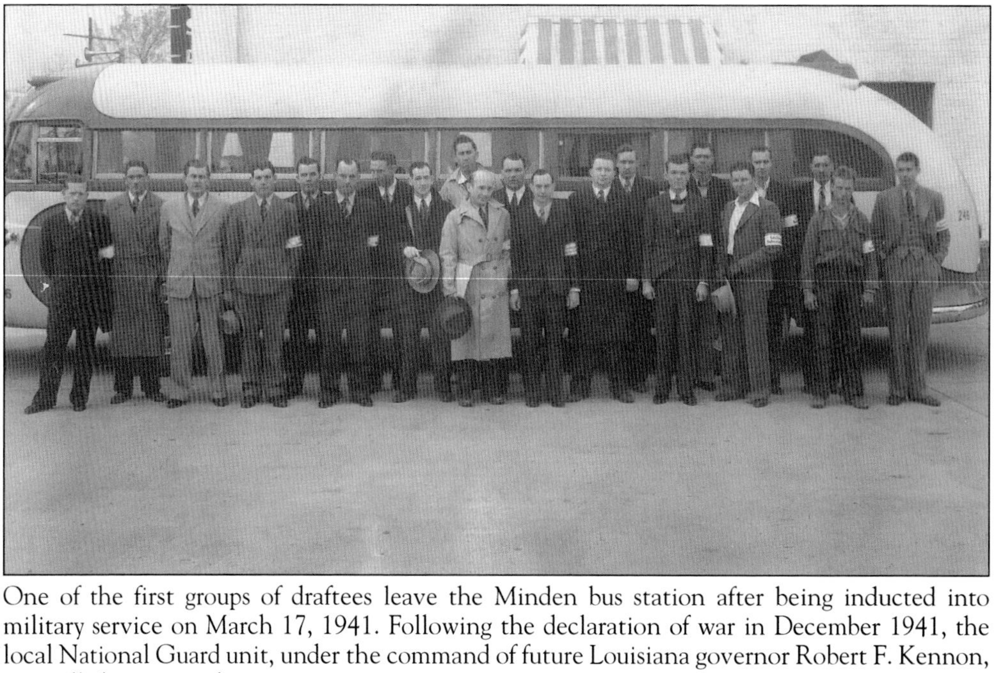

One of the first groups of draftees leave the Minden bus station after being inducted into military service on March 17, 1941. Following the declaration of war in December 1941, the local National Guard unit, under the command of future Louisiana governor Robert F. Kennon, was called to active duty.

Another son of R.H. Miller, Christopher Chaffe Miller, was a graduate of the U.S. Naval Academy and became the highest-ranking naval officer to call Minden home. A Navy career man, he retired as a rear admiral. Admiral Miller served in the Pacific during World War II as commander of the light cruiser USS *Mobile*, during which time he received the Silver Star and two Bronze Stars. (Courtesy of Thad Andress.)

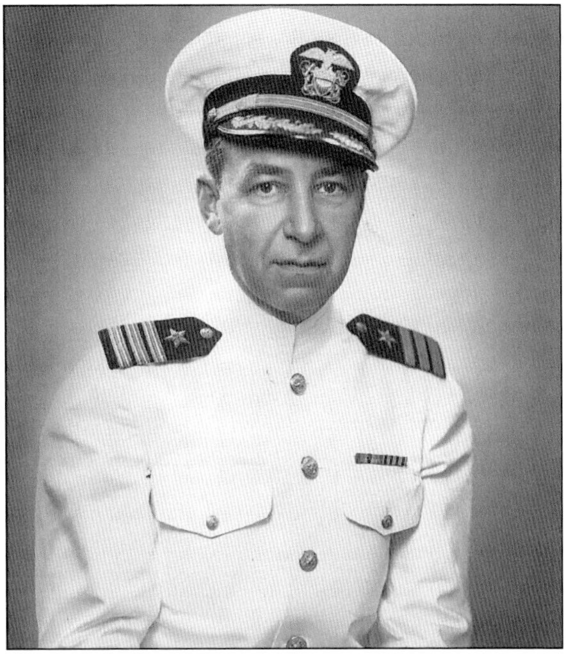

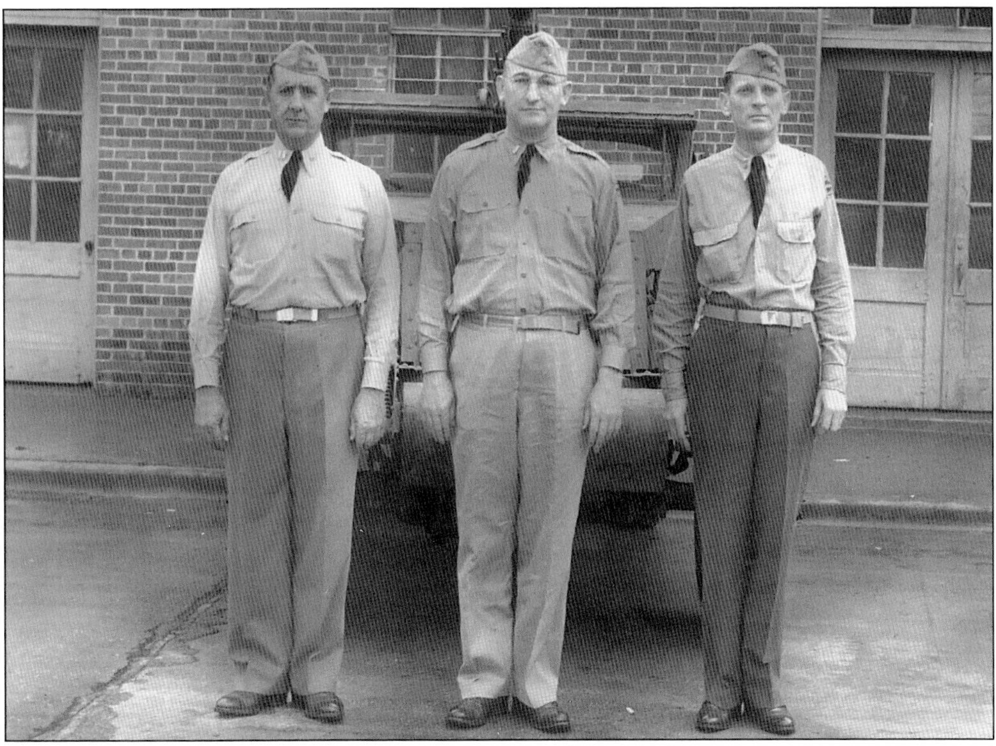

With the younger men away at war, the older married men of the community were summoned to duty as part of the home guard. In this picture are three officers of Minden's home guard, Capt. F.J. Van Peene, Lt. Harry C. Andress, and Lt. Byron Lumpkin. Because of the shortage of weapons, the home guard was equipped with dummy wooden guns. (Courtesy of Thad Andress.)

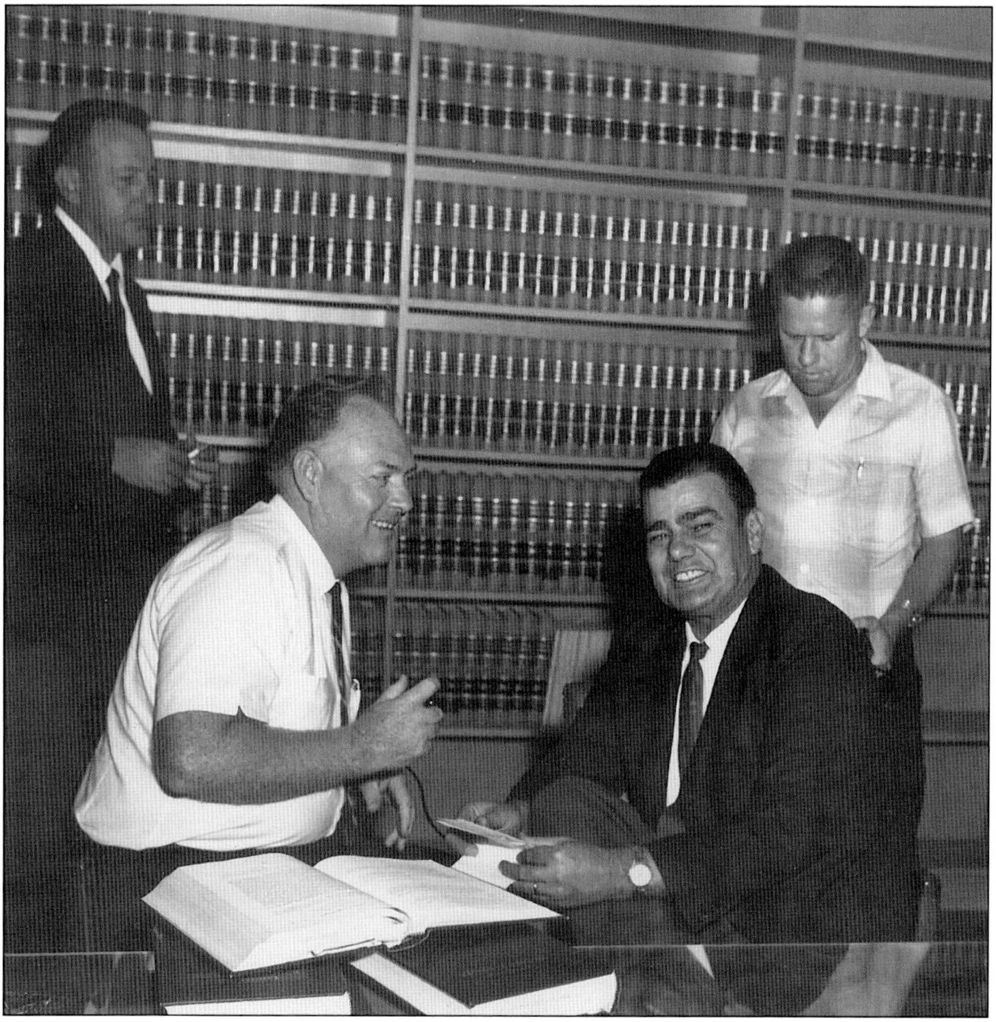

On election night, December 1963, O.H. Haynes Jr. followed in his father's footsteps by being elected sheriff of Webster Parish. The night before, the Haynes family had experienced another deja vu–type experience. O.H. Jr. had quarterbacked Minden High School to its first state football championship in 1938. On election eve 1963, his son, Fred Haynes, quarterbacked his undefeated Minden Crimson Tide team to a state championship. This picture shows a radio interview conducted by long-time Minden radio station owners and civic leaders, Harold "Boe" Cook and M.S. "Digger" O'Dell. Also pictured is district attorney John Benton. From left to right are John Benton, Boe Cook, O.H. Haynes Jr., and Digger O'Dell. (Courtesy of Mrs. O.H. Haynes Jr.)

The dean of the Minden bar, John T. Campbell, began his law practice in Minden in the 1927 after finishing at the top of his class at LSU law school. He continued his practice until his death in 1993. He earned a statewide reputation for excellence and was a participant in the most celebrated and significant trials in Minden during his lifetime. (Courtesy of Mrs. John T. Campbell.)

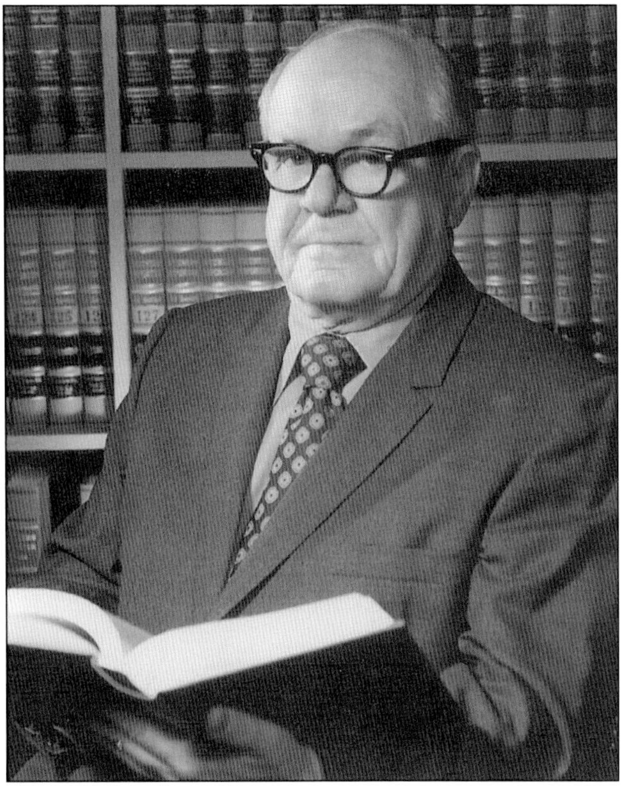

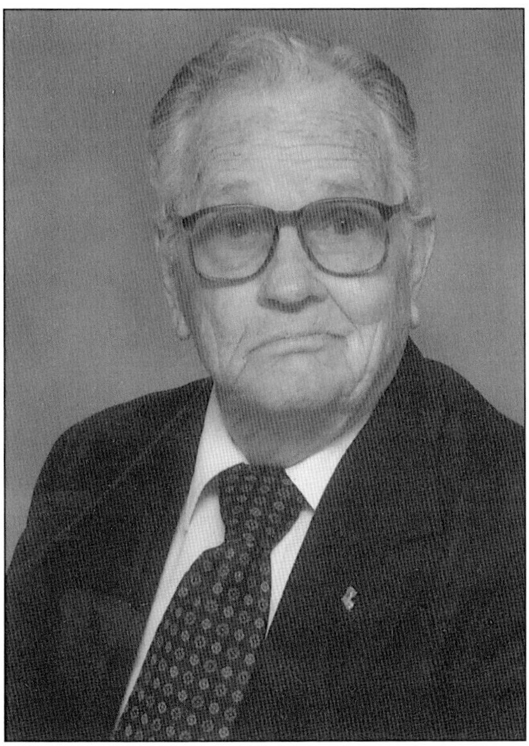

Frank Norman was an active leader in local civic organizations and a city councilman before being elected mayor of Minden in 1958. Mayor Norman served two terms before leaving office in 1966. (Courtesy of Mrs. Mildred Norman.)

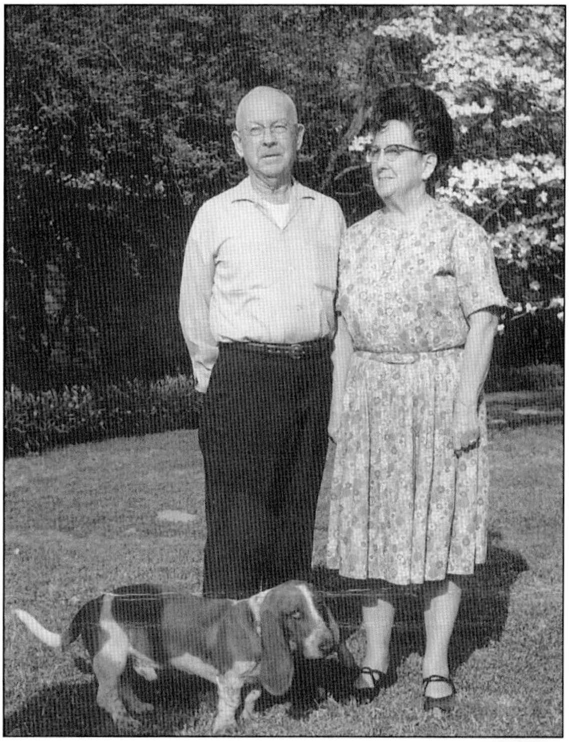

For nearly half a century, nearly all of the recreational activities for the young people of Minden were provided by one couple, Mr. and Mrs. Larry Hunter. Mr. Hunter, owner of the Minden Coca Cola Bottling Company, sponsored the summer baseball program and provided many other activities for the young people. He was supported in these efforts by his wife, Mrs. Gladys Hunter, who also served on the Webster Parish School Board. The Hunter family provided these activities free of charge to the children of Minden. (Courtesy of Ben Hunter.)

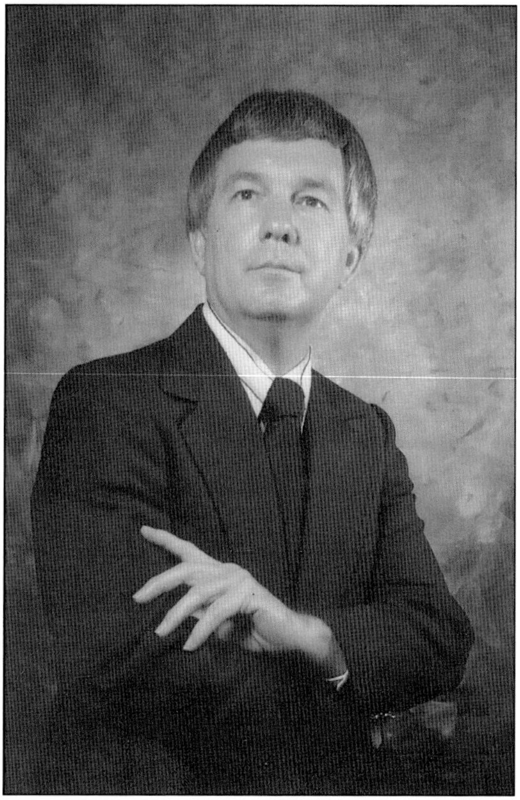

The Hunter family tradition of philanthropy is being carried out today by Larry Hunter's descendants, including Ben Hunter. Ben serves on many community boards and is always prepared to sponsor worthwhile activities that enrich the lives of the citizens of Minden, especially its young people. (Courtesy of Ben Hunter.)

Tom Colten came to Minden when he purchased the local newspaper in 1956. He soon became one of the most outstanding leaders in the community, and in 1966, he was elected mayor of Minden, the first Republican elected mayor in Louisiana since Reconstruction. During his term as mayor, Colten oversaw both a increase in efficiency and service in the local city government. A new power plant, street and park improvements, and the new city hall and civic center complex were completed during his two terms. He later served as CEO of the Minden Medical Center, before taking a job with the Louisiana state government. (Courtesy of *Minden Press Herald*.)

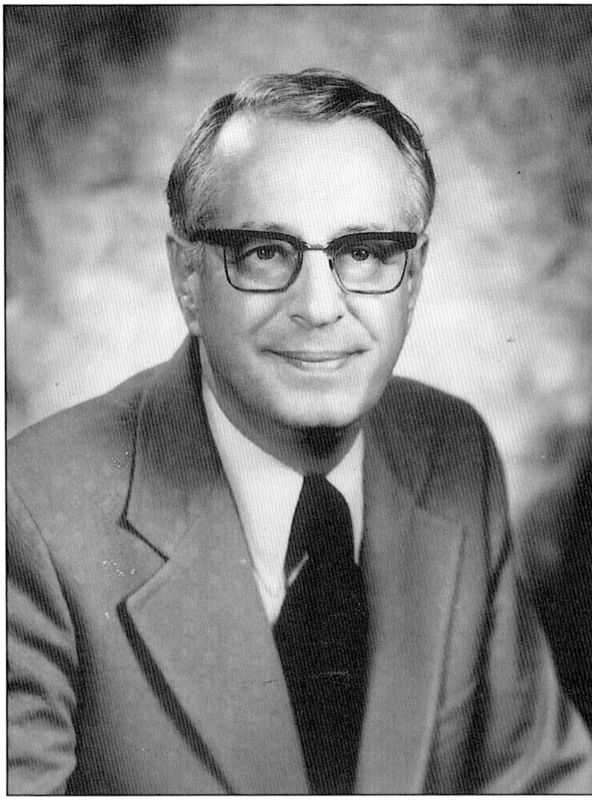

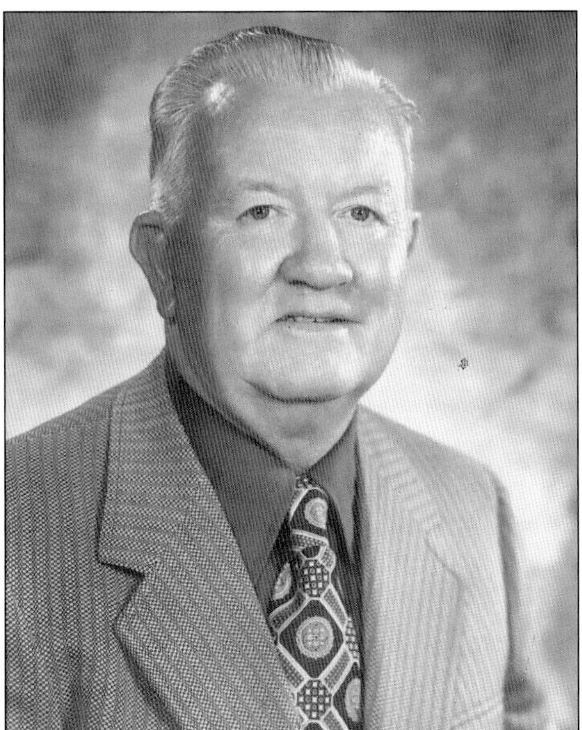

Jack Batton was the son of Bryan Batton, Minden police chief in the 1930s. He also operated a store in Minden, but was best known for his almost continuous service on the Minden City Council from the 1940s until the 1980s. His service to the city of Minden, which also included many years on the local volunteer fire department, culminated with two terms as mayor of Minden in the late 1970s and early 1980s. (Courtesy of *Minden Press Herald*.)

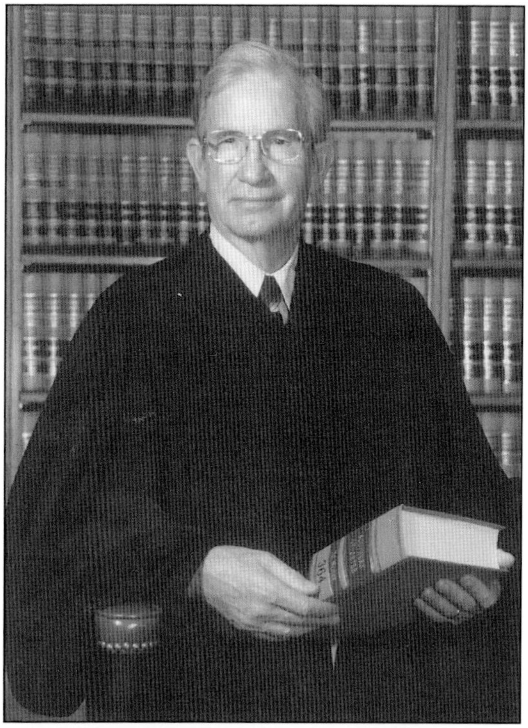

James E. Bolin was first elected to public office in the early 1940s, when he was chosen to serve in the Louisiana Legislature representing Webster Parish. After outstanding service with the Adjutant General Corps in World War II, he came home and gained election as a district judge. In later years, he was elected to the Louisiana Court of Appeals and capped his judicial career with several temporary stints serving on the Louisiana Supreme Court. (Courtesy of *Minden Press Herald.*)

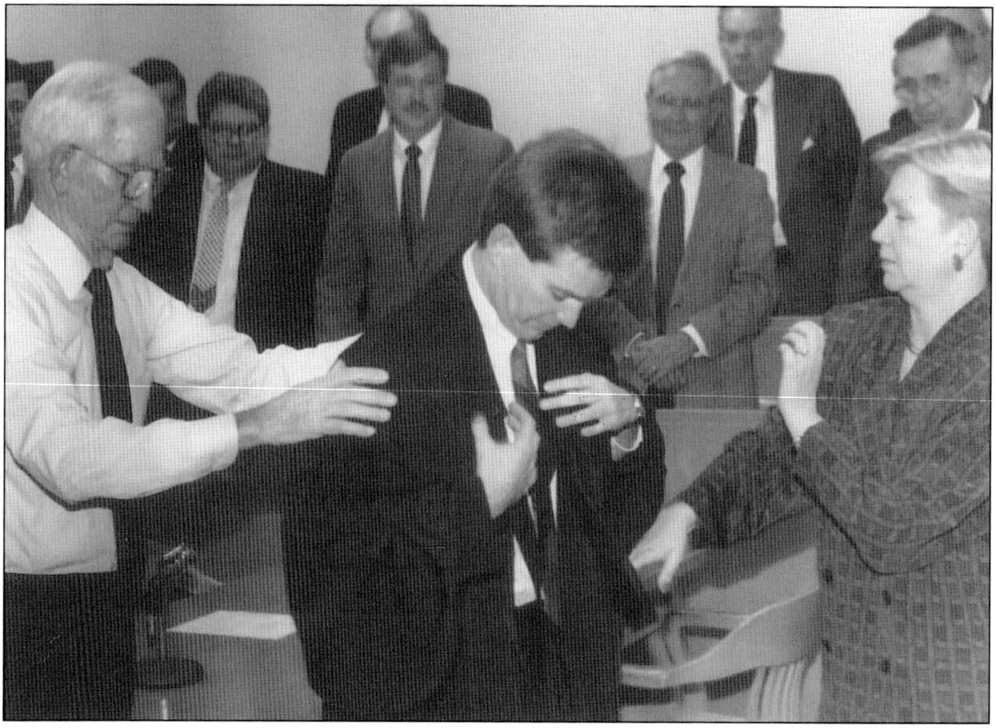

Following in his father's footsteps, Bruce Bolin was first elected as a state representative from Webster Parish. Then, he too was elected to a post as district judge. In this photo, he is receiving his judicial robes from his father, James Bolin. (Courtesy of *Minden Press Herald.*)

T.C. Bloxom began serving with the Minden Fire Department while still a teenager in the 1940s. Later, he served in various capacities with the Webster Parish Sheriff's Office including chief civil and criminal deputy. He has served as fire chief of Minden for more than 30 years and is currently serving his third term as Minden's chief of police. (Courtesy of *Minden Press Herald*.)

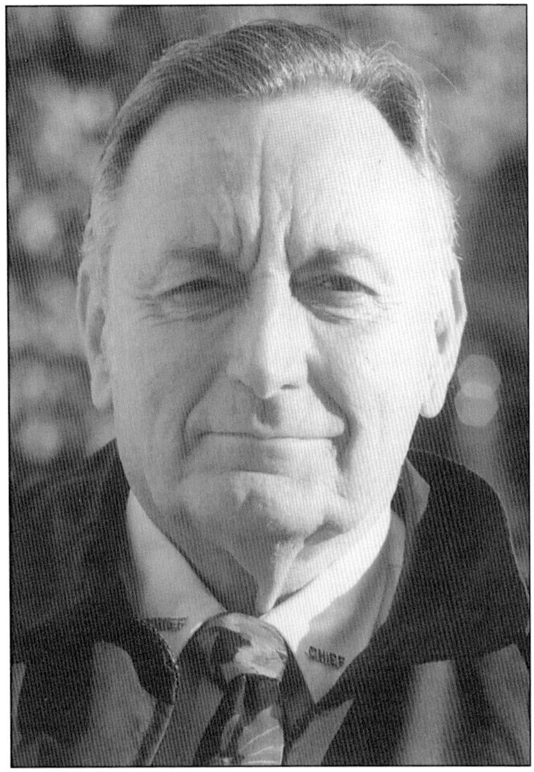

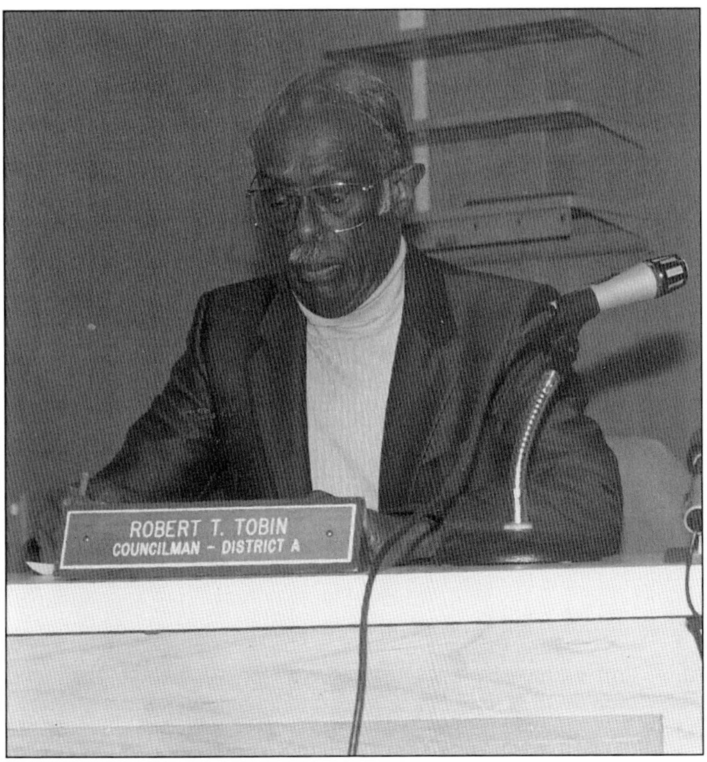

After retiring from a distinguished career as an educator, Robert T. Tobin was elected to the Minden City Council in the late 1970s, becoming one of the first two blacks elected to the Minden City Council since the 1880s. Later, he was serving as mayor pro-tem when the sitting mayor was recalled. He filled out the remainder of the term, becoming Minden's first black mayor. (Courtesy of *Minden Press Herald*.)

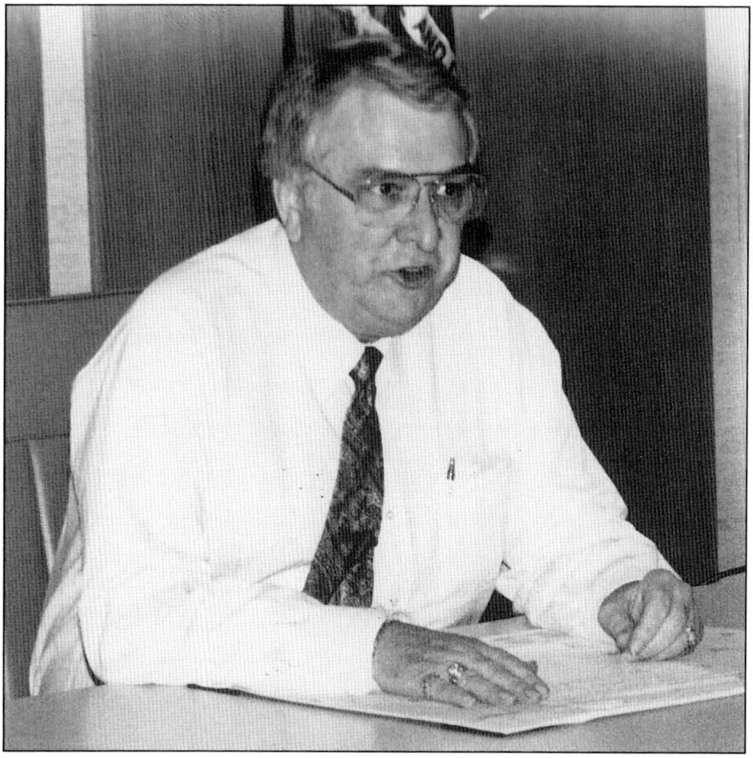

First gaining election to the Minden City Council and later serving on the Webster Parish Police Jury, Bill Robertson was elected to his third term as mayor of Minden in the fall of 1998. (Courtesy of *Minden Press Herald*.)

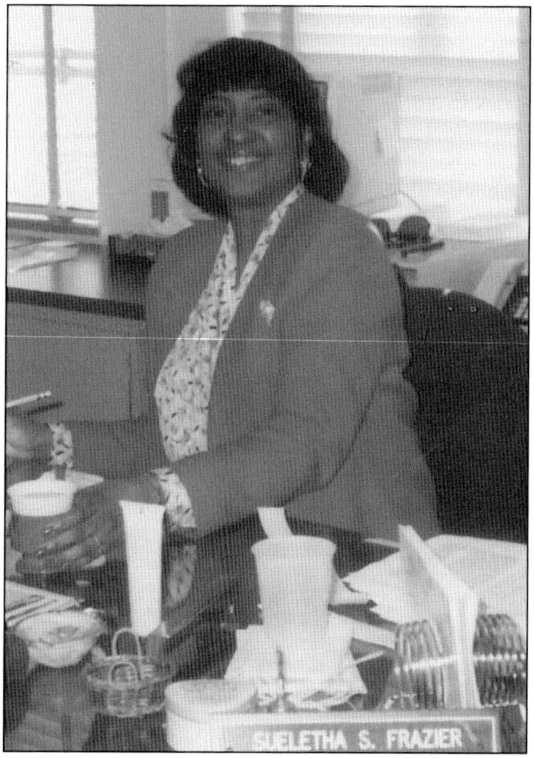

After serving as deputy clerk of court for many years, Sueletha Scott Frazier of Minden won election as Webster Parish clerk of court in 1999. She became the first black to ever gain election to a parish-wide office since the creation of the parish in 1871. (Courtesy of Sueletha Scott Frazier.)

Two

Community

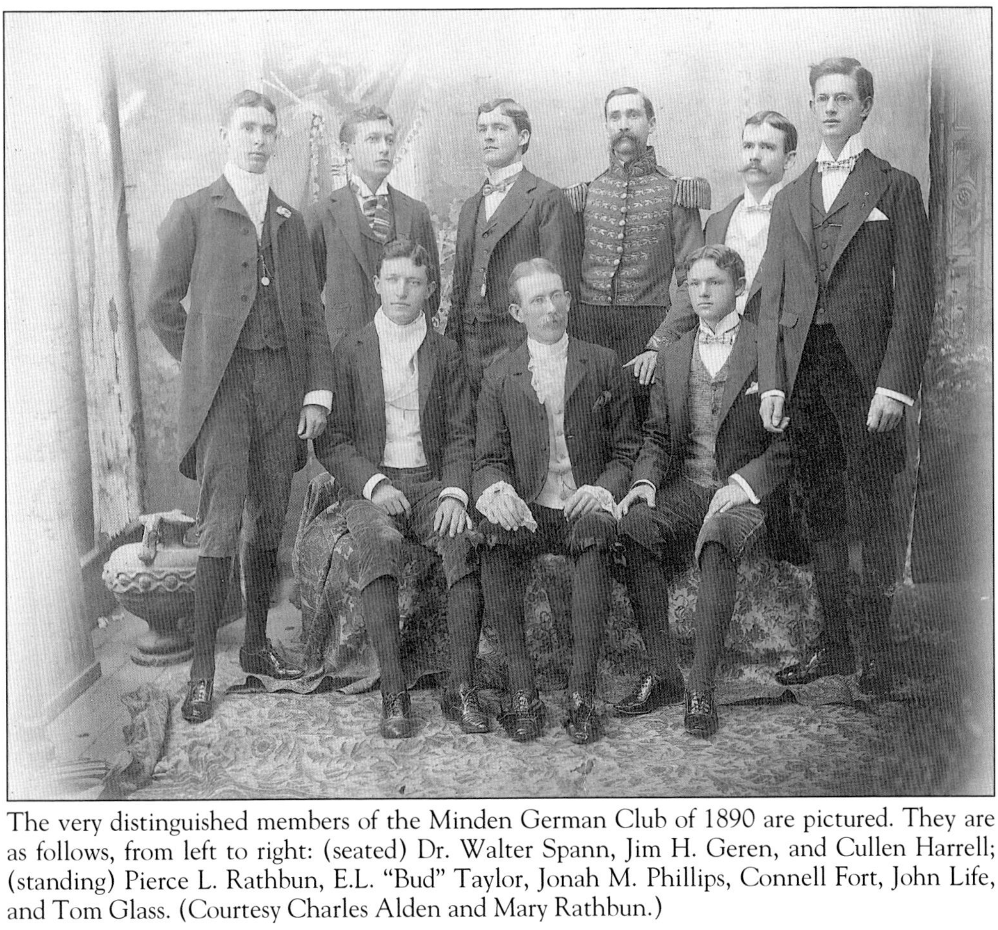

The very distinguished members of the Minden German Club of 1890 are pictured. They are as follows, from left to right: (seated) Dr. Walter Spann, Jim H. Geren, and Cullen Harrell; (standing) Pierce L. Rathbun, E.L. "Bud" Taylor, Jonah M. Phillips, Connell Fort, John Life, and Tom Glass. (Courtesy Charles Alden and Mary Rathbun.)

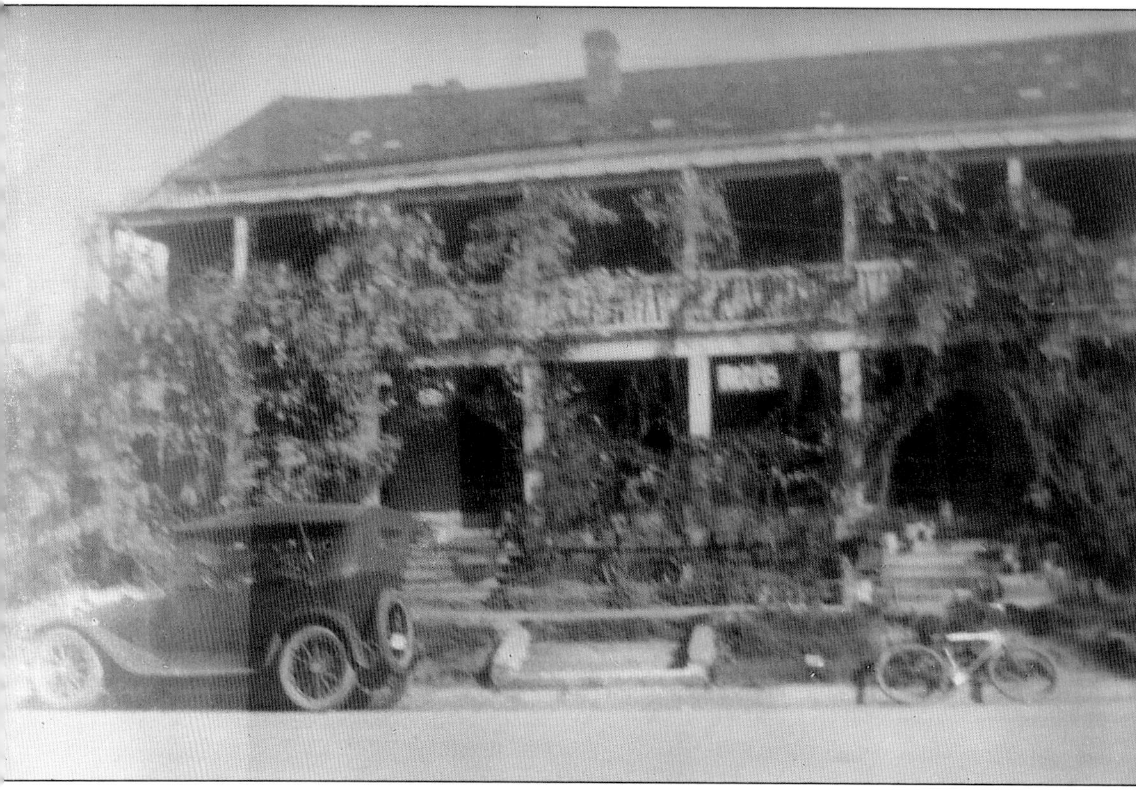

The original home of Christopher and Jane Chaffe, built about 1855, was located on the corner of Fogle and North Broadway where the Moss Eyecare Center is now located. Christopher Chaffe operated this building as an inn in addition to his blacksmith shop, foundry, and a stagecoach line, which at times ran as far east as Vicksburg and as far west as Nacogdoches, TX. He did not consider the inn a proper place to raise his young daughters and built a new home across the street in what is now the Minden Medical Center parking lot. (Courtesy of Thad Andress.)

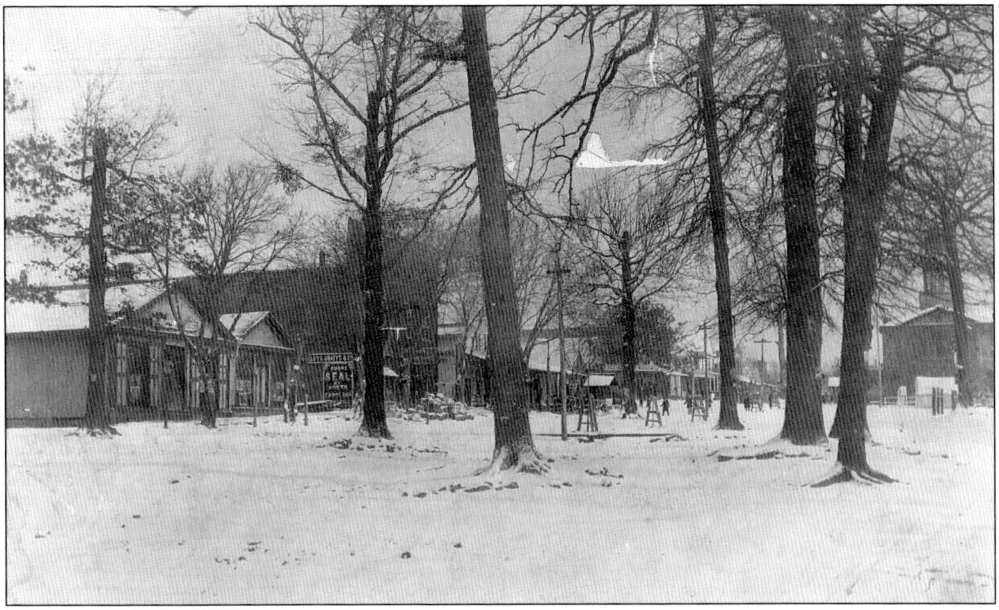

This image, of a snowy street scene in Minden, was taken in 1892. The area shown in this image is North Broadway (Main Street), looking north from Pine Street. Notice the 1872 Webster Parish Courthouse in the right background of the picture. Also notice the frame stores downtown, many of which burned in the disastrous fire of April 1902. (Courtesy of John S. and Lillian Life Willis.)

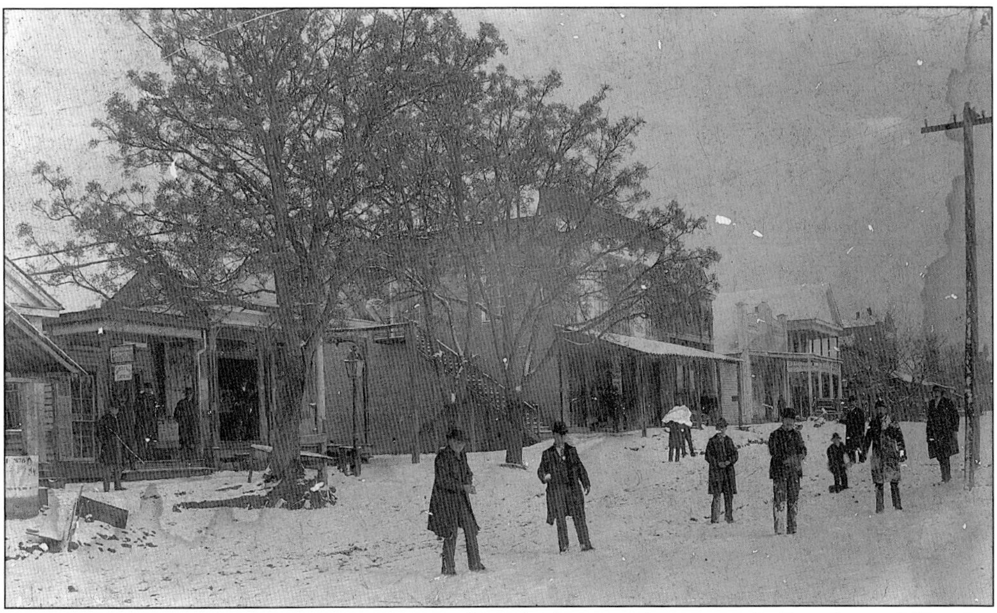

This image of the same snow storm was taken further north on North Broadway. The men pictured are apparently engaged in a snowball fight, based on the snowballs that can be seen in the hands of several. Notice the water well located in Main Street at the left edge of the picture. In those days, there were wells spaced throughout the downtown area.

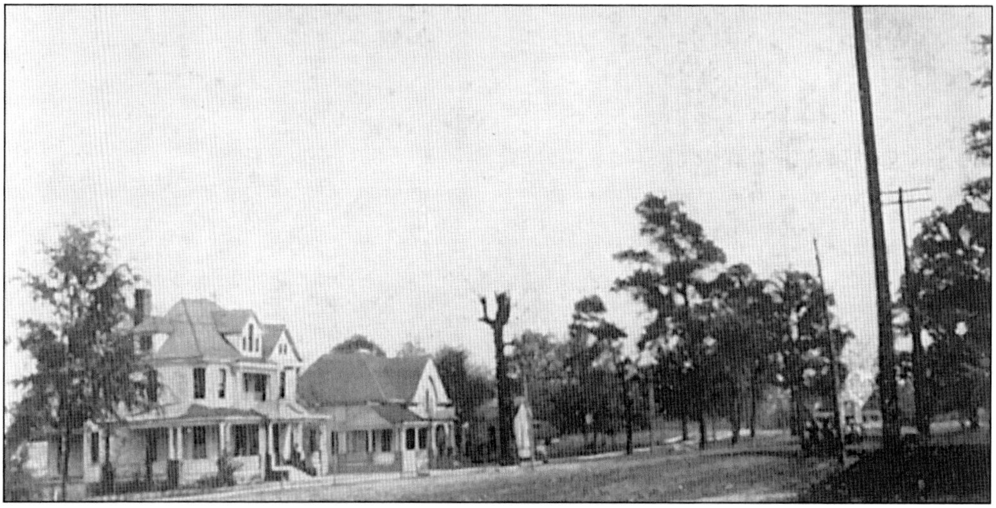

This image of the residential section of Broadway, looking north, was taken during the first decade of the 20th century. (Courtesy of Frank Griffith.)

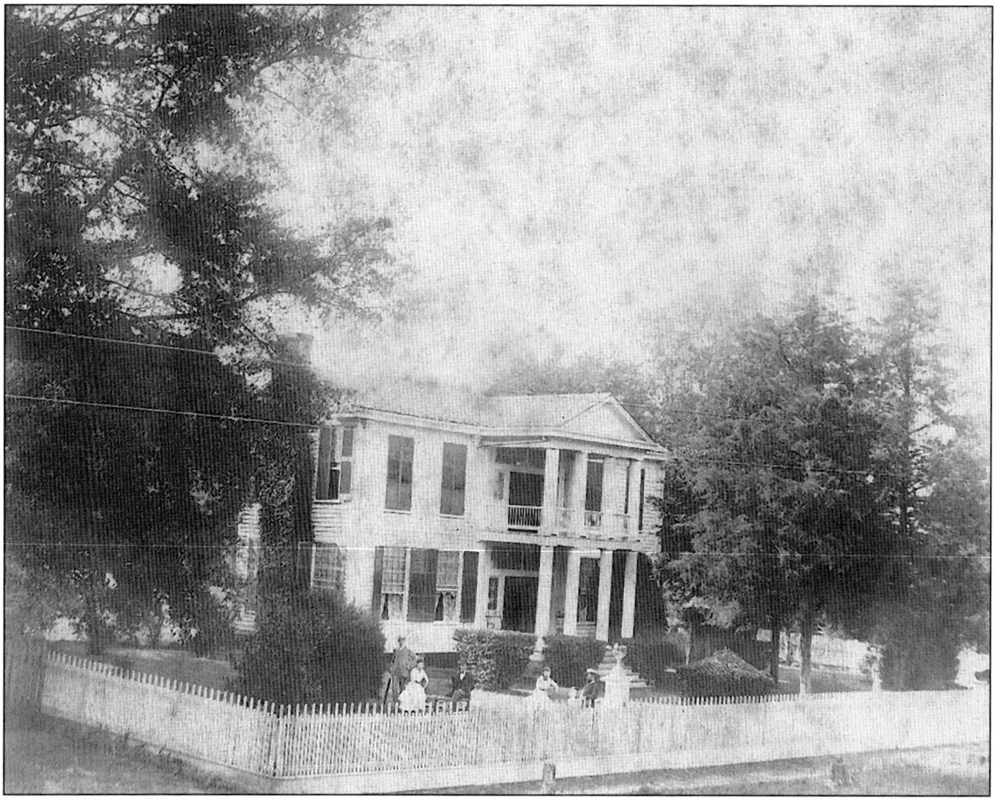

The antebellum home of Hervey Drake is pictured in the 1880s. Notice the dress of those in the picture and the Victorian-era yard decorations. Also of interest is the level of the street in front of the home. This was taken before Broadway Street was lowered several feet, creating the hills that flank the roadway today. Today, the home is owned by Hervey's great-great-granddaughter, Claire Drake Moore, and her husband, Luther Moore. (Courtesy of Luther & Claire Moore and Charles Alden & Mary Rathbun.)

The First Methodist Church was erected in 1905. The church had been located on another portion of this lot since the land was donated by W.A. Drake in 1839. Shortly after this building was completed, the old church, sitting next door to the pictured building, burned. (Courtesy of Frank Griffith.)

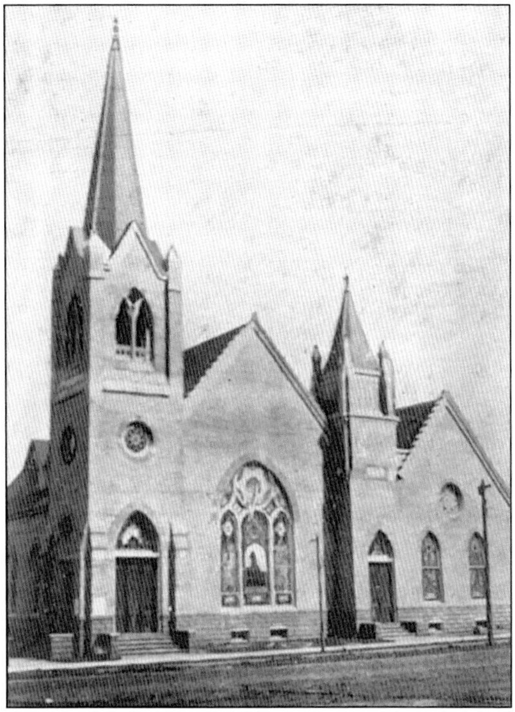

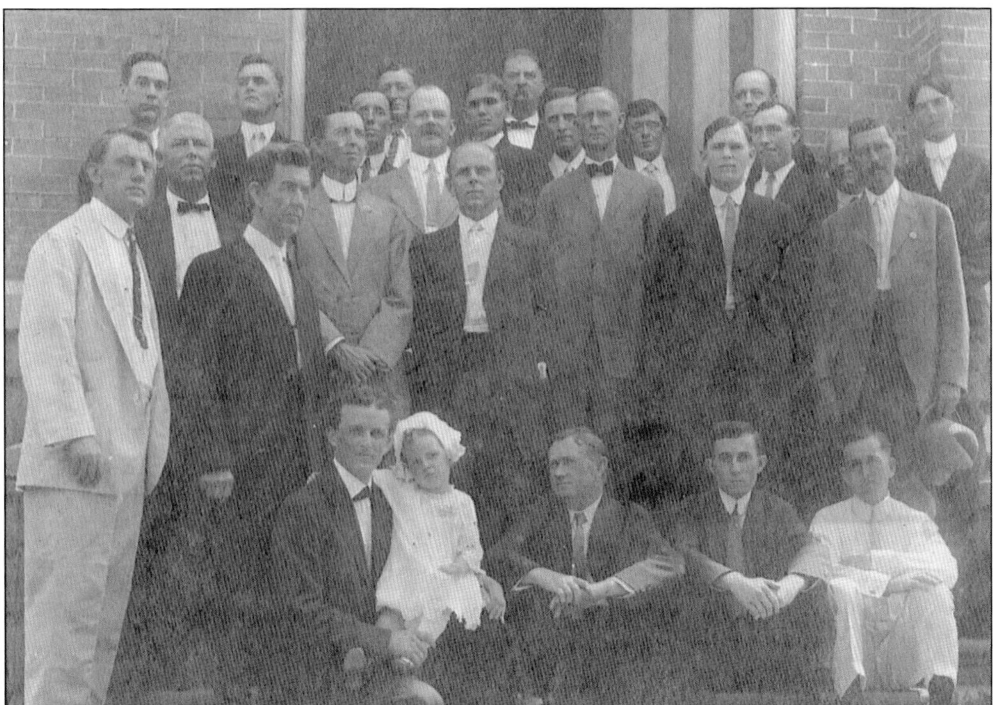

The cornerstone of the First Methodist Church building was laid in 1905. The chairman of the finance committee for this structure was Sheriff B.F. Griffith, who is shown in this picture with other members of the congregation. (Courtesy of Frank Griffith.)

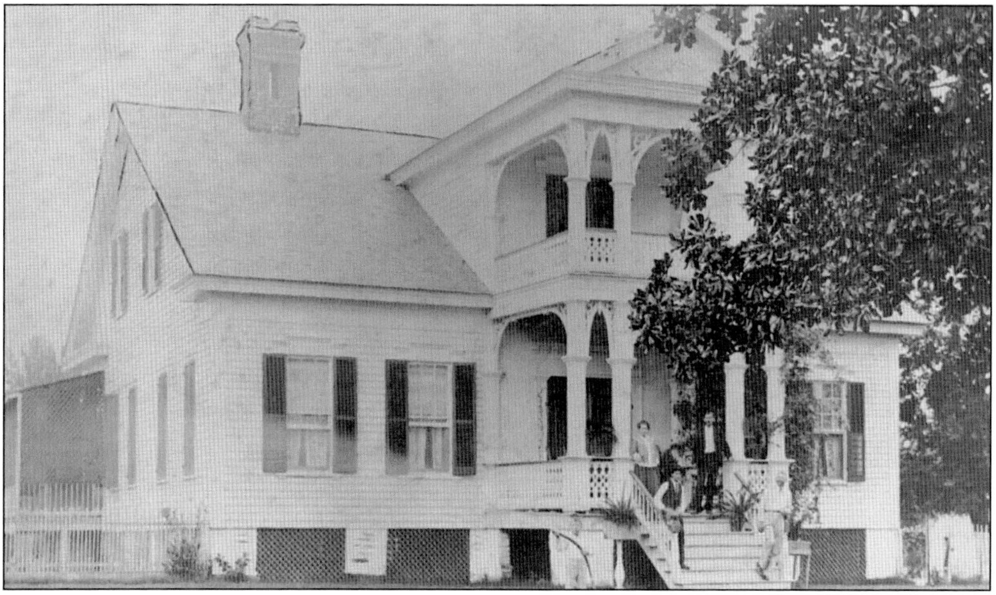

This is the home built by early Minden businessman Drury Murrell. The street that ran to the home was named in his honor. It is pictured during the time that it was the home of B.F. Griffith. The Griffith family later sold it to a Hortman family, and eventually, the home served for many years as the Green-Kleinegger and later Rose-Neath Funeral Homes. The house was moved to serve as the Dorcheat Historical Association Museum in the mid-1970s, but was destroyed by fire before the museum could be created. (Courtesy of Frank Griffith.)

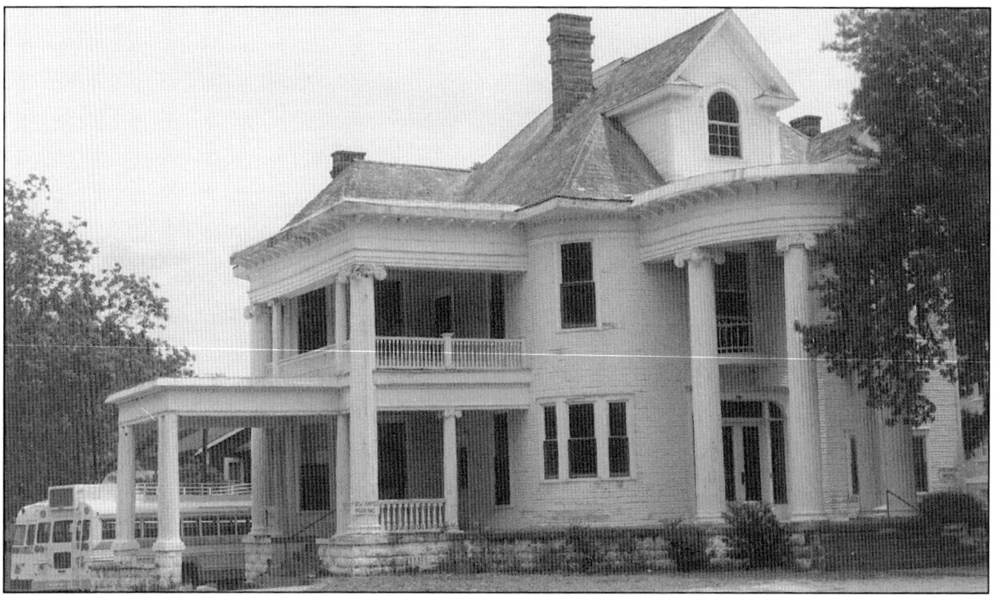

Built about 1905 as the home of Mr. and Mrs. Jack Crichton, this house was home for more than 50 years to Congressman John N. Sandlin, who married Mrs. Crichton in 1916 after her husband's death. After Congressman Sandlin died in 1957, the property was eventually acquired by the First Baptist Church, which was located just across First Street. The church used the home for Sunday school classrooms for 16 years before it was torn down to make way for a parking lot.

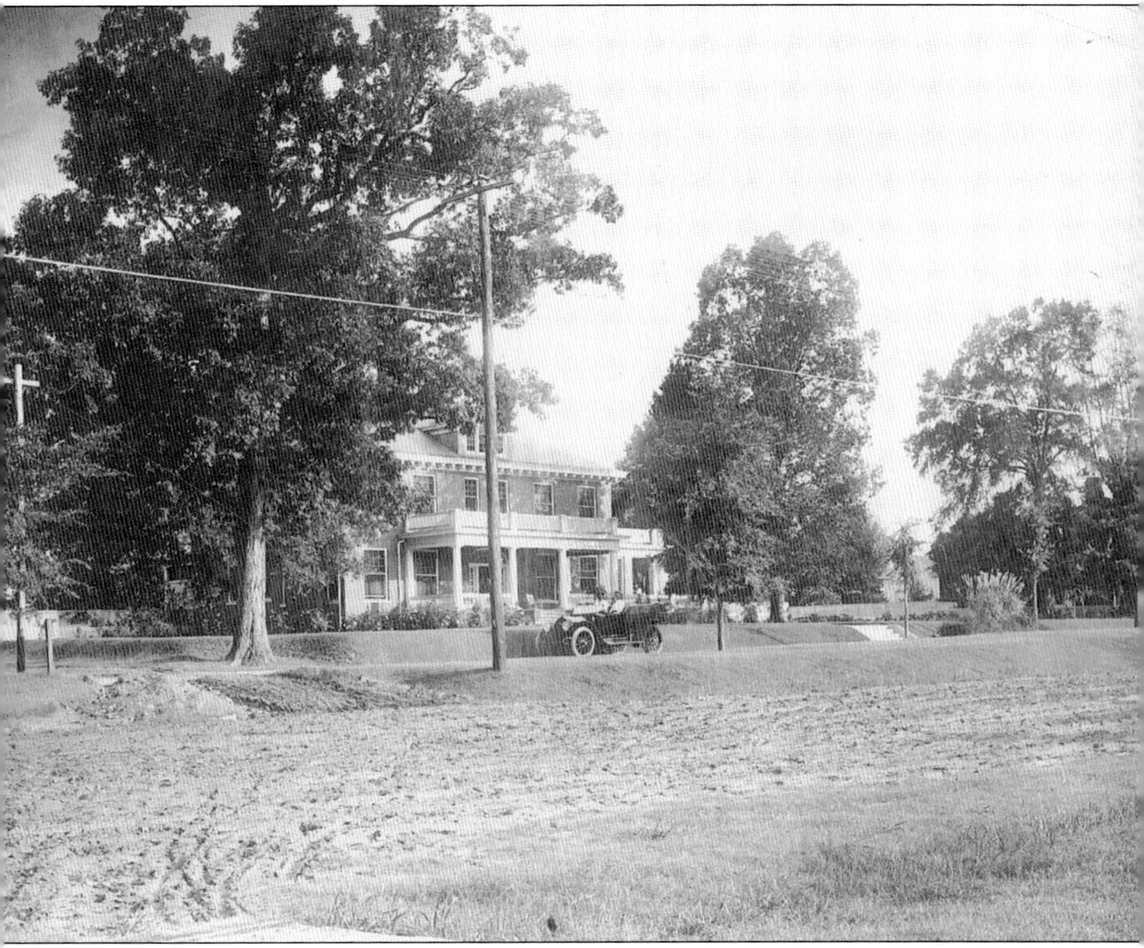

This is the home of Samuel G. Webb, pictured about 1915. The home was built about 1909. Notice that the grading of Broadway Street has begun, as the front layer of street is noticeably lower than the level where the car is parked. This home was later occupied by Mr. Webb's daughter Juliet and her husband, C.M. Hutton. They passed it on to their daughter, Juliet Hutton, who married Charles Alden Rathbun Sr. Today, the home is occupied by Charles and Juliet Hutton Rathbun's son, Charles Alden Rathbun Jr., and his wife, Mary. (Courtesy of Charles Alden and Mary Rathbun.)

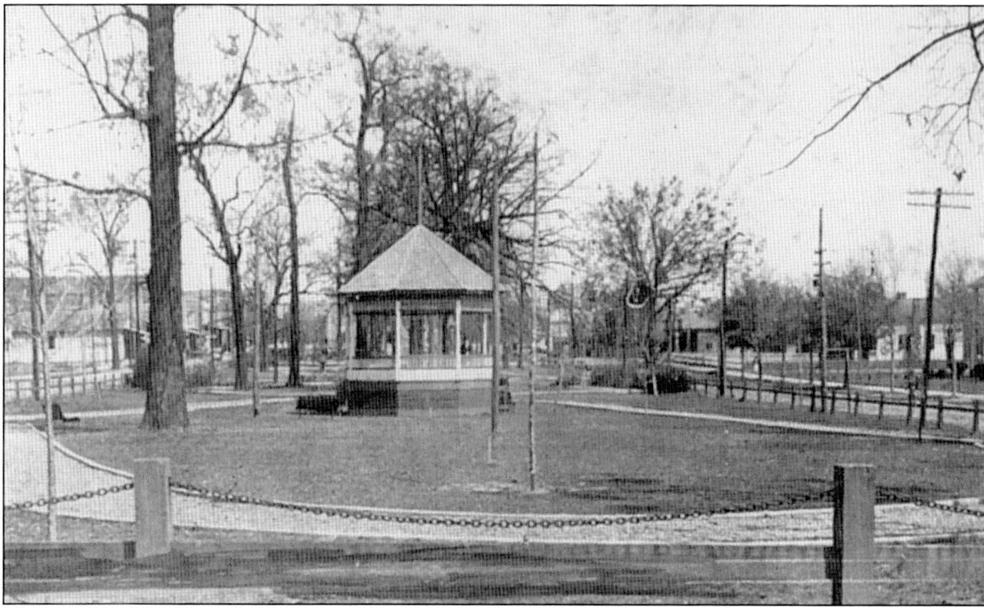

This postcard image is of the Minden City Park in the early years of the 20th century. Today, the site of this park is occupied by the Webster Parish Courthouse, constructed in the early 1950s. (Courtesy of Frank Griffith.)

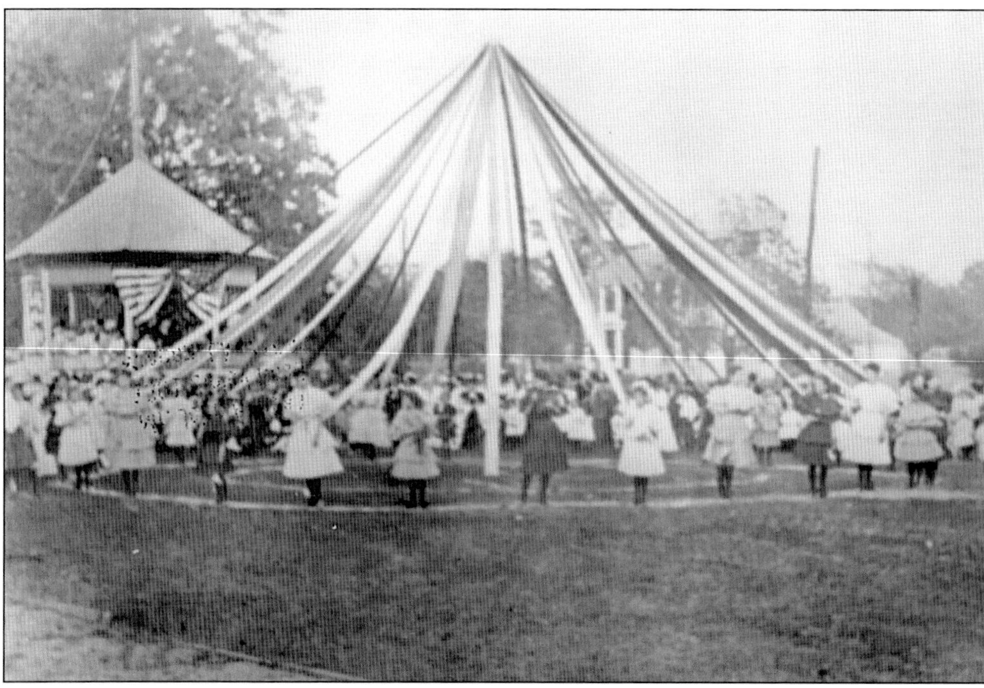

Here is another image of the City Park during a May Day celebration in 1909. The children are dancing around the Maypole. Notice in the background the antebellum Miller-Inabnett home that still stands behind the Webster Parish Courthouse today.

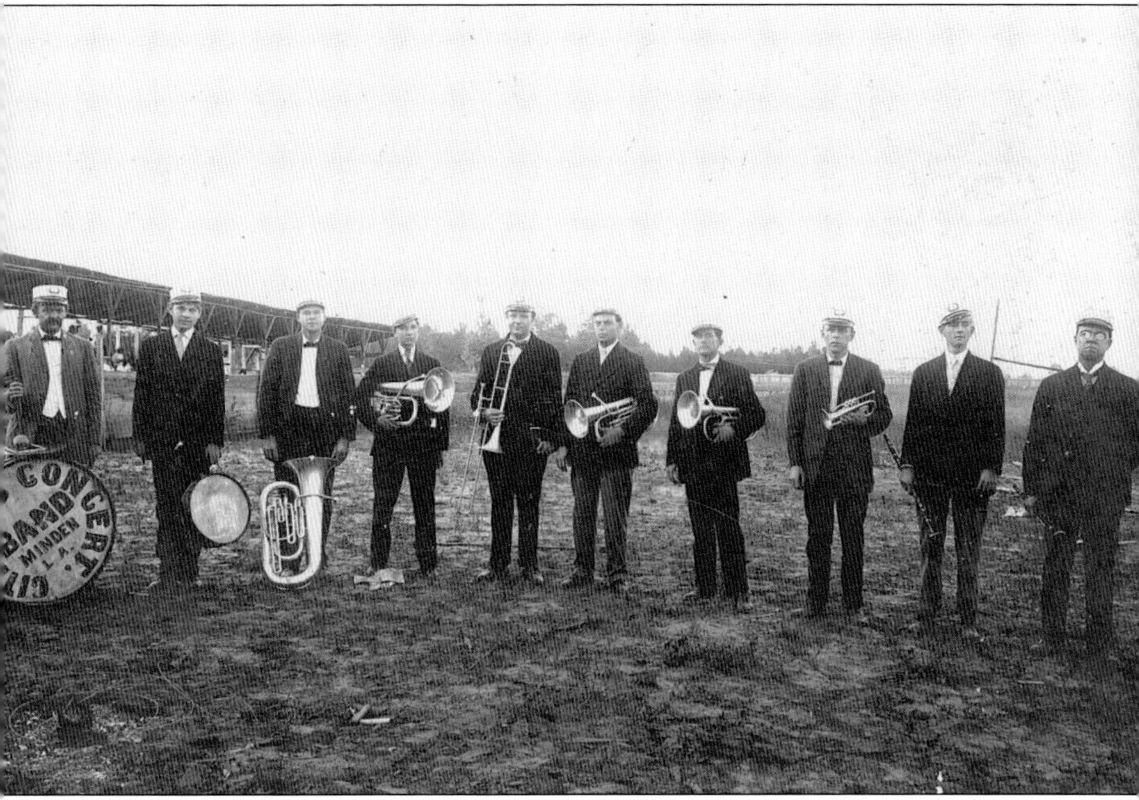

The Minden Concert Band is pictured in 1907 at what is perhaps the football field of that day, based on what appears to be goal posts in the background. It is also possible that this structure could be B.F. Griffith's racetrack, which was standing at that time. (Courtesy of John S. and Lillian Life Willis.)

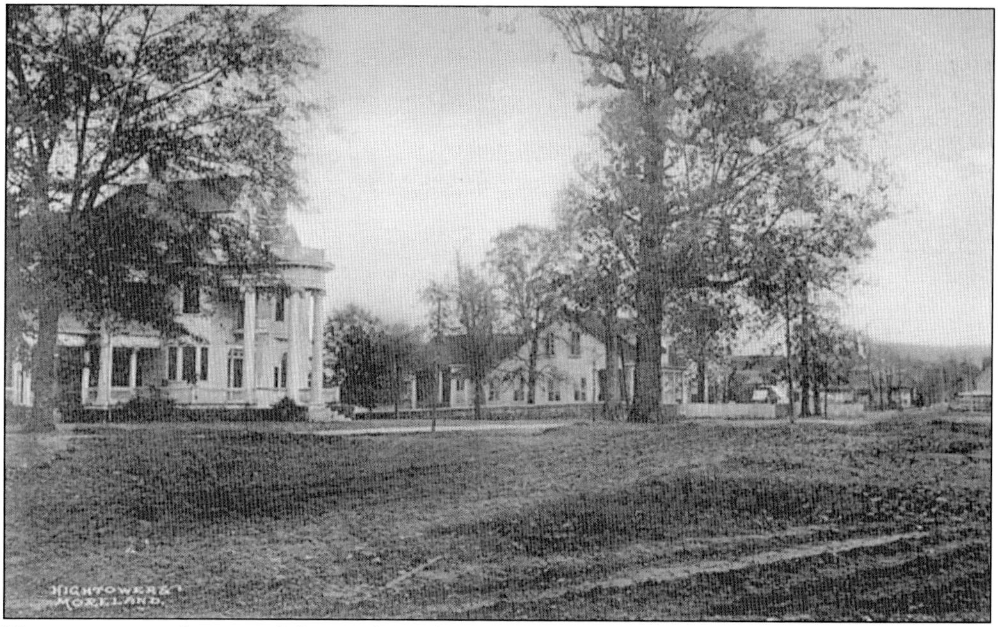

Here is a postcard image of the residential section of Minden in about 1908. Pictured are what was at the time the Jack Crichton home (better known as the Sandlin home) and the English home across First Street, which was demolished in 1925 when the First Baptist Church built a new building on that site.

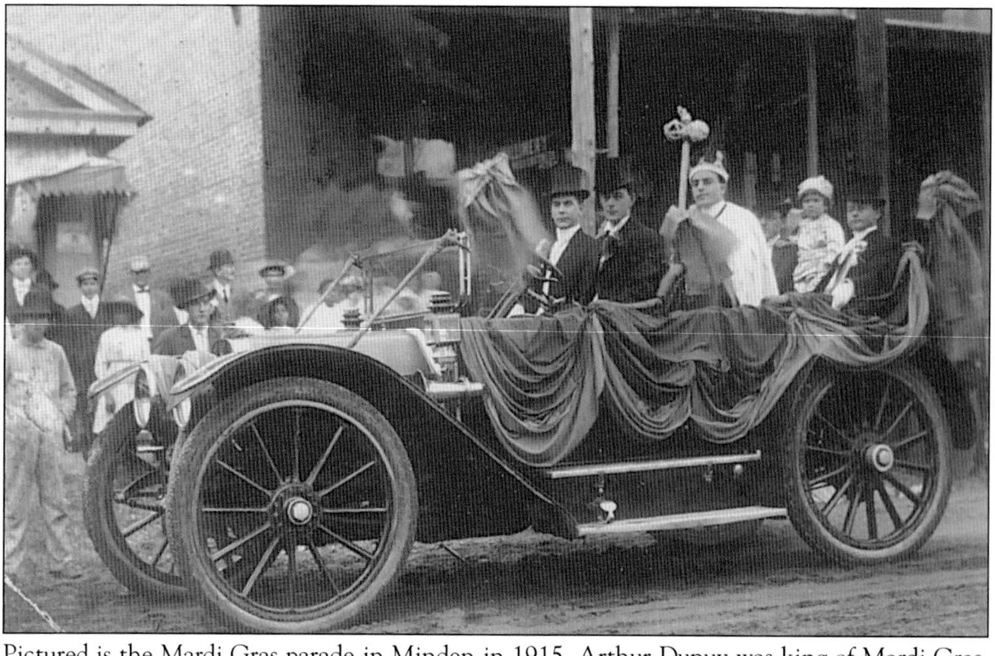

Pictured is the Mardi Gras parade in Minden in 1915. Arthur Dupuy was king of Mardi Gras, and Jules Dupuy served as page. Ardis Moreland is with the king, while Charles Beard drives the car. Also in the vehicle is Dr. Edgar Butler. The Mardi Gras queen that year was Joan Chaffe Miller, pictured earlier in the previous chapter. (Courtesy of Thad Andress.)

Young George Calvit is pictured standing in front of his home on South Broadway in about 1923. The home was located where the Cox Communications office is today. Notice the frame homes lining the street, which has been entirely commercial for about 70 years. (Courtesy of George Calvit.)

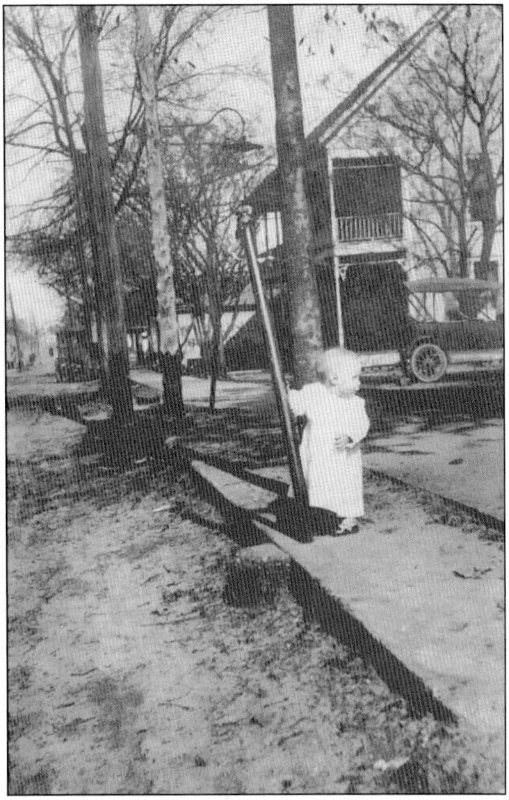

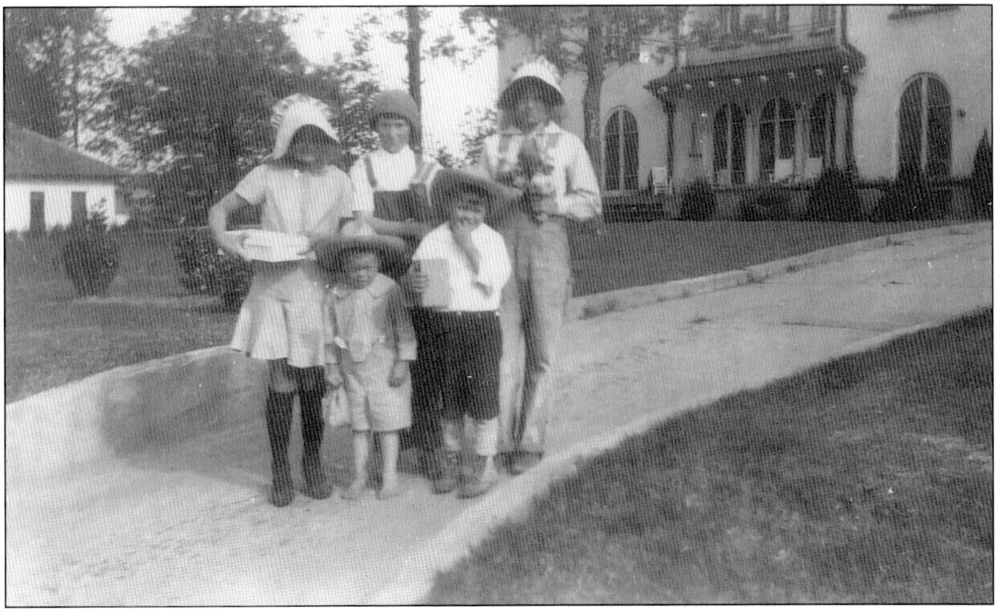

Several children are seen in the driveway of the J.G. Ferguson home in the 1920s. The Ferguson home later served as the Webster Parish Library from 1964 to 1997 and today is the Library Annex. Among the children are Albert Talton, Ted Talton, Grace Gruner, and Alma Lou Gruner. (Courtesy of Peggy Wise Jones.)

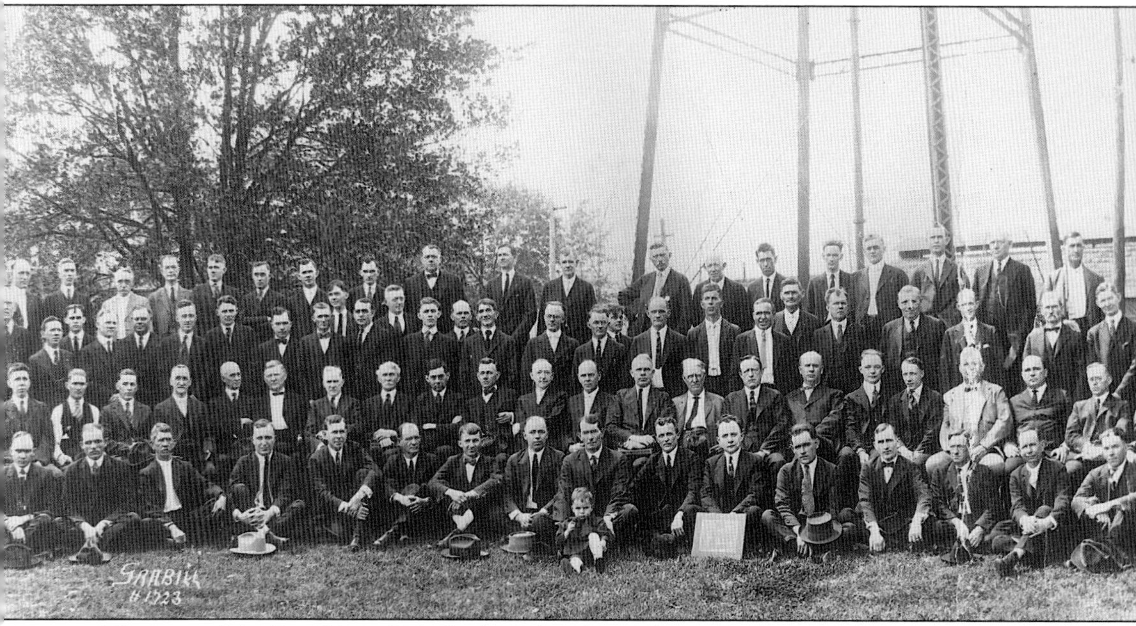

The men of the First United Methodist Church are shown in about 1921 or 1922. The men are seated below the first downtown water tower, which was torn down in the late 1960s. In the background, you can see Fuller's Garage, Minden's first auto repair shop, which still stands on the site today. (Courtesy of Lonnie Maddry.)

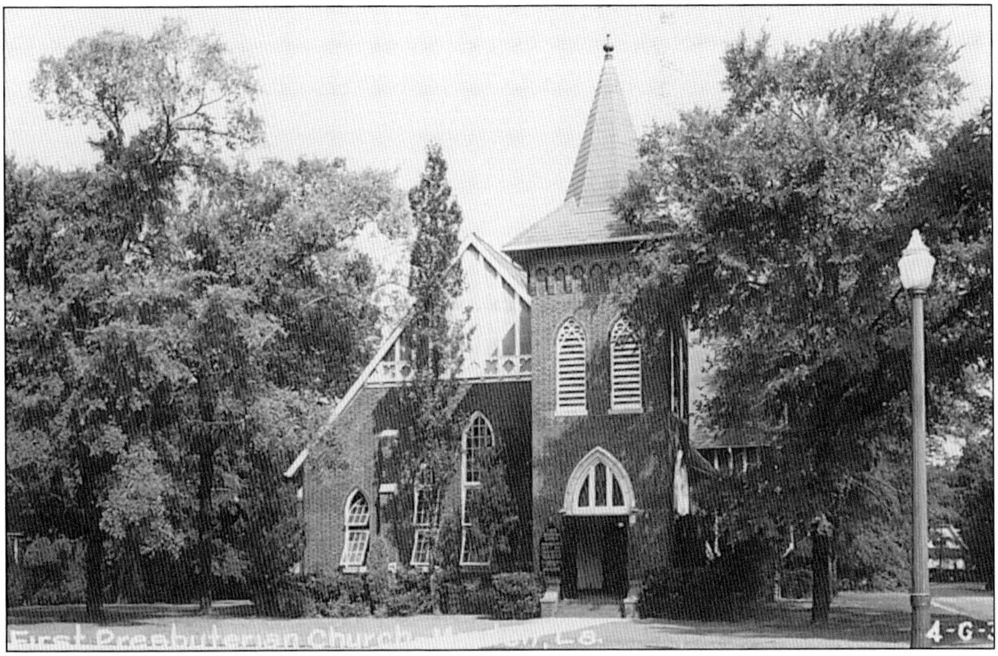

The 1924 Minden Presbyterian Church is shown in this postcard from the 1940s. This was the second church built on the site, which had been donated to the congregation by Hervey Drake in the 1800s. (Courtesy of George Calvit.)

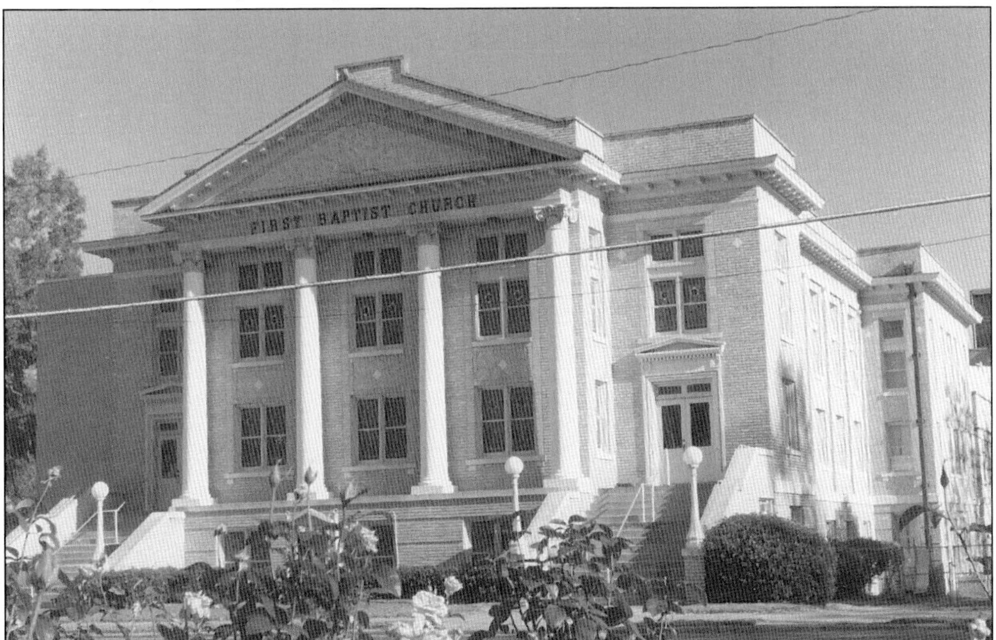

Built in 1925, this building was the third home for the First Baptist Church congregation, which had been founded in 1844. The first event held in this building was the funeral of eight-term congressman John T. Watkins, a prominent Baptist layman and former president of the Louisiana Baptist Convention. This building was used until it was torn down and a new building was built in 1977.

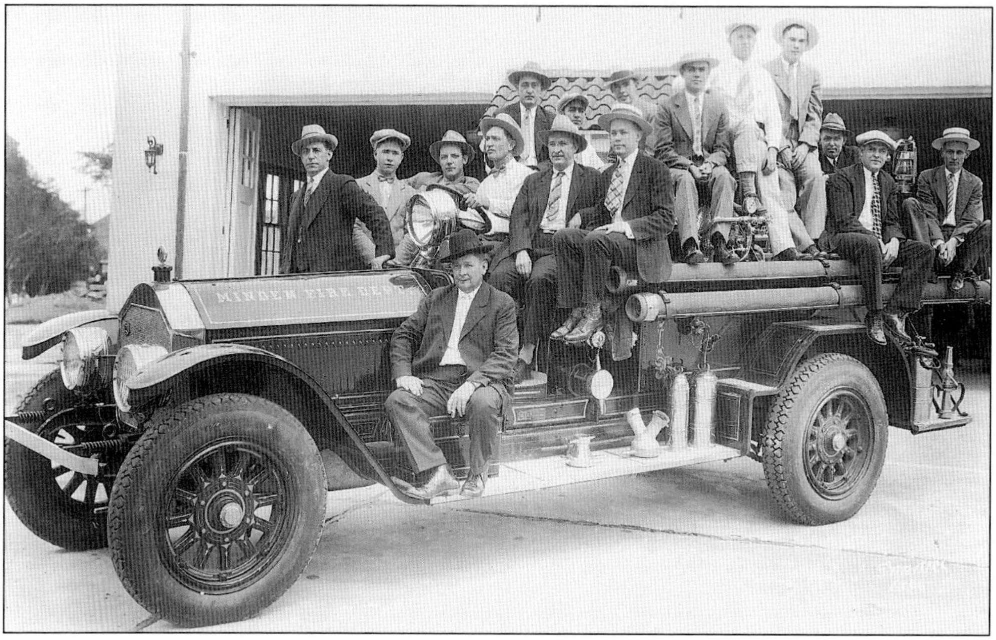

The Minden Volunteer Fire Department of 1926 is pictured in front of the new combination city hall/fire station. The building sat at the corner of Pearl and Monroe and today is a parking lot for the post office and Spillers Appliance and Furniture. (Courtesy of John S. and Lillian Life Willis.)

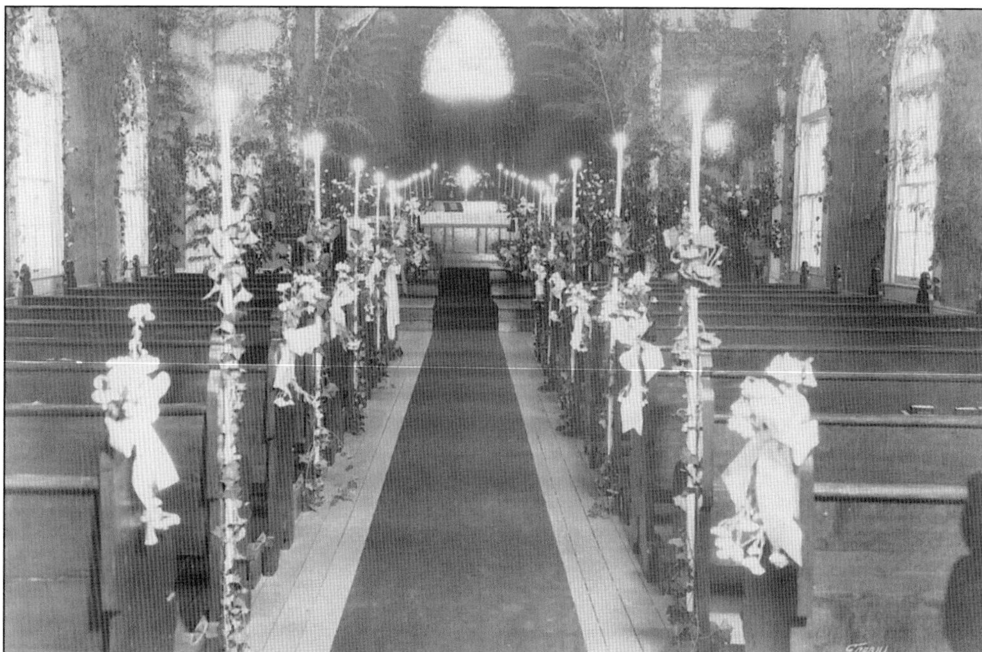

Shown is the interior of the St. John's Episcopal Church—built in the 1870s—decorated for the wedding of Treeby Miller and Harry Carter Andress in 1931. This church was located next to the 1909 Webster Parish Jail on South Broadway, or "Back Street," in Minden from the 1870s until the early 1950s. (Courtesy of Thad Andress.)

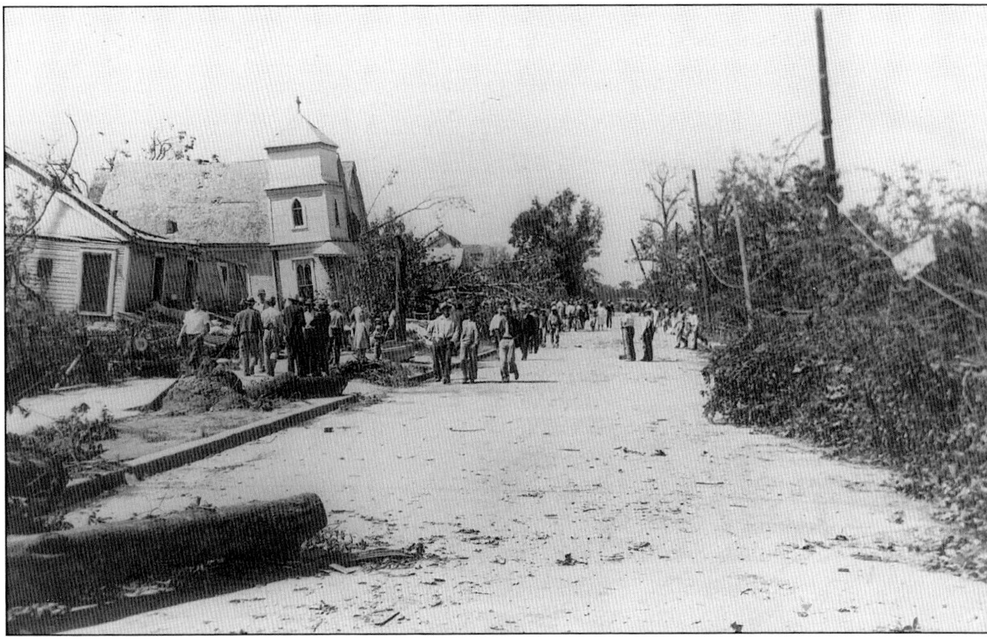

Shown in the aftermath of the powerful tornado of May 1, 1933, is the St. Anne's Catholic Church and the parish house next door. This picture was taken from behind the site of the current Webster Parish Courthouse at about the point where the tornado turned to the south and east.

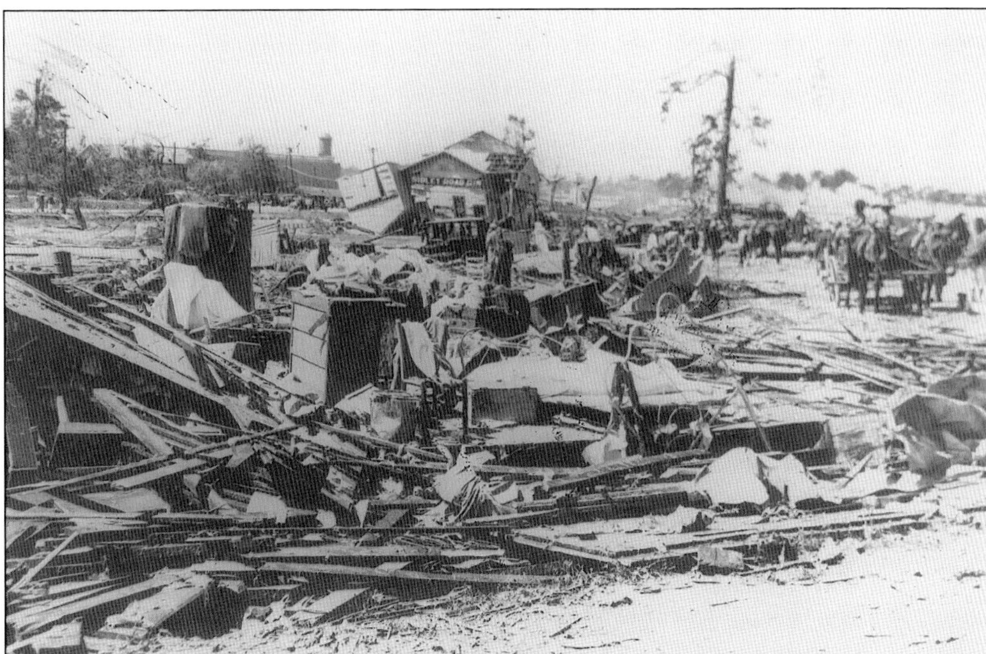

Above is a home on the Sibley Road demolished by the tornado. In the background, the Sibley Road Cotton Gin can be seen. Further in the background, the L&A Railroad shops can be seen, along with the water tower in the rail yard. The tornado killed at least 28 people, injured more than 400, and inflicted more than $1.25 million in damages.

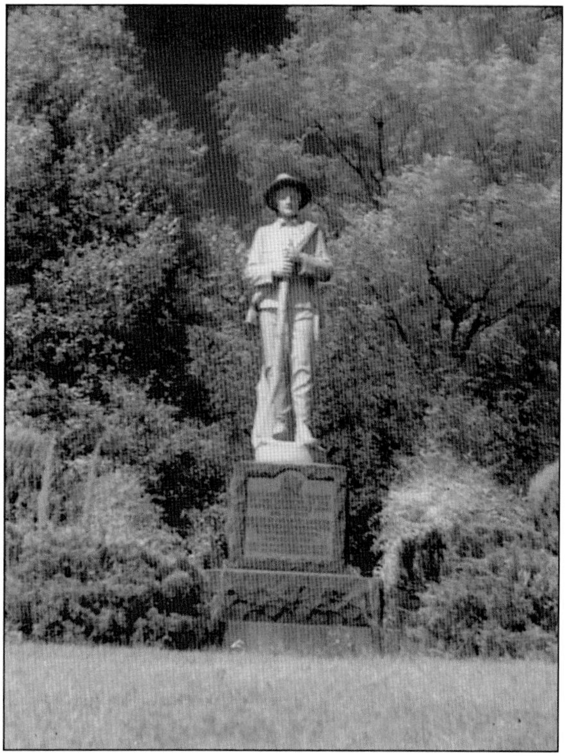

The Confederate Memorial Statue was erected by the United Daughters of the Confederacy in January 1933. This picture was taken after the May 1, 1933 tornado, as the storm toppled the statue from its base and broke the bayonet off the gun the soldier is holding. Notice the missing bayonet in this picture.

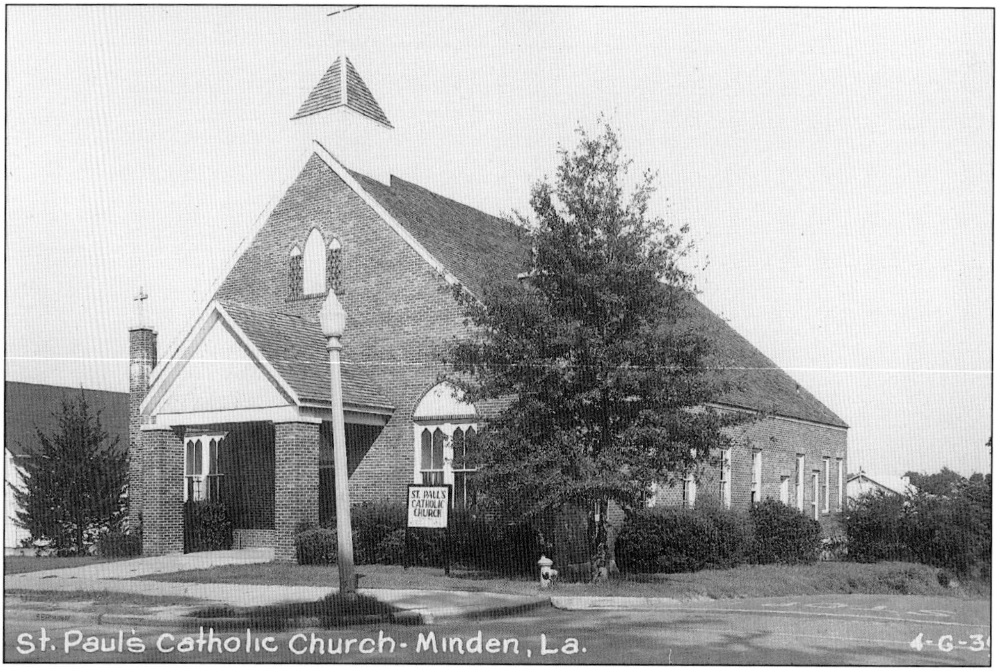

St. Paul's Catholic Church was constructed at the corner of Miller and South Broadway to replace the old St. Anne's Church that was destroyed by the tornado. The church occupied this site until recent years, when it relocated. It sat on the site of the original First Baptist Church, constructed *c.* 1846. (Courtesy of George Calvit.)

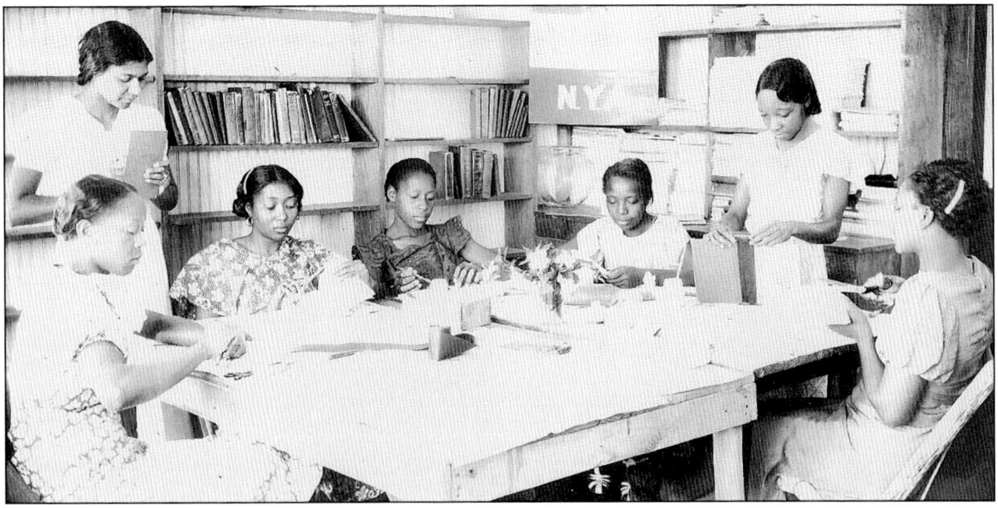

The National Youth Administration book repair project was held at the Webster Training School, forerunner of Webster High School. This was one of the many New Deal programs that provided income for parish residents during the years of the Great Depression.

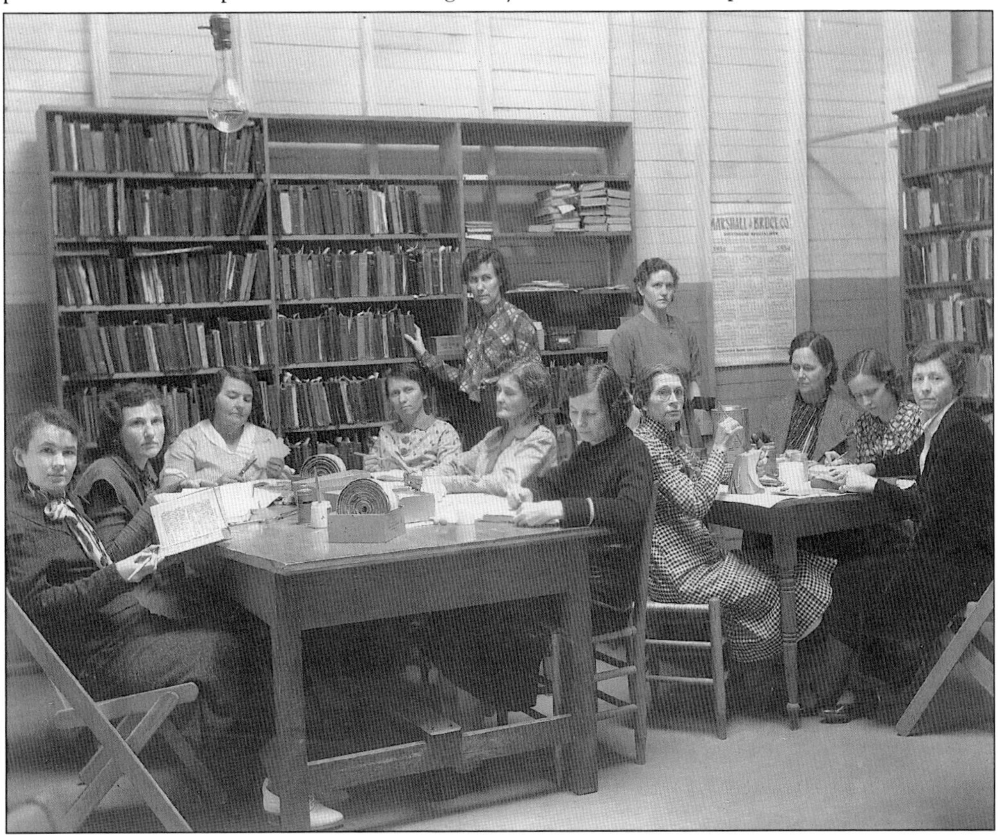

Pictured is another book-binding project for ladies, sponsored by the Works Progress Administration in 1934. This project continued for several years and was conducted in several different locations as the government attempted to provide income by paying the unemployed to accomplish needed tasks.

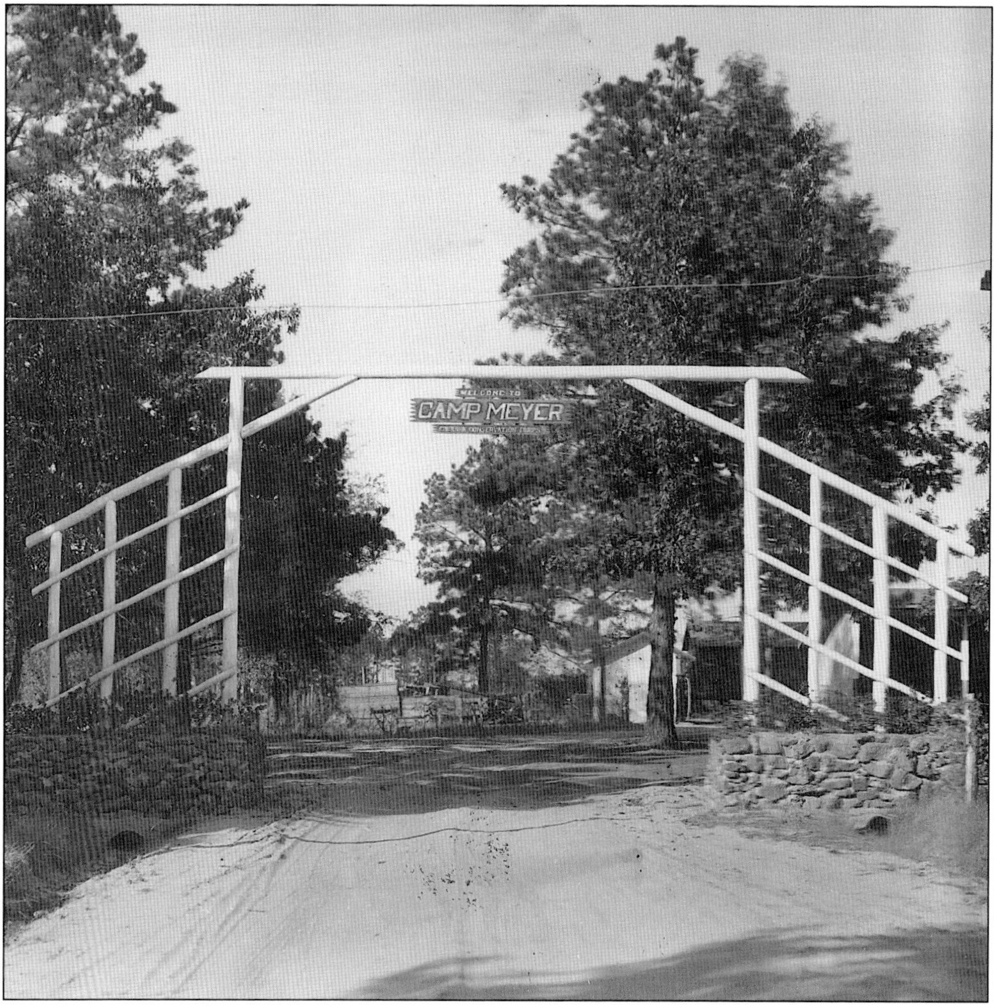

Another New Deal program that benefited Minden was the Civilian Conservation Corps (CCC). This is a picture of the front gate of Minden's CCC installation, Camp Meyer. The camp operated for several years. Its first occupants were given a rapid introduction to Southern life, as they were brought from New Jersey to work on the various reforestation and soil conservation projects of the CCC. Today the North Louisiana Technical College is located on the site of Camp Meyer.

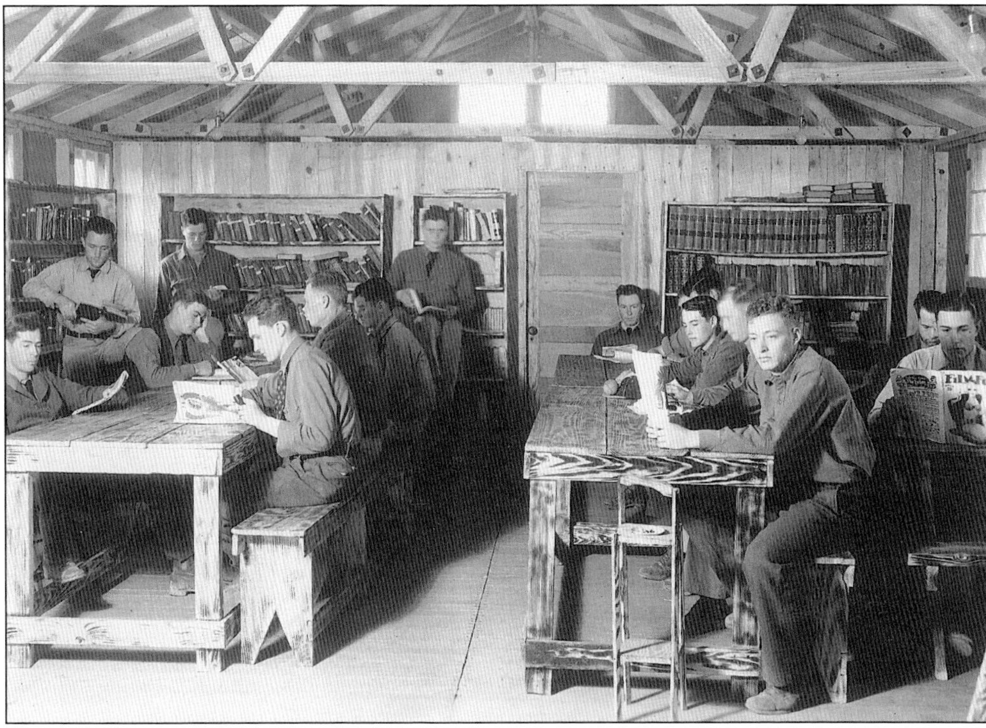

Among the entertainment opportunities provided for the cadets at Camp Meyer was a reading room. In this image, taken about 1936, more than a dozen cadets are taking advantage of the facility to pass the time reading, or at least have been told to pose as if they are reading.

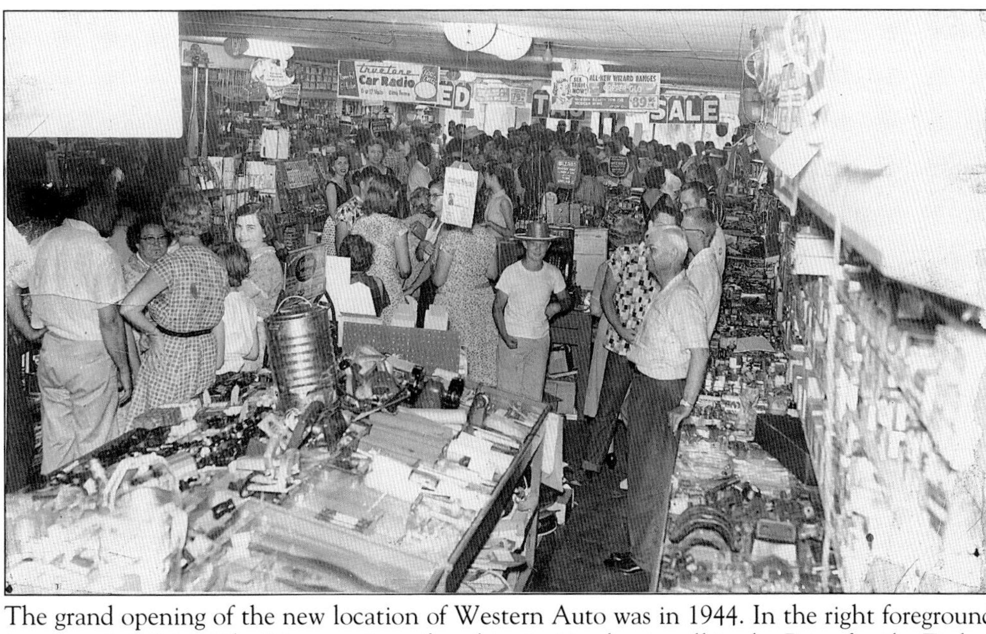

The grand opening of the new location of Western Auto was in 1944. In the right foreground is owner A.J. Price. The Western Auto franchise in Minden is still in the Price family. Today, it is operated by his grandson, John Price Collins. In addition, the Western Auto franchise in Springhill, in northern Webster Parish, is held by A.J. Price Jr. (Courtesy of John Collins.)

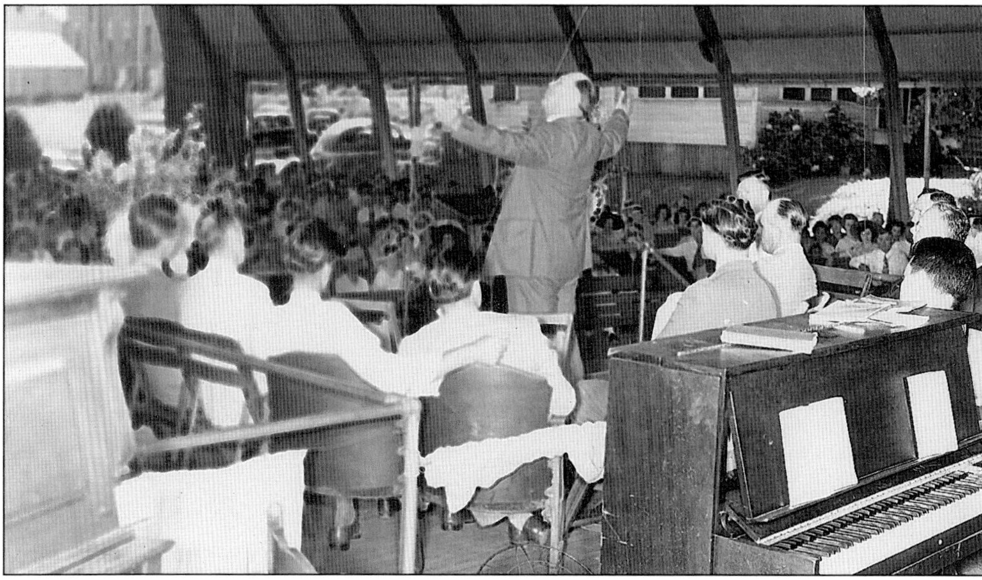

The Ferguson Memorial Tabernacle of the First Baptist Church is shown during a revival service in the 1930s. The tabernacle was used for Sunday evening church services, revivals, special events, and town meetings. It was the largest structure of its type in the world when it was built in 1927, after the funds were donated by Mrs. Nancy Mullins Ferguson. The tabernacle was torn down in 1977 during construction of the fourth home of the First Baptist Church. (Courtesy of Paul and Bertha Mae Mattingly.)

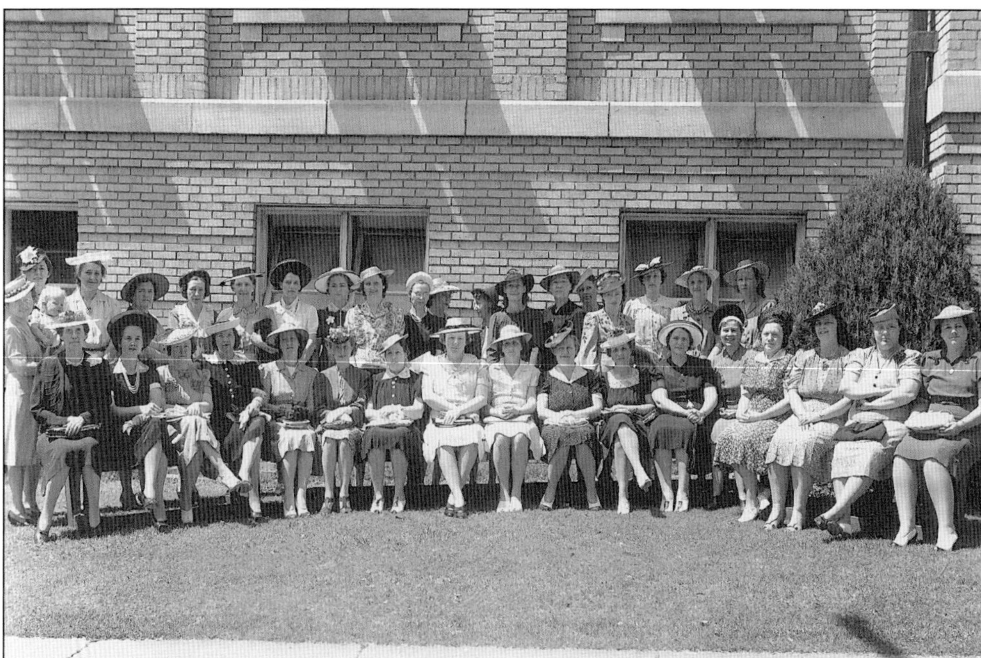

A group of ladies from the First Baptist Church of Minden are pictured on May 17, 1941. They are gathered on the First Street side of the 1925 building. The open windows on the second floor are in the church auditorium. (Courtesy of George Calvit.)

A shoeshine boy is pictured on the streets of Minden in the 1930s. Street vendors with regular locations were rather common in that era. Several other individuals, including Jack Jarrell and a Mr. Green, sold peanuts and popcorn while Jim Lyons sold his famous hot tamales on the streets in those years. (Courtesy of Lonnie Maddry.)

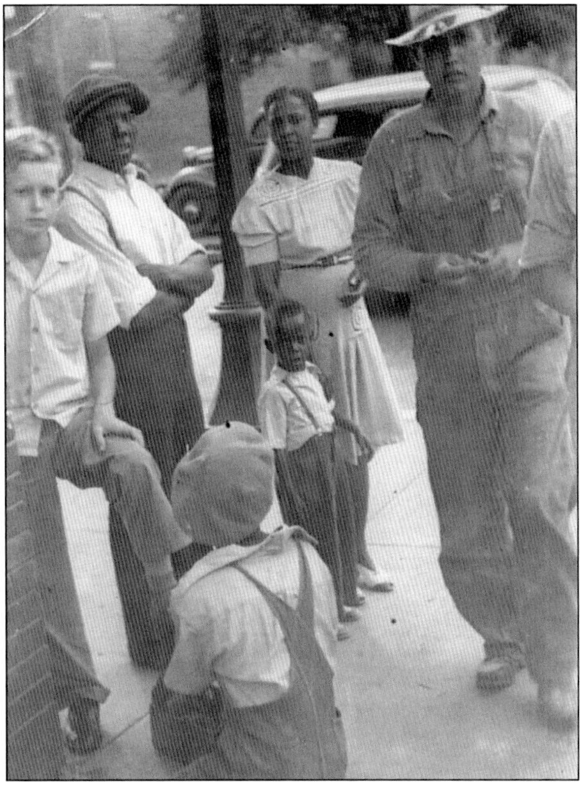

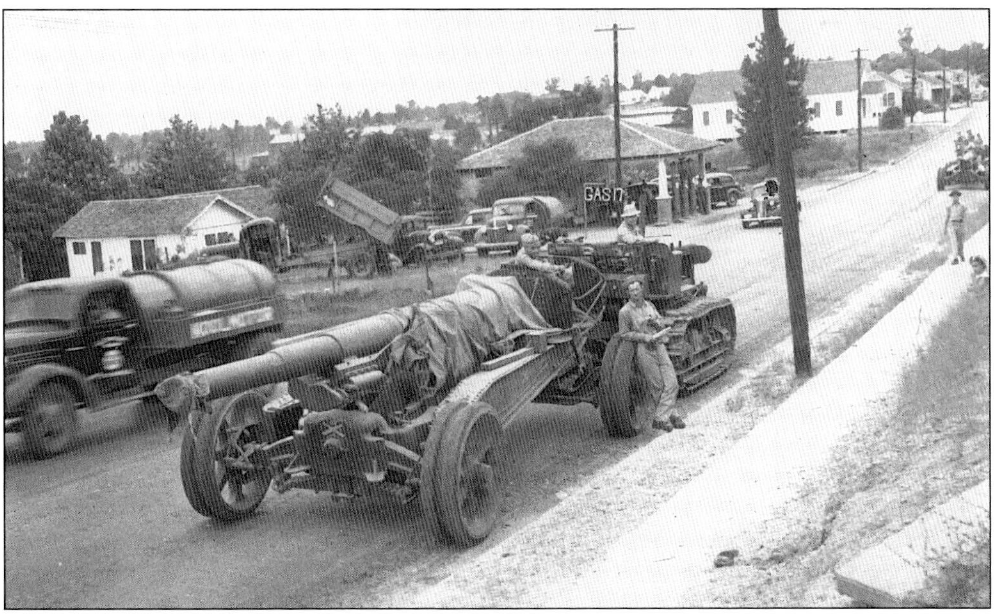

In June 1941, the troops of the Louisiana War Games or Maneuvers came through Minden. A convoy more than 50 miles long went through Minden on U.S. Highway 80, passing through downtown on the first day of the exercises. Among those in that convoy was Gen. George Patton. Pictured is an artillery piece parked on a Minden street as part of the convoy. (Courtesy of Lonnie Maddry.)

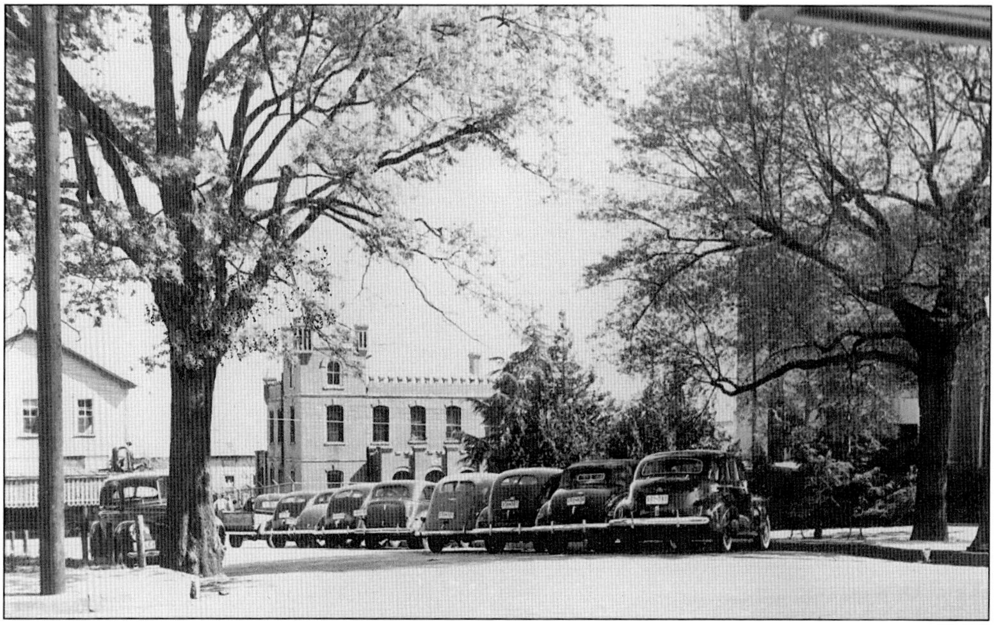

Shown here is the parking area between the Webster Parish Courthouse and the Minden Post Office in the 1930s. The 1909 Webster Parish Jail can be seen in the background. The tree in the right foreground was nicknamed the "Tree of Knowledge," as the benches under its branches were a favorite gathering place for older men of the town, who met there to "solve the problems of the world." The "Tree of Knowledge" was blown down during a spring thunderstorm in 1955.

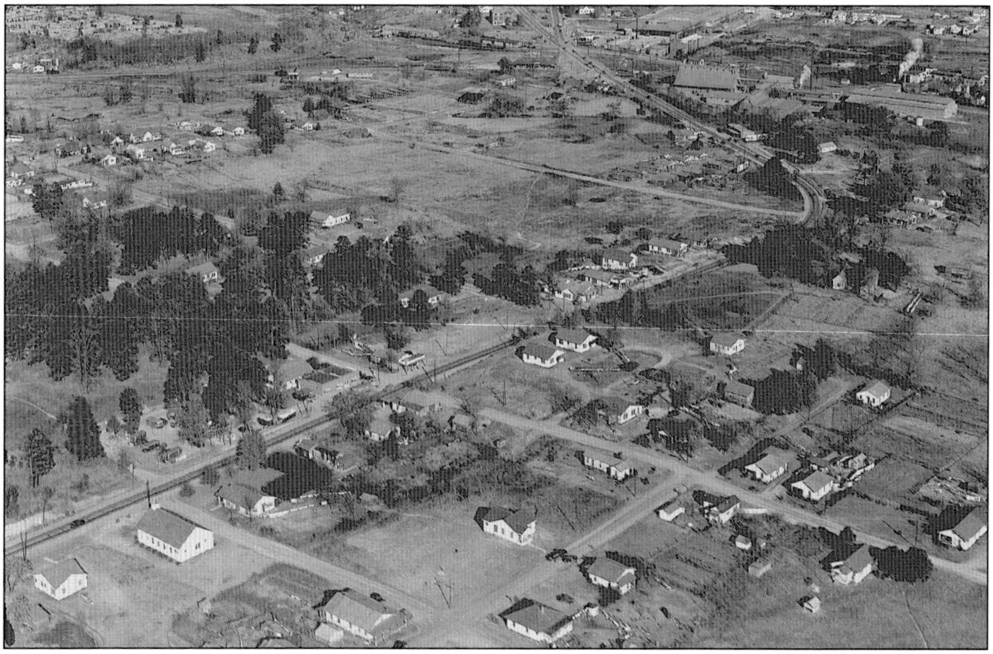

Here is an aerial view of Minden, taken from the west on December 13, 1941. Landmarks visible include the Minden Cotton Oil & Ice buildings at the right center, along the railroad tracks.

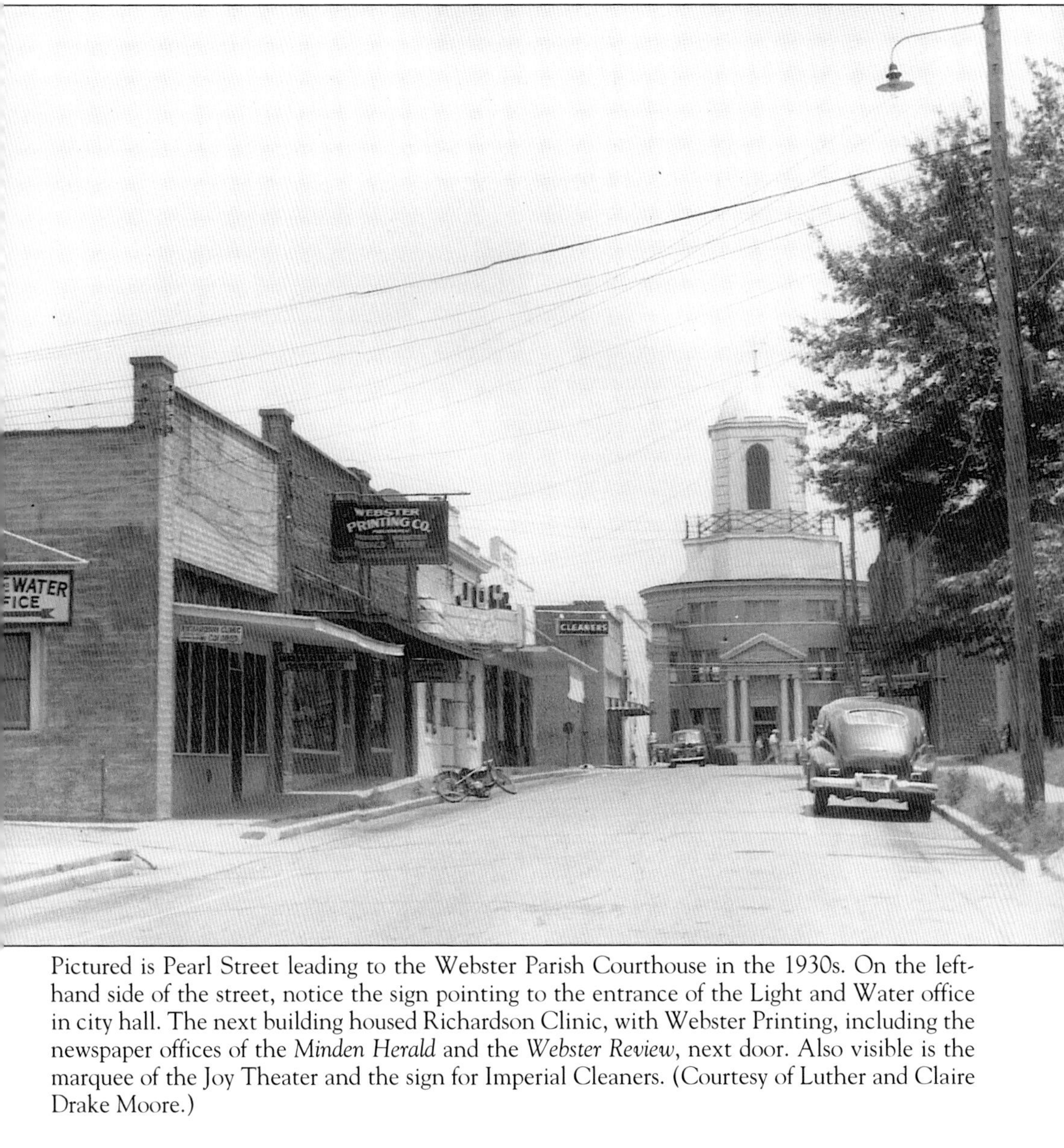

Pictured is Pearl Street leading to the Webster Parish Courthouse in the 1930s. On the left-hand side of the street, notice the sign pointing to the entrance of the Light and Water office in city hall. The next building housed Richardson Clinic, with Webster Printing, including the newspaper offices of the *Minden Herald* and the *Webster Review*, next door. Also visible is the marquee of the Joy Theater and the sign for Imperial Cleaners. (Courtesy of Luther and Claire Drake Moore.)

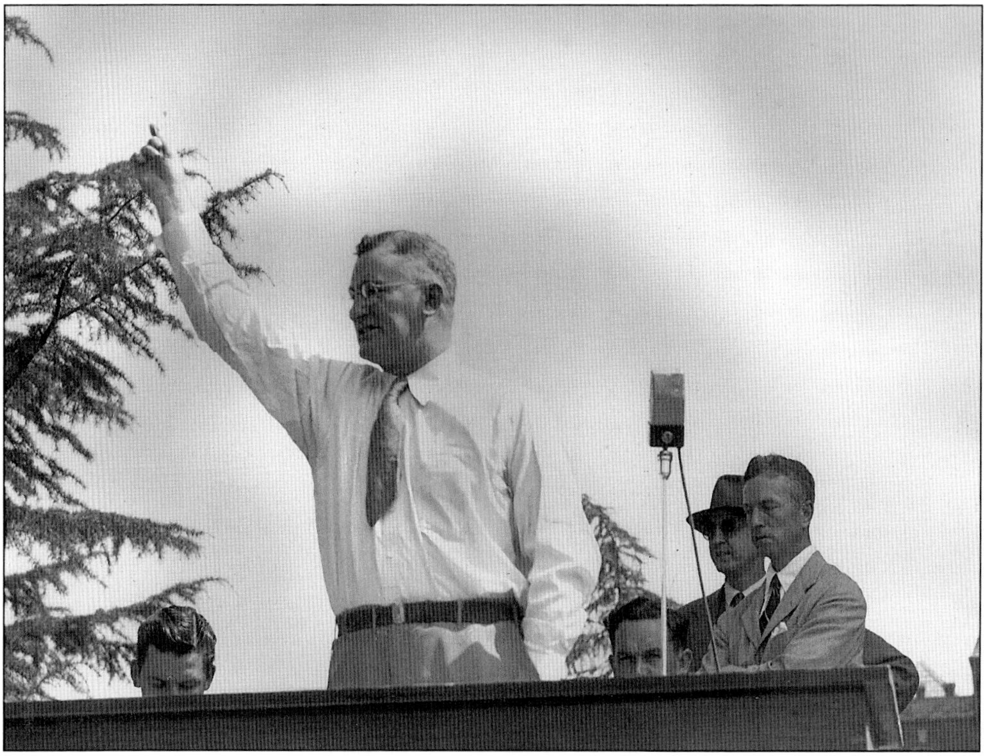

A war bond rally in Minden was held in 1943. Exhorting the crowd is Harry Andress, local Ford dealer. Among those visible in the background are local attorney Graydon Kitchens Sr., in the hat and sun glasses, and Minden businessman Willard Roberts, to the left of Kitchens. (Courtesy of Thad Andress.)

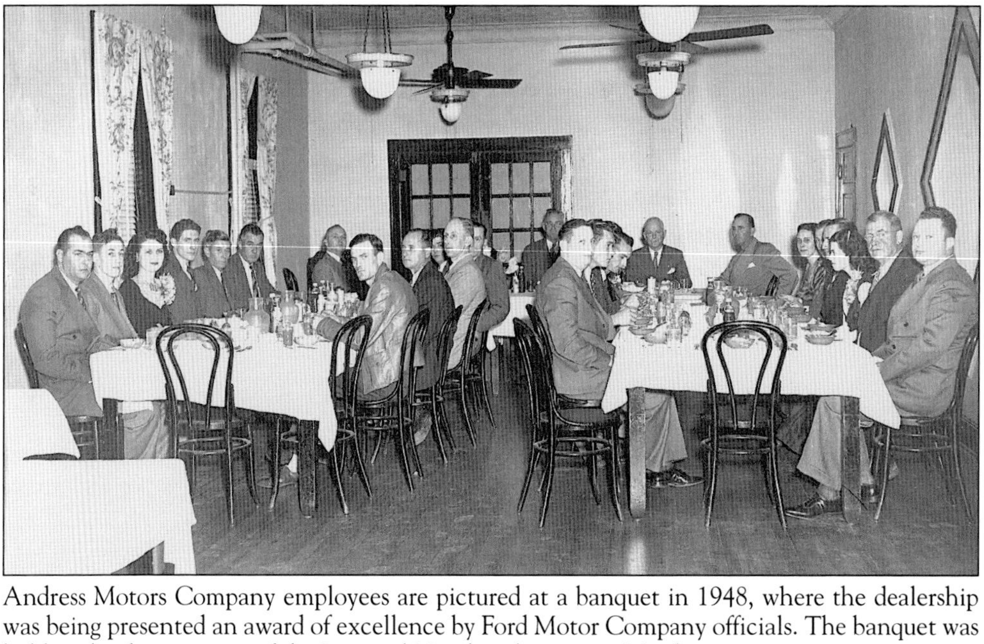

Andress Motors Company employees are pictured at a banquet in 1948, where the dealership was being presented an award of excellence by Ford Motor Company officials. The banquet was held in the dining room of the Imperial Hotel in downtown Minden.

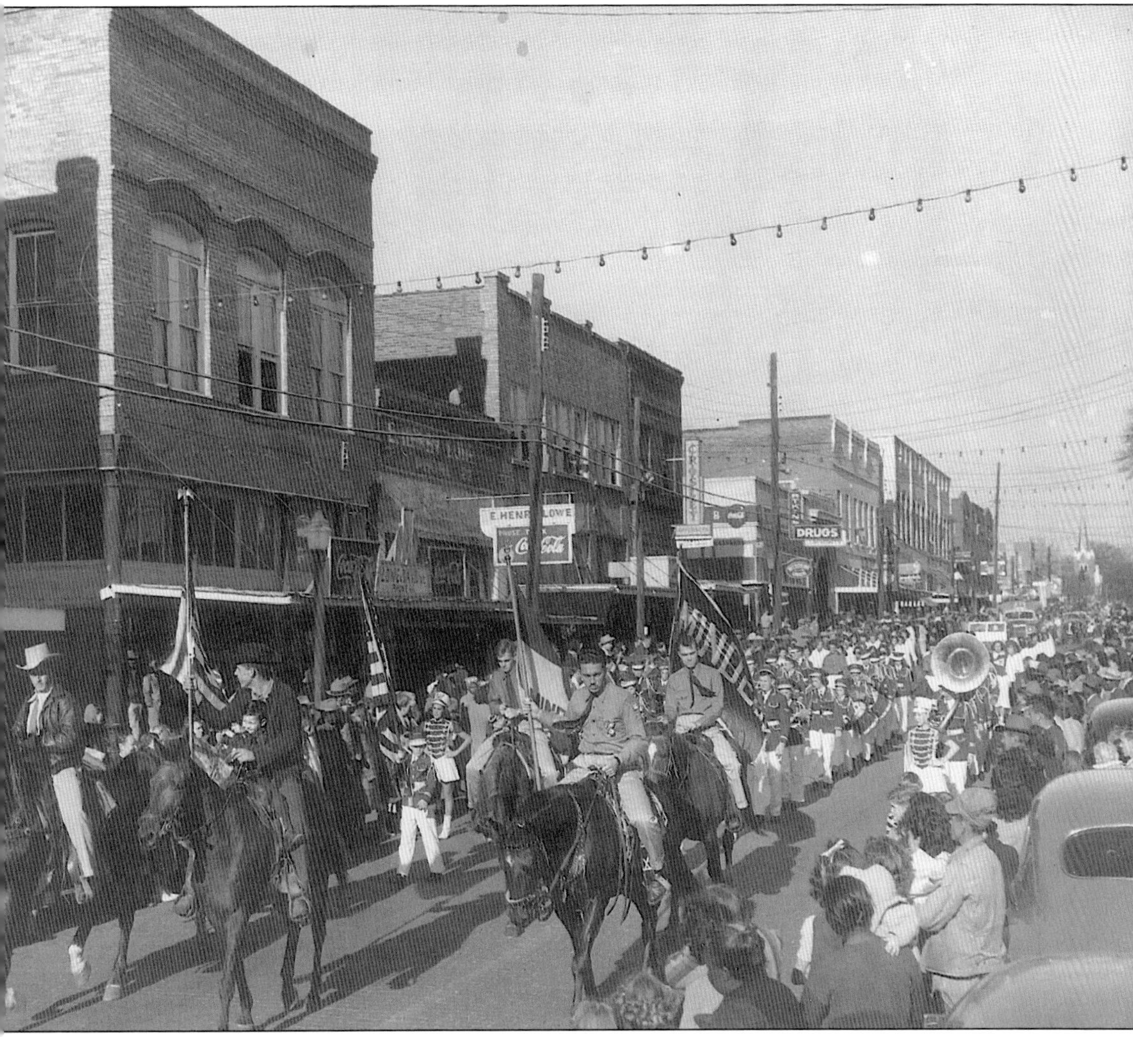

A parade in downtown Minden in the late 1940s is pictured. The Minden Riding Club is leading the parade, followed by the Minden High School band. The picture was taken on North Broadway in the block between Pearl and Pine Street. In addition to the signs for the long vanished businesses on the left, the steeple of the 1905 First Methodist Church is visible in the extreme background. (Courtesy of Luther and Claire Drake Moore.)

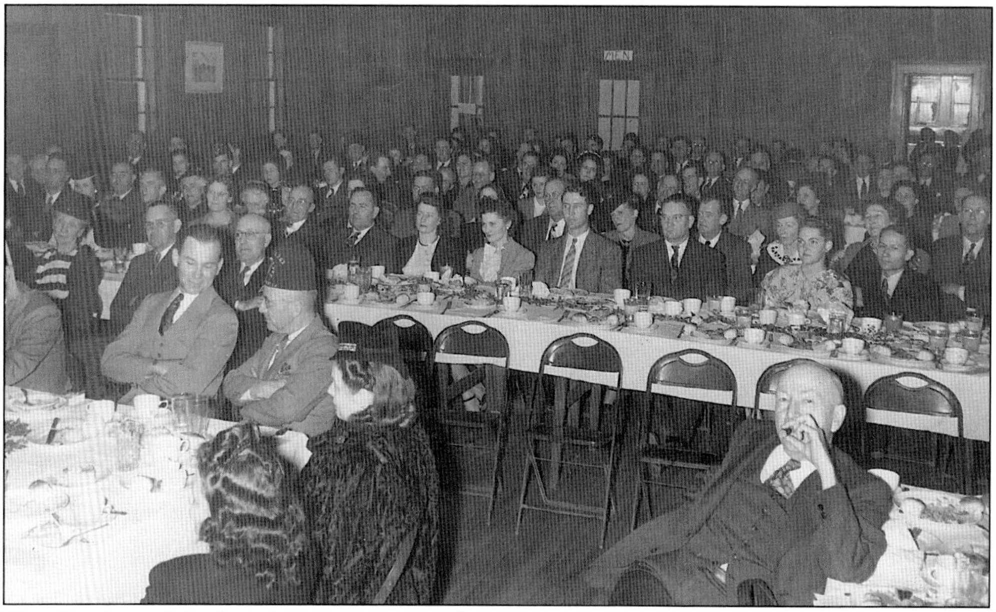

The Knights of Pythias banquet was held in the Minden Community House, located in Victory Park, in about 1950. At the right front, with the cigar, is Judge J. Frank McInnis. He served as Webster Parish clerk of court in the early 1920s, while reading law at night. After being admitted to the bar, he rose to a position as a court of appeals judge. (Courtesy of George Calvit.)

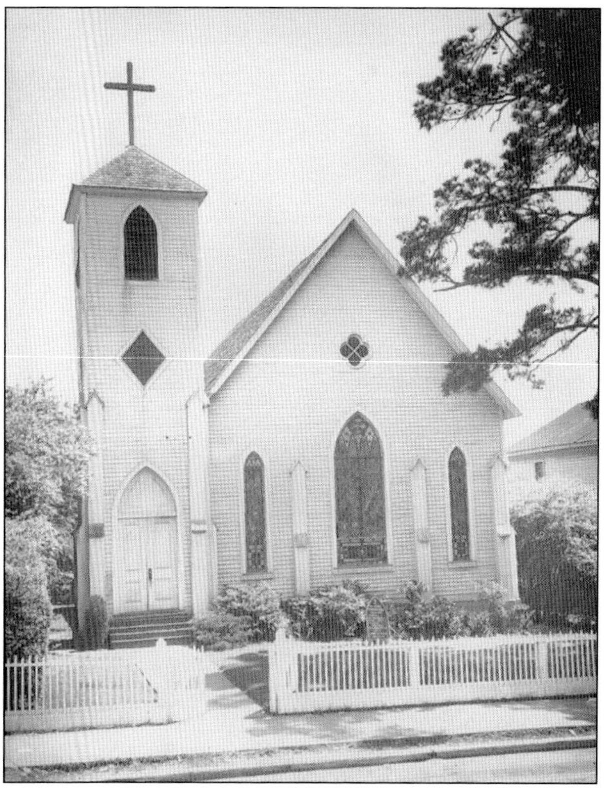

The old St. John's Episcopal Church was located behind the Minden Post Office on South Broadway. This church was built in the 1870s and was used until about 1950. The earlier image of the decorations for the Miller-Andress pictured the interior of this church. (Courtesy of Charles Alden and Mary Rathbun.)

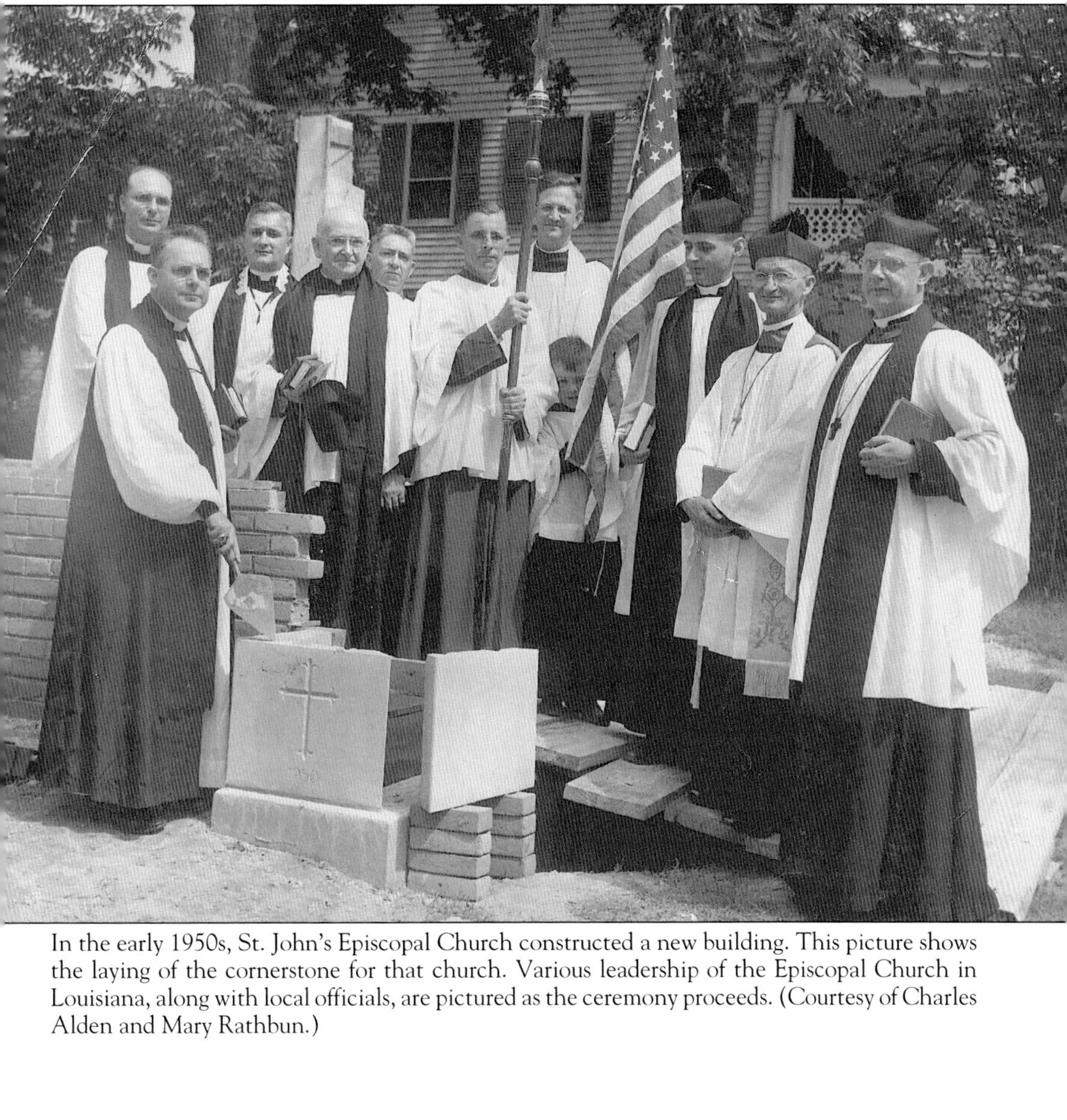

In the early 1950s, St. John's Episcopal Church constructed a new building. This picture shows the laying of the cornerstone for that church. Various leadership of the Episcopal Church in Louisiana, along with local officials, are pictured as the ceremony proceeds. (Courtesy of Charles Alden and Mary Rathbun.)

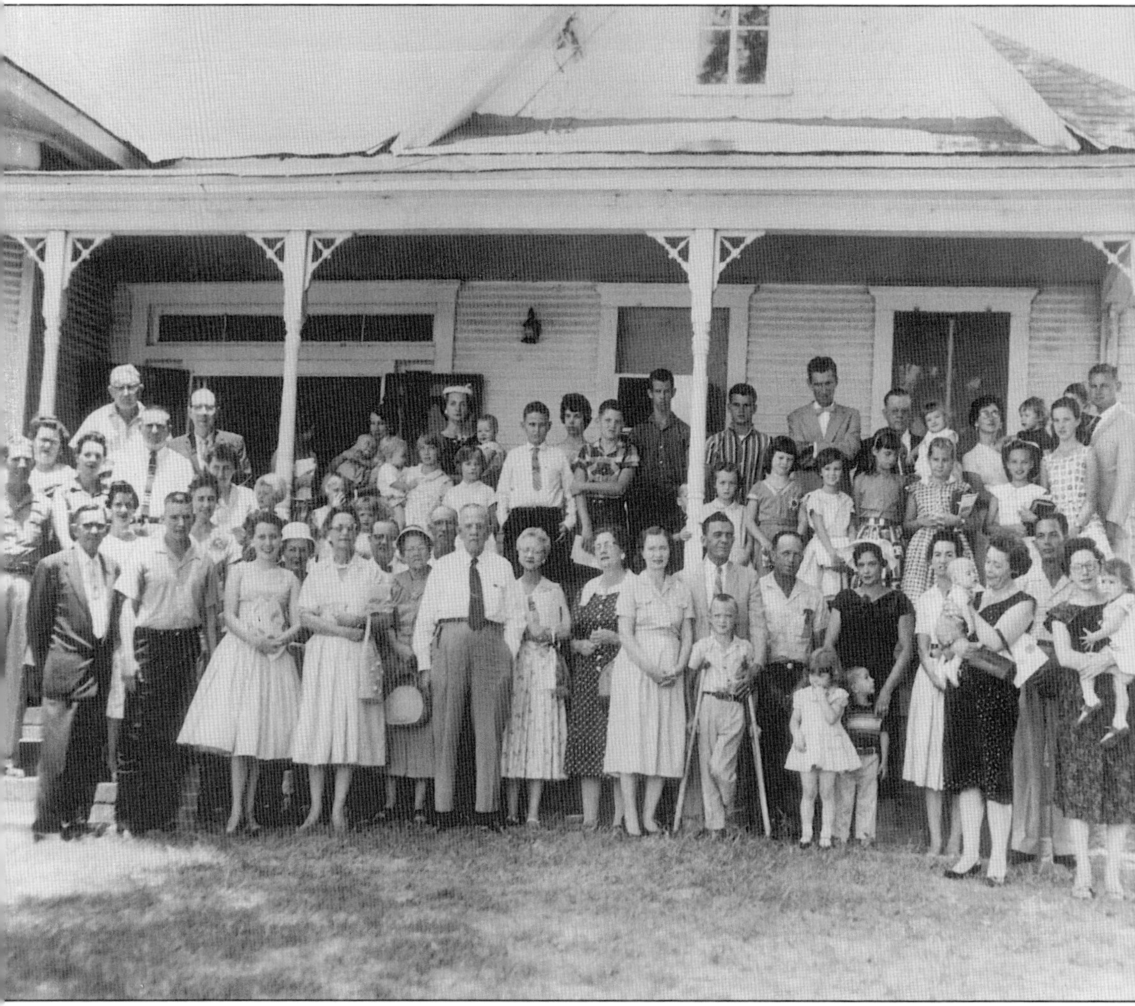

On June 4, 1959, charter members of the newly formed Emmanuel Baptist Church assumed ownership of their new church building, formerly the home of the Tom David family, on the Homer Road in Minden. At the left-hand end of the front row is Rev. Tom Leachman, pastor of the new church. At the center front of the picture in the white shirt and tie is Tom David, former owner of the home. (Courtesy of Mrs. Melba Jones Lowery.)

Three

Business and Industry

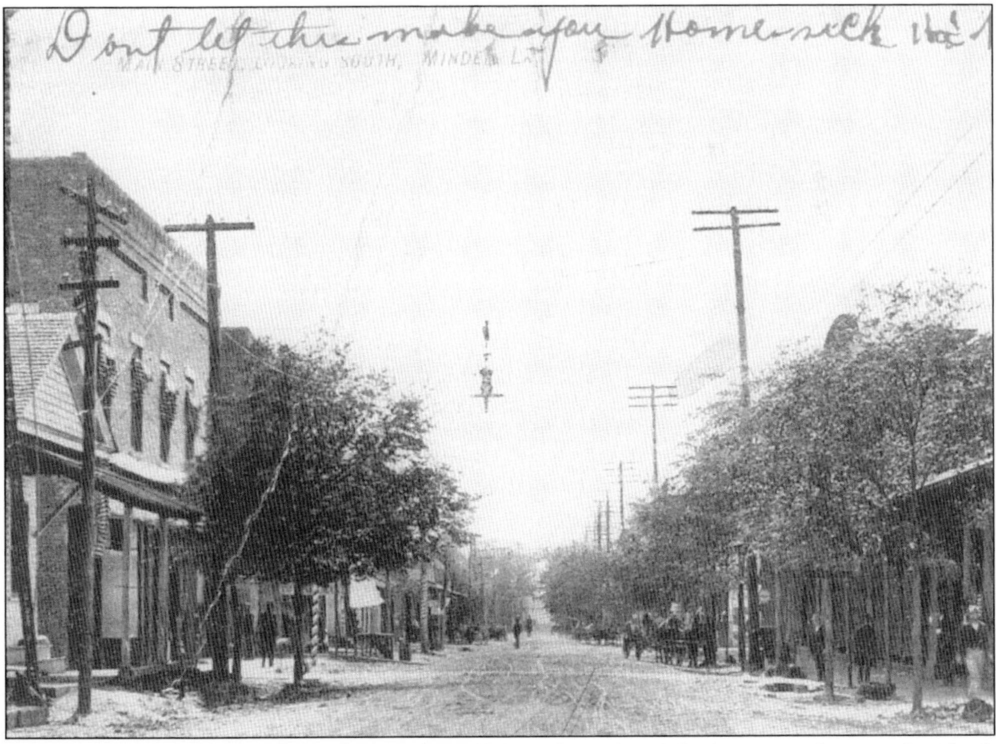

This 1880s street scene of North Broadway (Main Street) in Minden was taken in the block between today's Fogle Street and East Union. Visible in the left foreground is the store building owned by Drury Murrell, which served for many years as the lodge building of the Knights of Pythias and which still stands today. It has now been purchased and remodeled by the Mealey family. (Courtesy of Wanda Pittman.)

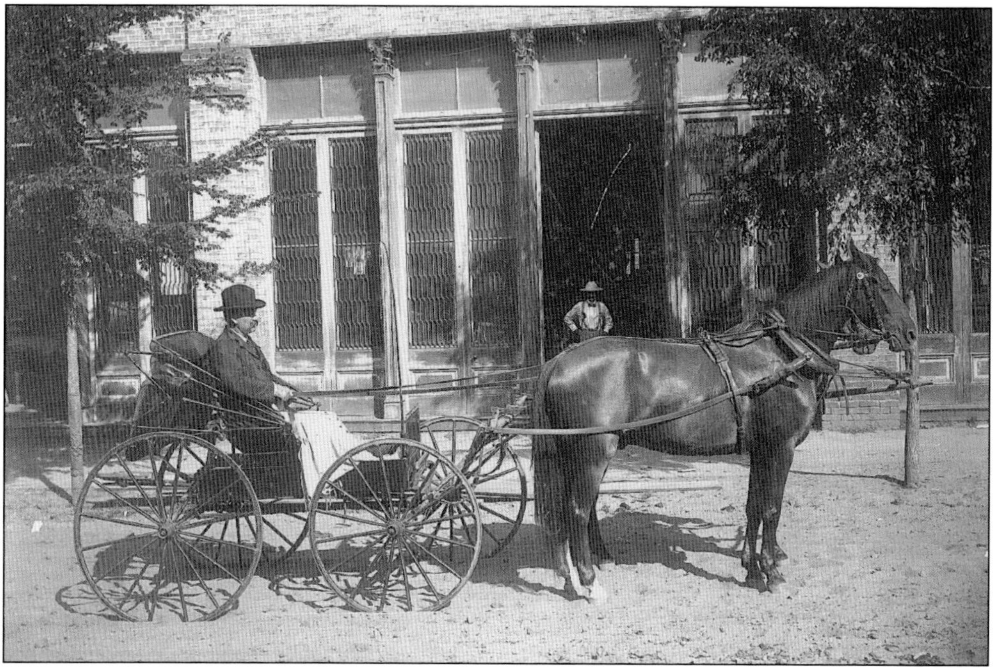

An unknown man in a buggy is pictured in front of the Goodwill Store in Minden in about 1900. Owned by Capt. Alfred Goodwill, great-grandfather of Louisiana governor Mike Foster, the store had the largest square footage of any in Louisiana when it was opened in 1880. It was the "super store" of its day. It included a pharmacy and offered everything from clothing to buggies and hardware to coffins and funeral services.

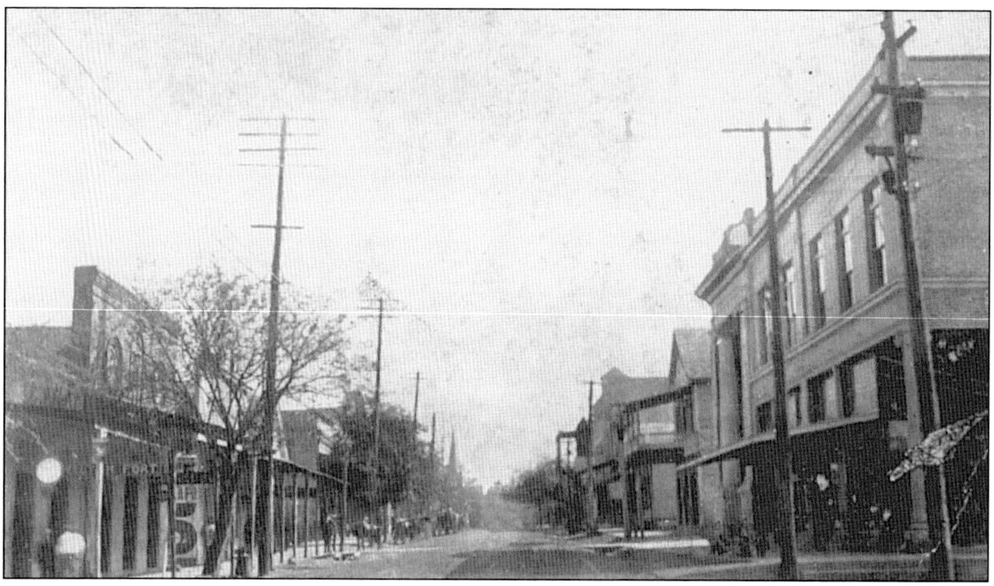

Pictured is North Broadway in Minden in the late 1890s, looking north from East Union Street. The Bank of Webster building is visible as the second building on the right of the picture. Again, notice the large number of frame buildings, many of which would be destroyed in fires by 1902, when any further frame structures in downtown were banned. (Courtesy of Frank Griffith.)

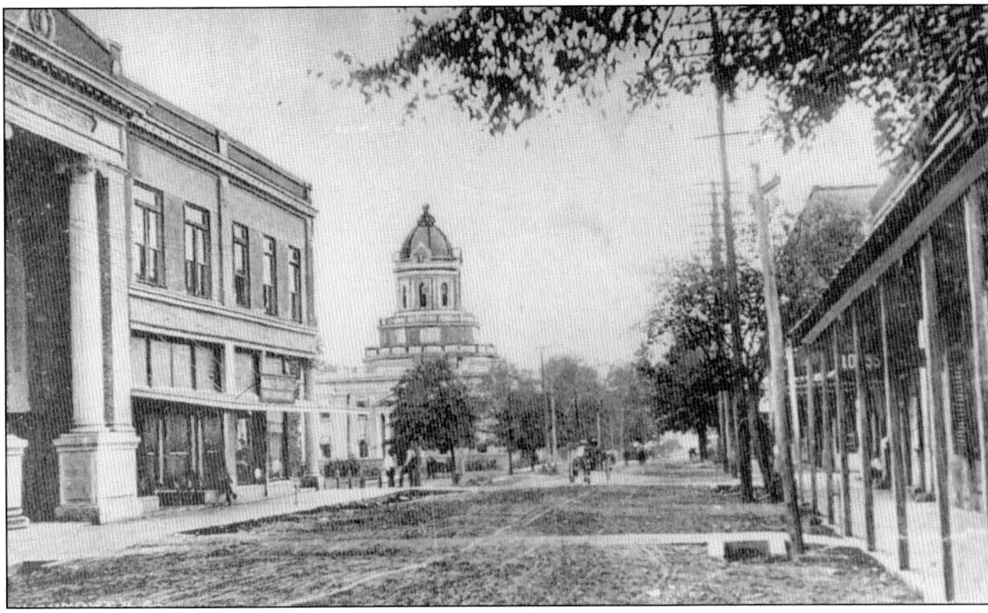

Here is another view of North Broadway, taken between 1905 and 1916. The Bank of Webster building is again visible in the left foreground. The vacant area between the business structures and the 1905 Webster Parish Courthouse had been the site of the 1872 courthouse and would become the location of the 1916 post office. Notice the raised wooden walkway over the muddy streets in the foreground. (Courtesy of Wanda Pittman.)

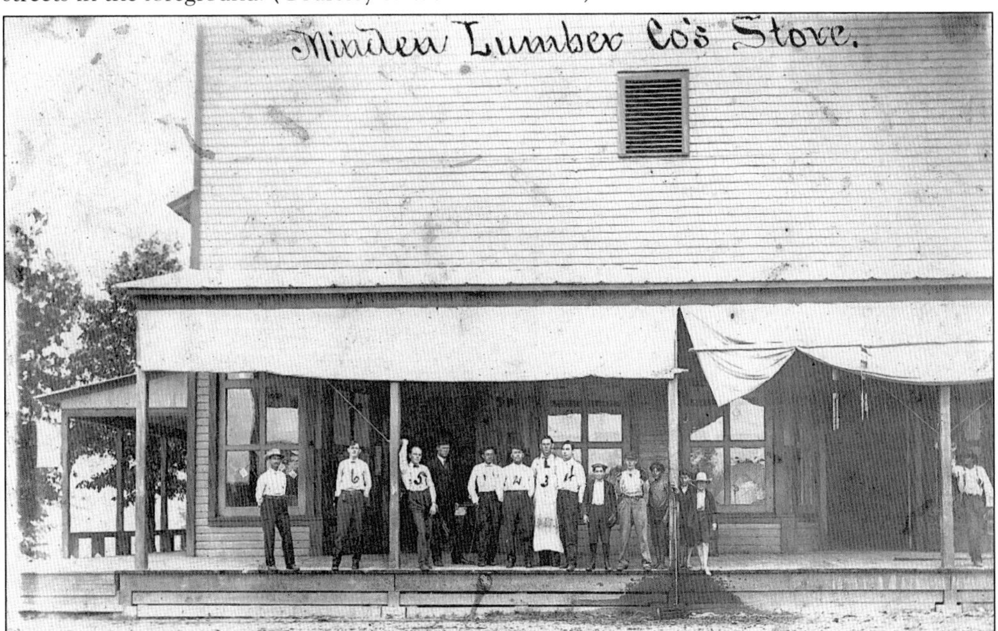

Shown is the commissary of the Minden Lumber Company in a picture taken on May 10, 1907. The numbered individuals are as follows: 1) E.L. "Bud" Taylor, manager; 2) H.M. Jones; 3) A.H. Hubbard, butcher; 4) F.B. Overstreet, bookkeeper; 5) Leroy Rathbun, dry goods department; and 6) G. Alden Rathbun, gentlemen's department. G. Alden Rathbun later became clerk of court of Webster Parish. (Courtesy of Charles Alden and Mary Rathbun.)

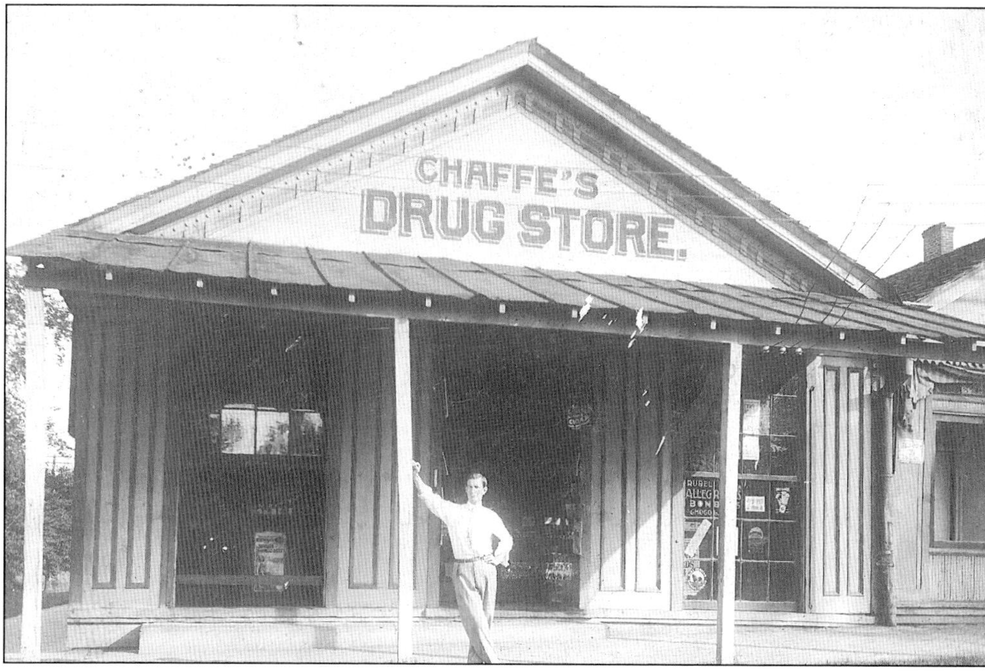

Chaffe's Drug Store stood for many years on the corner of Pine and North Broadway and marked the unofficial west end of the business district. In addition to its business function, the Minden Post Office was located in the building for several years around the turn of the 20th century, before the first officially designated post office building was built in 1916. (Courtesy of Charles Alden and Mary Rathbun.)

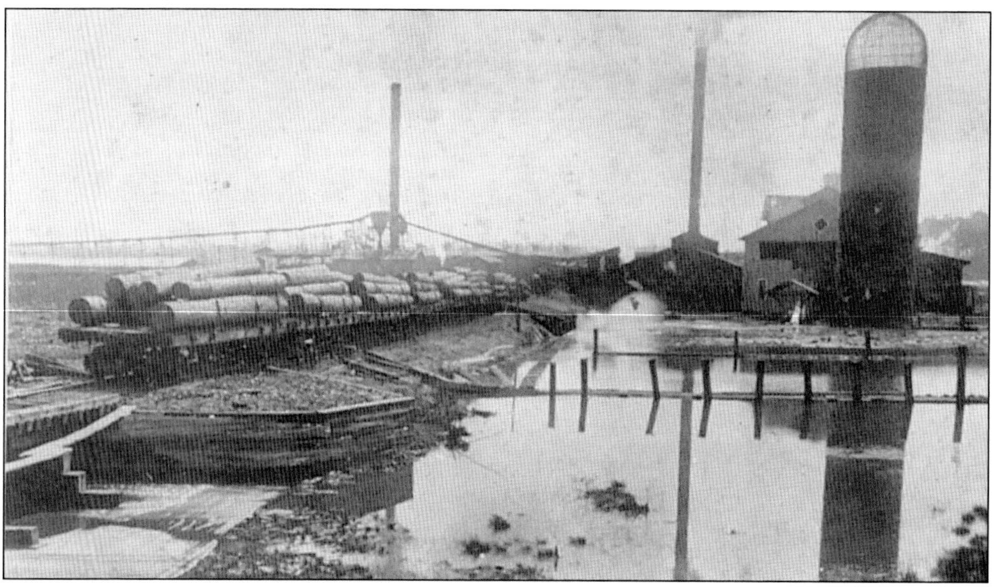

Built in 1901, the Minden Lumber Mill of the Bodcau Lumber Company was the leading industry in Minden for nearly 20 years, and was one of the largest capacity mills in the world. It provided electric lights for the city and led to the addition of natural gas service to the town. When the mill was destroyed by a mysterious fire in May of 1918, the economic life of Minden was severely impacted. (Courtesy of Frank Griffith.)

Pictured are the front display windows of Webb Hardware in Minden in the early 1900s, including the peanut vending wagon at the right foreground. Webb Hardware opened in 1890 and served the Minden community for nearly 100 years. At the far left in the hat is Will Life, longtime manager and, for many years, owner of the company. (Courtesy of John S. and Lillian Life Willis.)

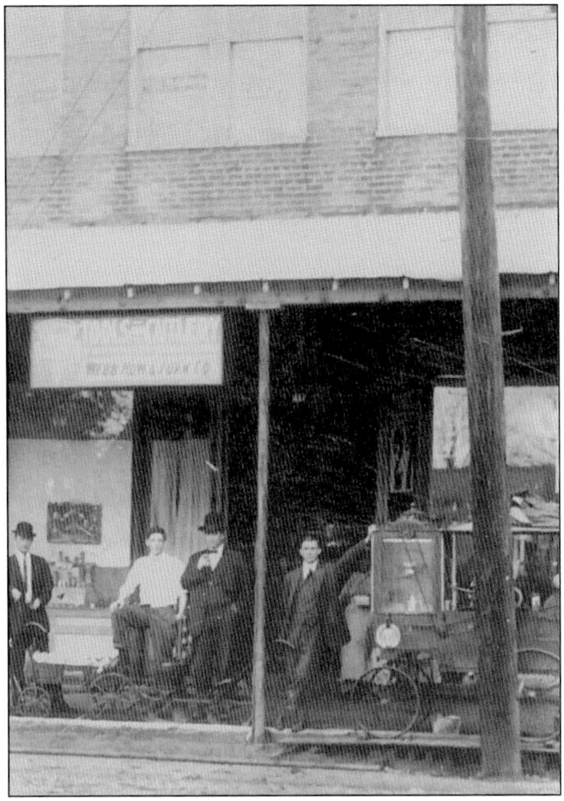

Here is an interior view of Webb Hardware in the early 1920s. Pictured from left to right are Will Life, his brother, Sam Life, and an unidentified hardware salesman. Notice the glass display cases, the many hardware drawers, and the upstairs gallery of the structure. (Courtesy of John S. and Lillian Life Willis.)

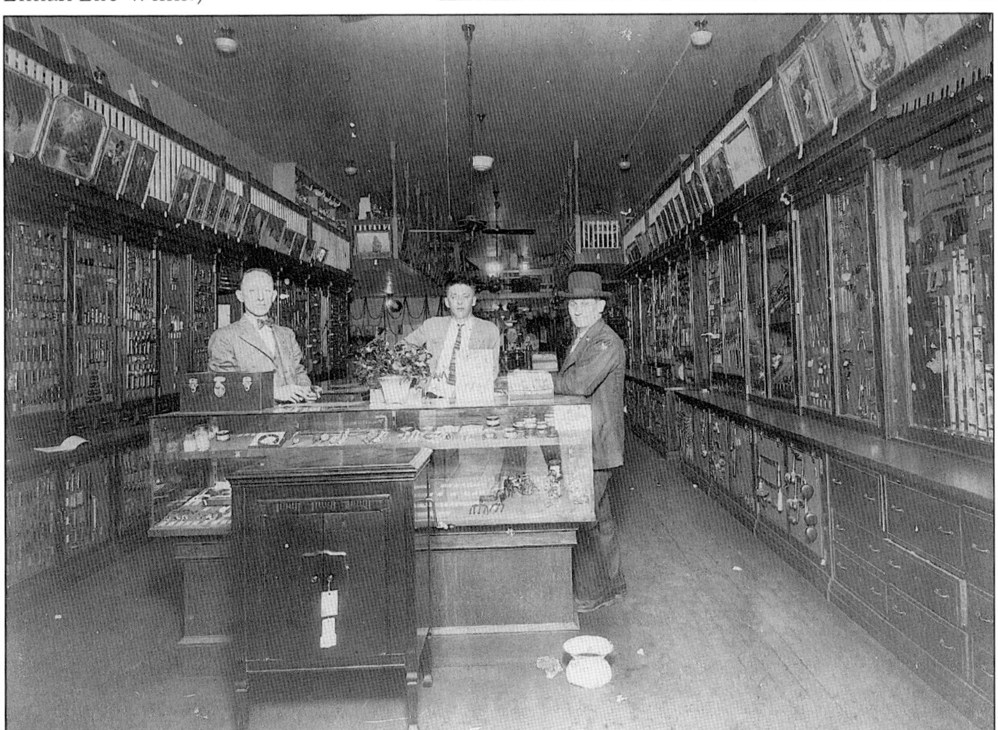

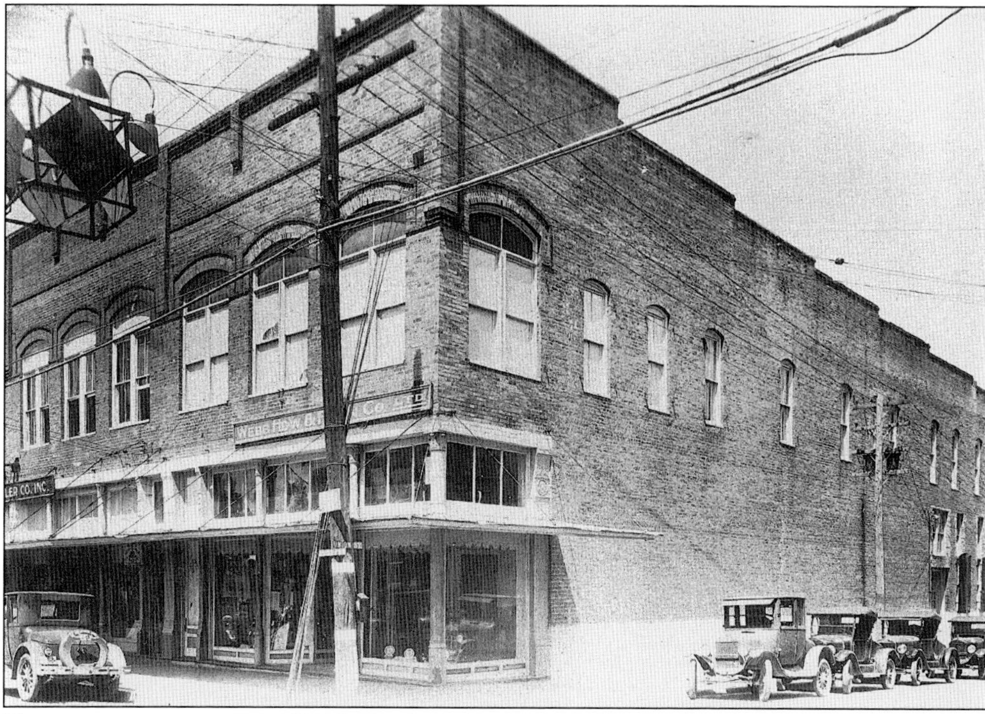

Here is an exterior view of Webb Hardware in 1925. In later years, display windows would be added along the Union Street side of the building where the row of vintage automobiles are parked in this image. (Courtesy of John S. and Lillian Life Willis.)

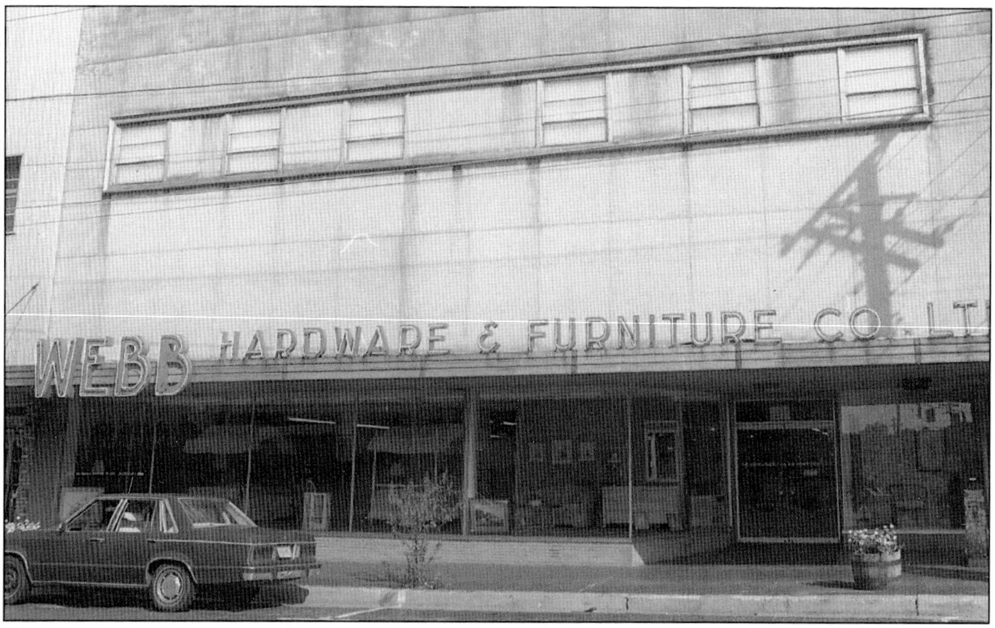

This image of the expanded storefront of Webb Hardware was taken in the 1970s. Eventually, Webb Hardware purchased the upper floors of the buildings to its west and had furniture display rooms that extended two-thirds of the distance down the block and three stories high. (Courtesy of John S. and Lillian Life Willis.)

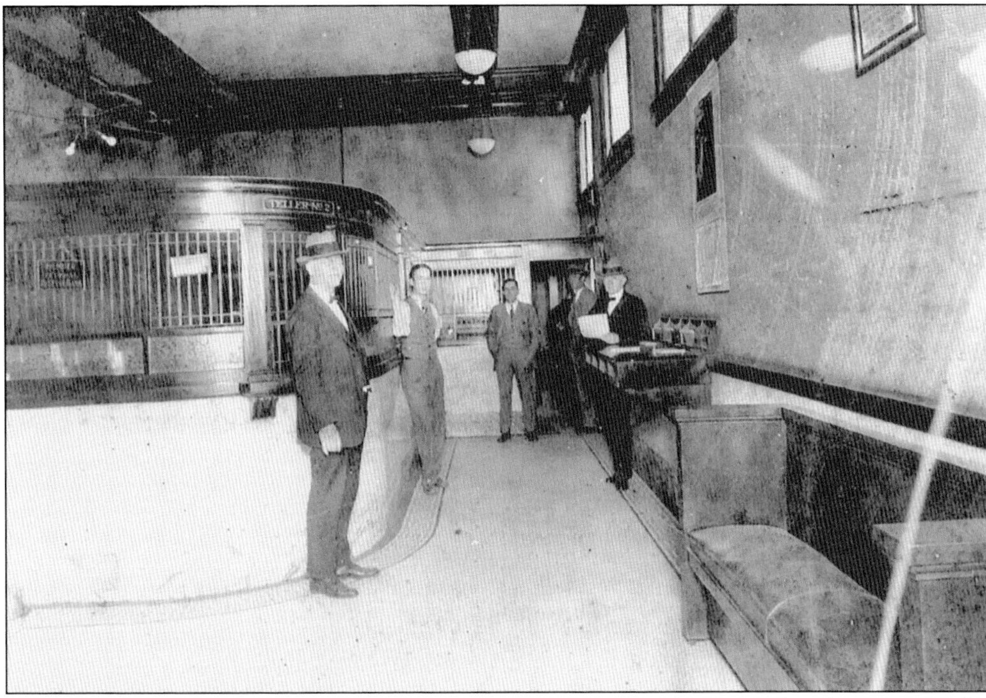

The First National Bank of Minden was founded in 1910 and remained in business until it failed and was acquired by the Bank of Webster in 1929. Through the years, various businesses, including appliance and drug stores, have been in the building. Today, it is occupied by Vivian's House of Fashion. This is an interior view of the bank taken about 1920. The man in the foreground is former Webster Parish sheriff B.F. Griffith. (Courtesy of Frank Griffith.)

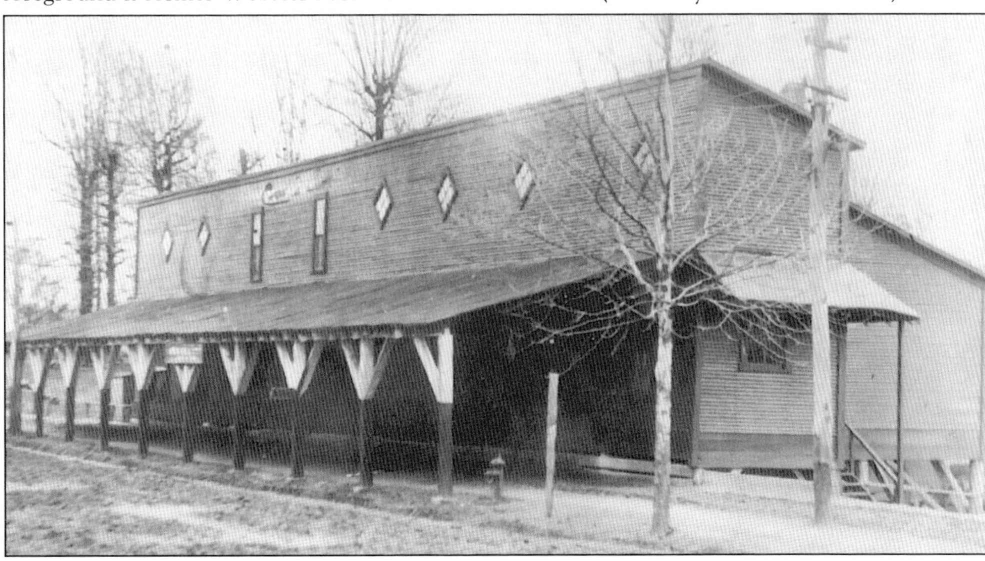

The 1914 bottling plant of the North Louisiana Bottling Works, Ltd., forerunner of the Minden Coca Cola Bottling Company, is pictured. The company, founded by W.S. Hunter in the early years of the 20th century, has remained in the Hunter family until the present. This plant was used until 1925 and also operated a gristmill and a wood yard through 1919. (Courtesy of Ben Hunter.)

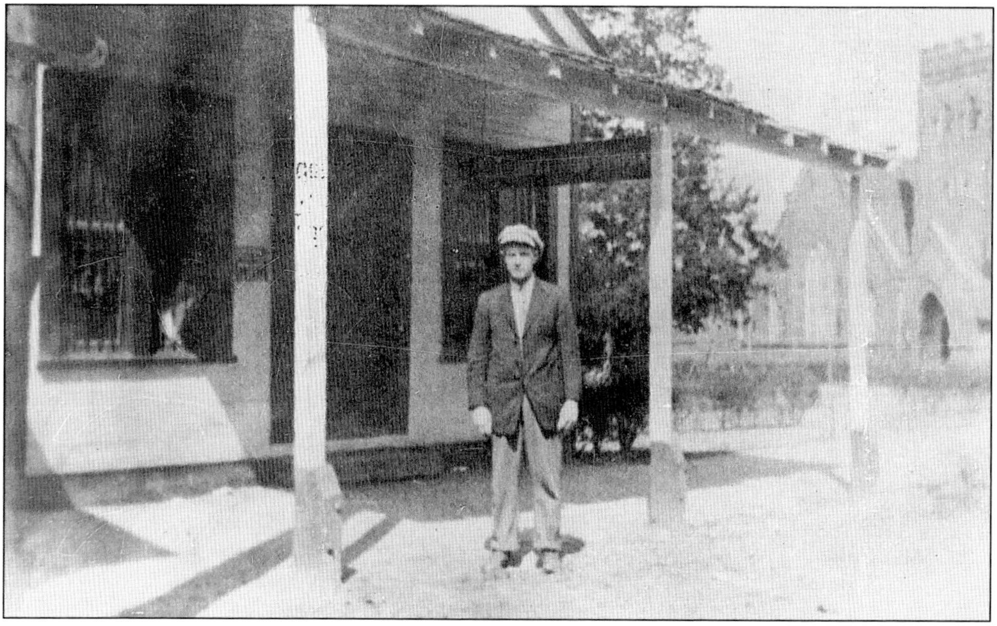

An Express Delivery boy is shown in front of the delivery office in about 1920. This site was later home to Fort's Newsstand, a Minden landmark for half a century. In the background is the 1902 building of the First Baptist Church, which was later converted into the Rex Theater, images of which are contained later in this book.

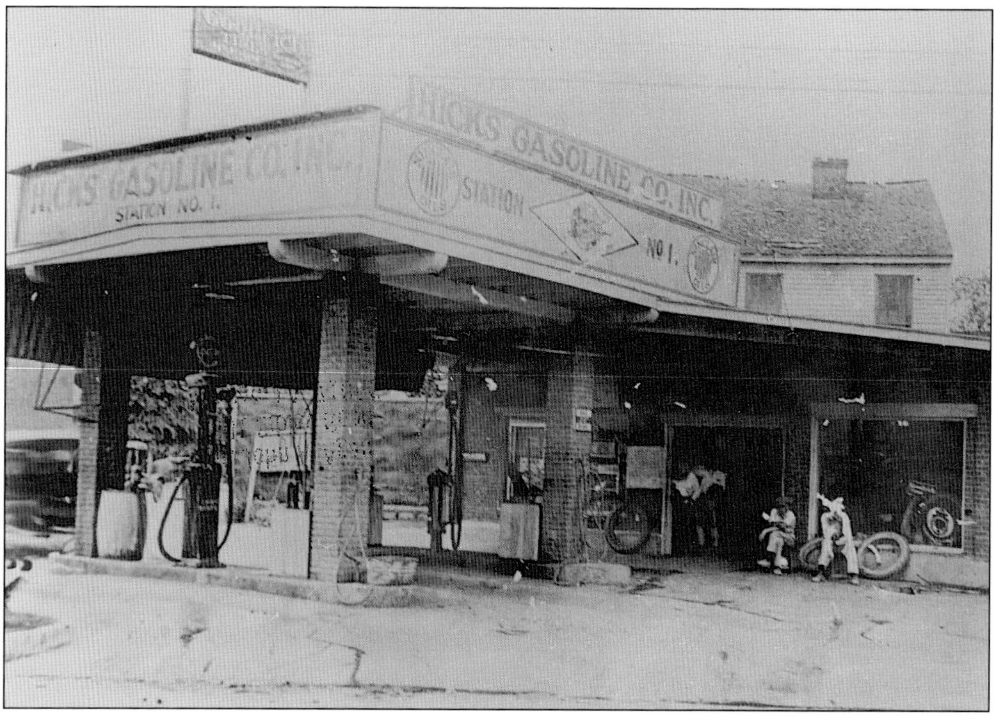

Hicks Gasoline Co., Station #1, the first service station in Minden, is pictured here. Prior to this time, gasoline was available from other sources, but this business, opened in 1922, was the first dedicated strictly to gasoline sales.

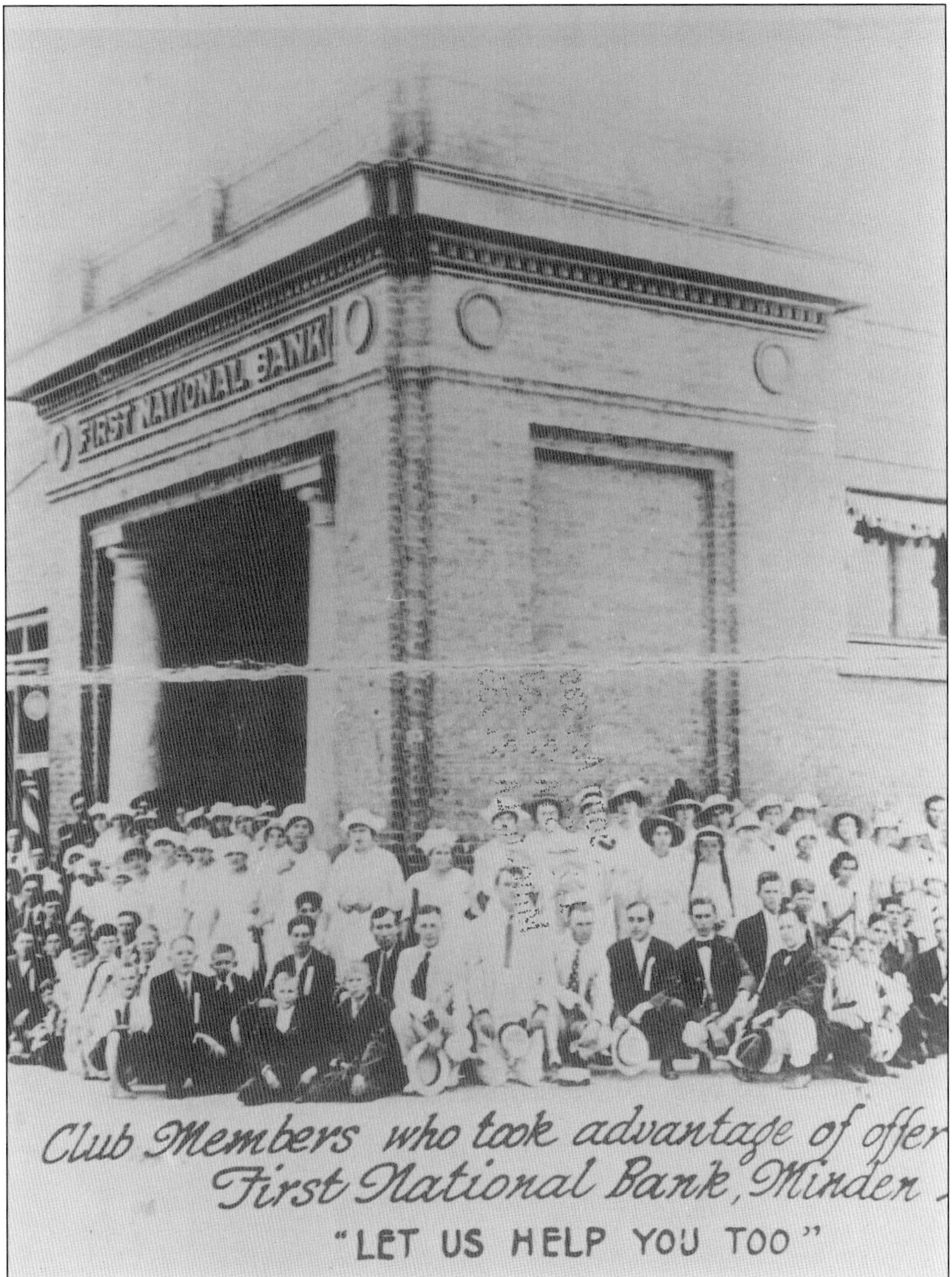

An advertisement is shown from the mid-1920s for a special club promotion of the First National Bank of Minden, showing the exterior of the building on the corner of Pearl and North Broadway when it was a bank. Whatever the promotion might have been, it was ultimately unsuccessful, as the bank failed in 1929.

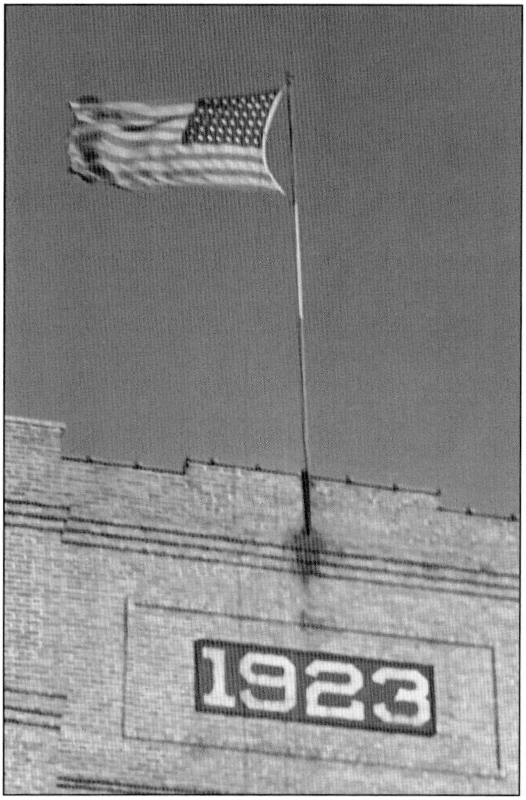

The United States flag is displayed over the brand new L&A Railroad shops in 1923. The transfer of the railroad shops to Minden from Stamps, AR, was a economic boost that helped overcome the loss of the Minden Lumber Mill in 1918. (Courtesy of Paul and Bertha Mae Mattingly.)

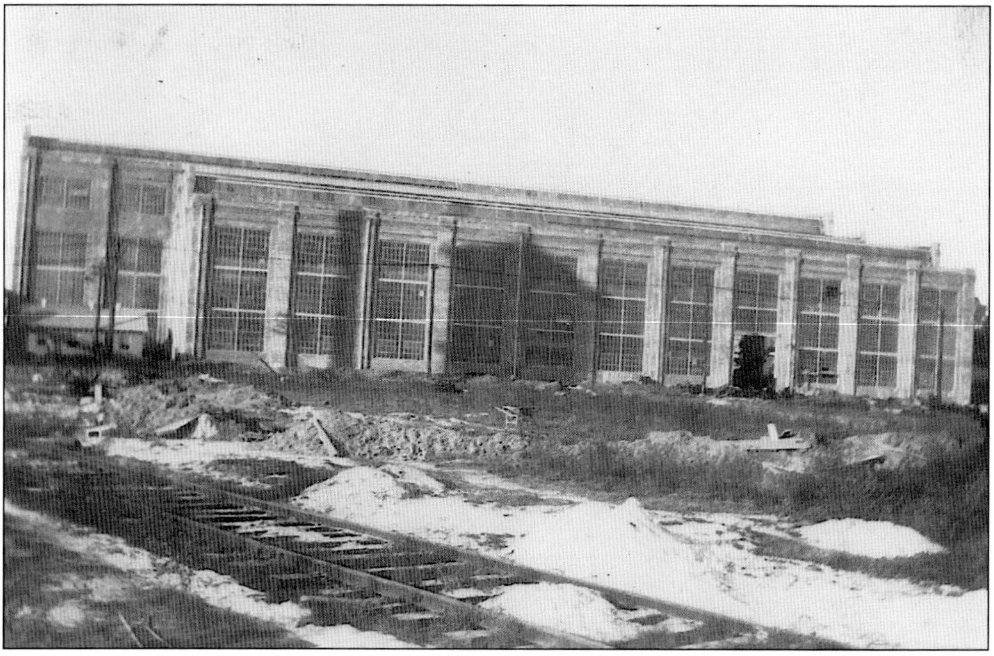

Here is an exterior view of the newly completed shops. Construction began on these facilities in late 1922; however, a region-wide brick shortage delayed completion for several months. (Courtesy of George Calvit.)

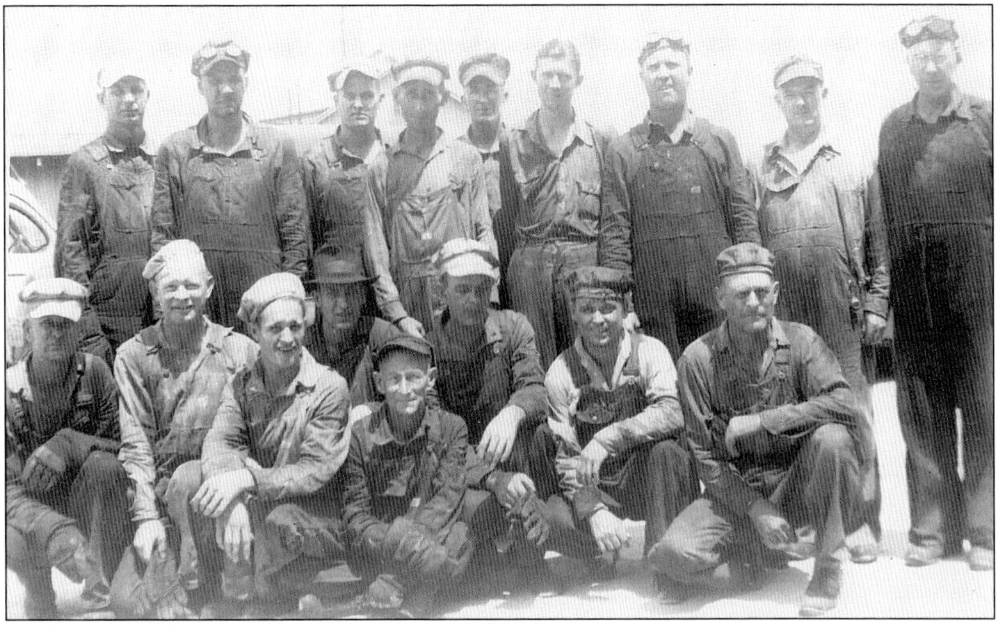

A group of railroad car men from the L&A shops are pictured in about 1926. These men worked repairing the cars and engines, doing work including carpentry and welding. (Courtesy of Paul and Bertha Mae Mattingly.)

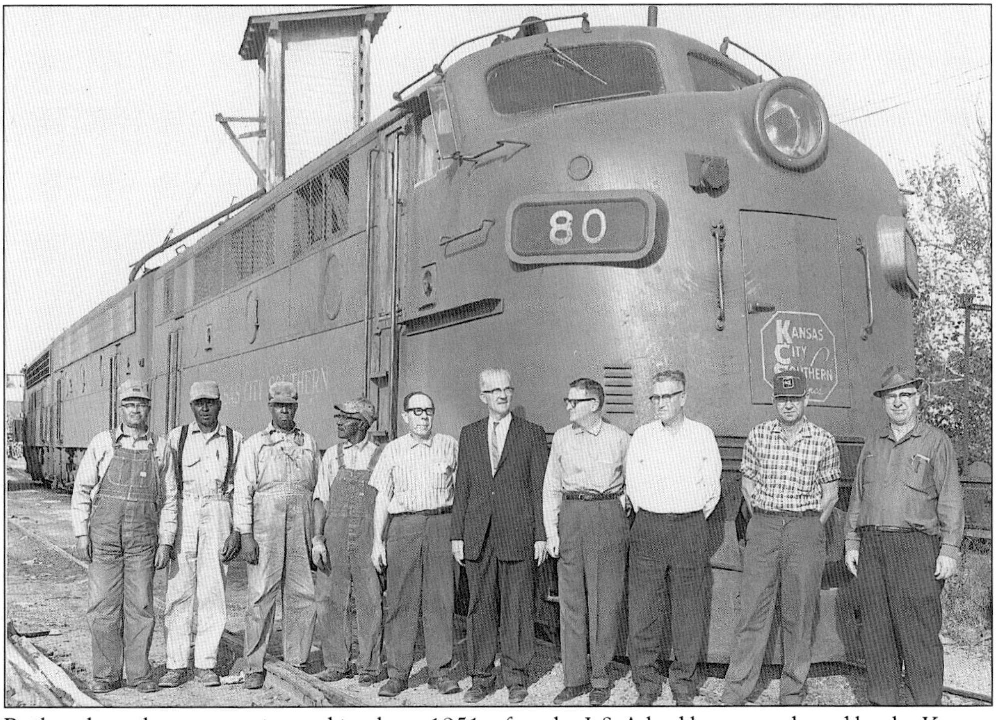

Railroad employees are pictured in about 1951, after the L&A had been purchased by the Kansas City Southern Railroad, which would later move the railroad shops from Minden. Among those in this picture are G.L. Frye, U.H. Gardner, Jesse L. Miller, and Albert Talton. (Courtesy of Paul and Bertha Mae Mattingly.)

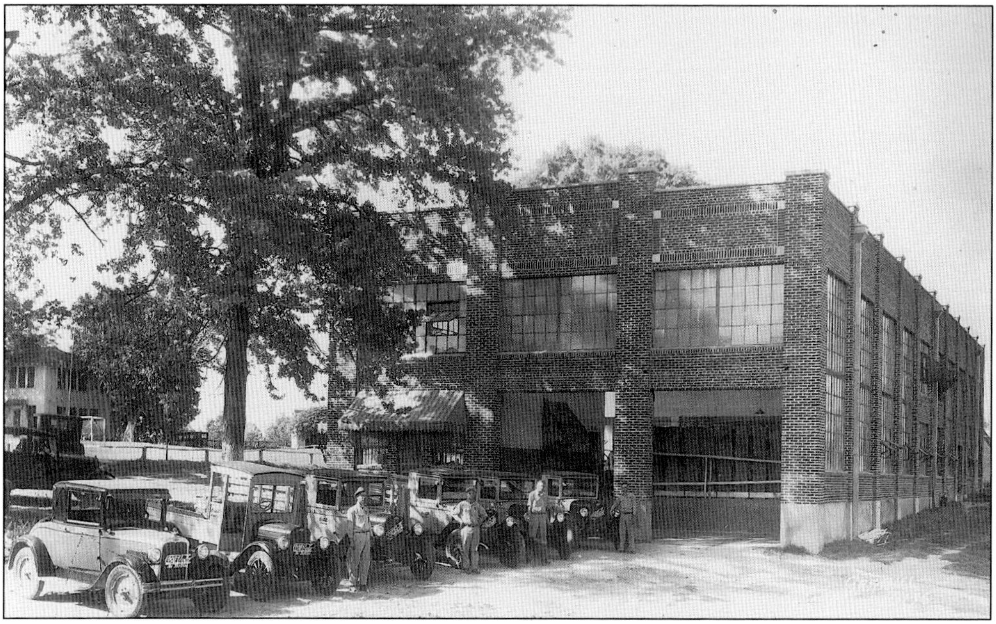

Delivery drivers for the Coca Cola Bottling Company are pictured in 1926. From left to right are Lester Lee, Whit Wall, Henry Lane, and Harfield McDow. The home of Mr. Larry Hunter can be seen in the background. (Courtesy of Ben Hunter.)

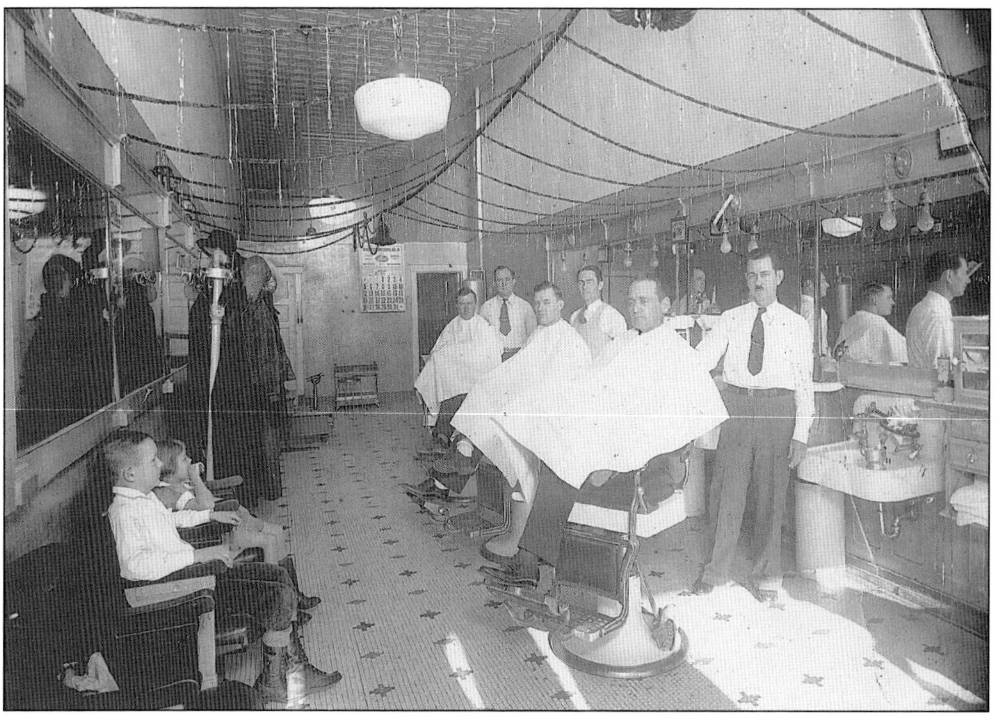

The interior of Almond's Barber Shop in Minden is shown in the 1930s. The barbers from left rear are Arnold Almond, Eddie Johnson, and Mr. Hardy. The two children waiting are Aubrey Drake Jr. and Sybil Drake. Based on the coats and decorations, the picture was apparently taken during the Christmas season. (Courtesy of Luther and Claire Moore Drake.)

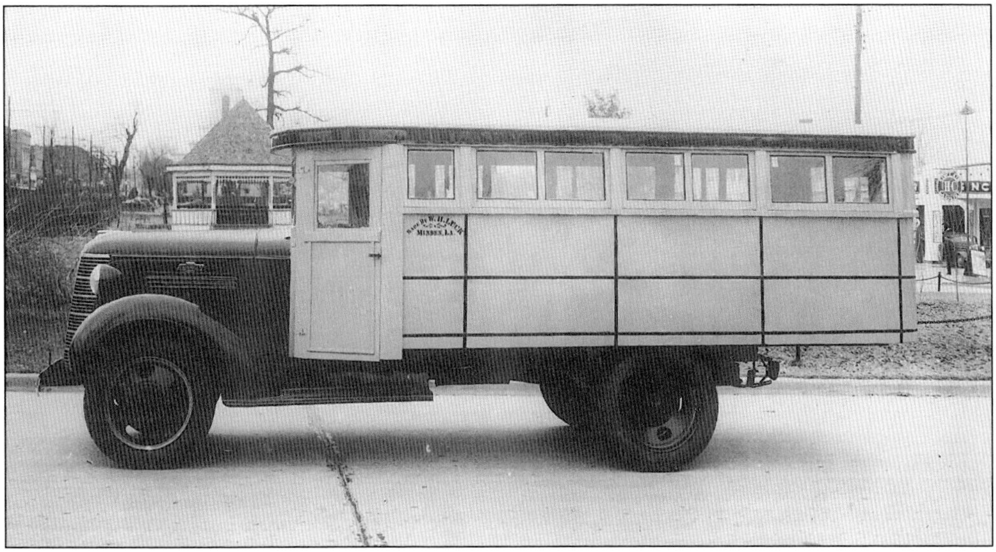

Pictured is one of the school "trucks" or buses built by the W.H. Luck Company of Minden. Webster Parish pioneered in the use of school buses to bring rural students to larger consolidated schools. Notice the City Park Gazebo and the Webster Parish Courthouse in the background.

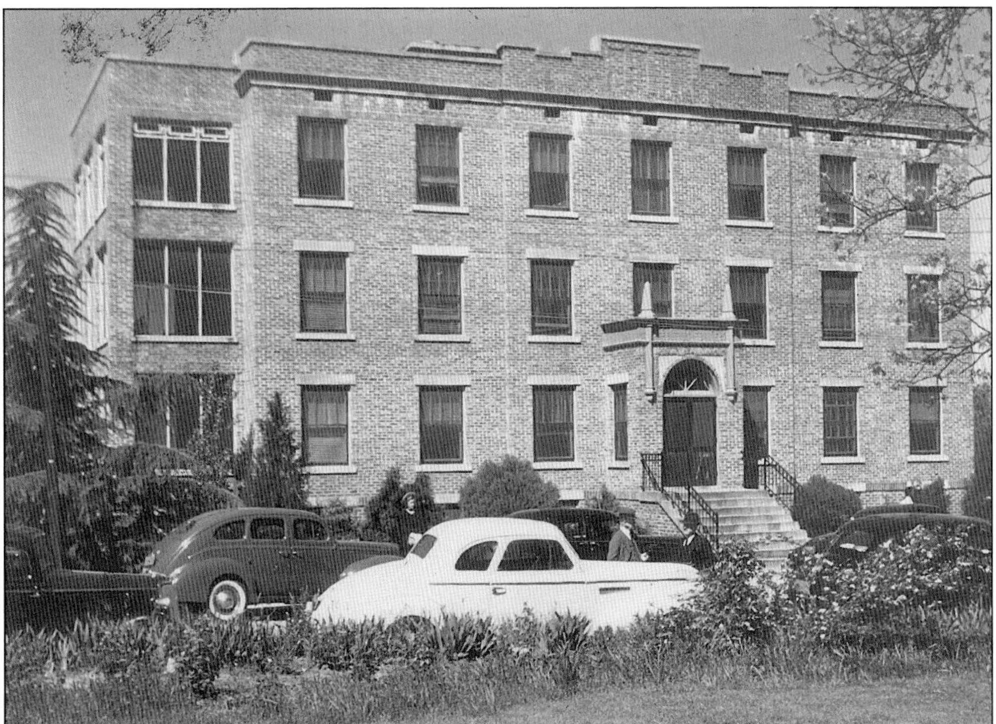

The 1926 Minden Sanitarium is shown during the 1930s. Founded by a group of local doctors, the hospital has grown into today's Minden Medical Center, which is part of a large nationwide hospital chain. This original 1926 building has not been torn down, but has been incorporated into the renovations and is still "inside" today's modern building.

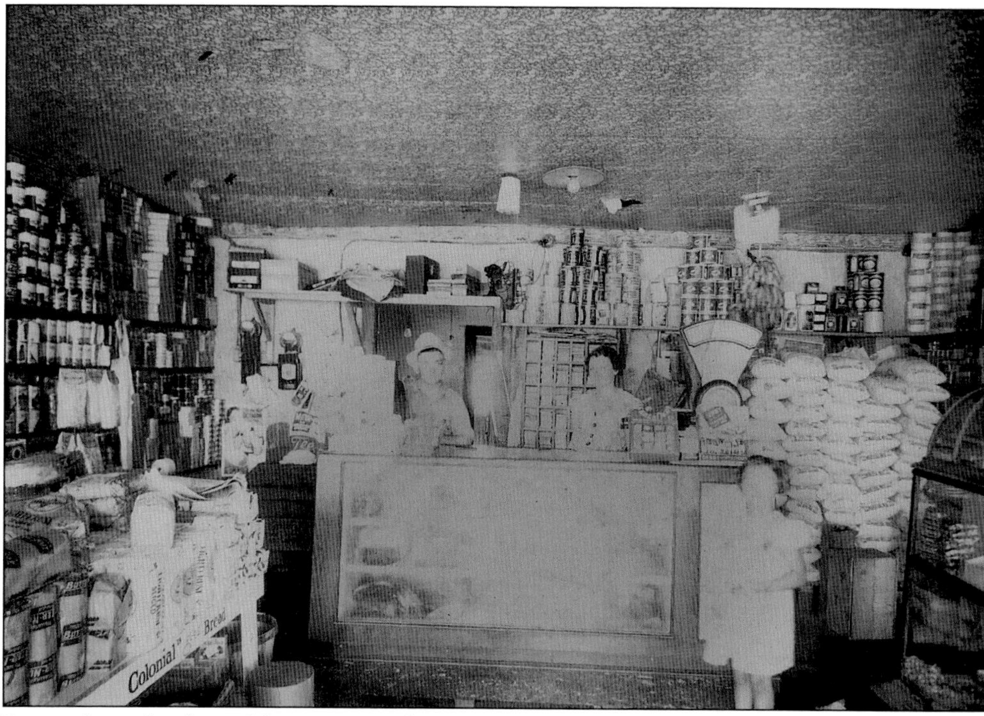

Pictured are the first of four separate locations of the G.V. Wise Store on Shreveport Road in Minden. Shown in this picture are the owner, Gilbert Wise, sales clerk Grace Gruner, Mr. Wise's sister-in-law, and Mrs. Gruner's daughter, Doris Gruner (today Mrs. Tony Elzen). (Courtesy of Peggy Wise Jones.)

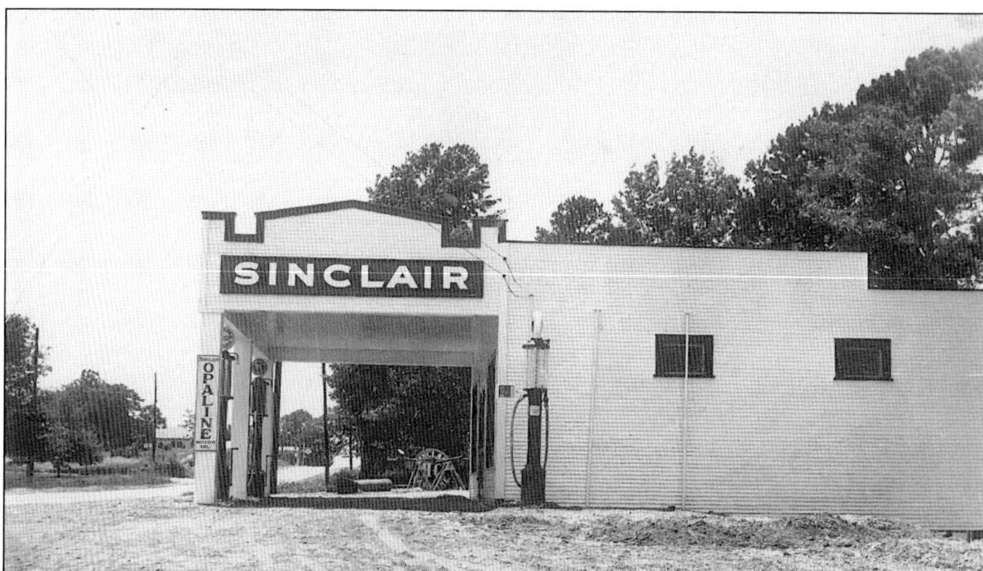

Here is an exterior view of the second Wise Grocery in 1939. The store became an institution in the Shreveport Road community, famous for its service, which included delivery service years after all other stores had stopped offering this benefit to customers. (Courtesy of Peggy Wise Jones.)

The third Wise Grocery store had living quarters attached to the back of the store. This picture was taken in the early 1940s, and when compared to the earlier picture, you can see that Mr. Wise has switched from Sinclair gasoline to Gulf. (Courtesy of Peggy Wise Jones.)

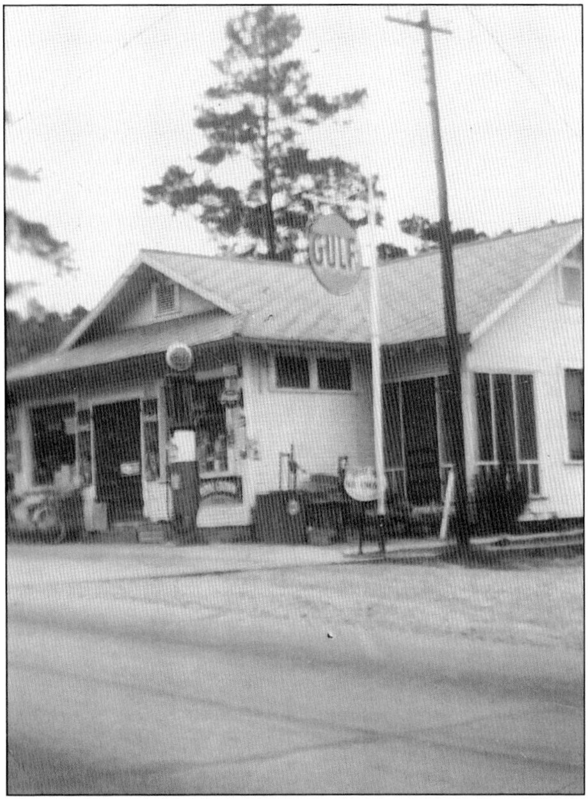

Here is the fourth and last Wise Grocery, with Gilbert V. Wise standing outside the store. Mr. Wise earned a well-deserved reputation for having the best beef available for sale in the area. He raised his own cattle and also butchered the animals. Customers came from wide-ranging areas to purchase their beef from Wise's Grocery. (Courtesy of Peggy Wise Jones.)

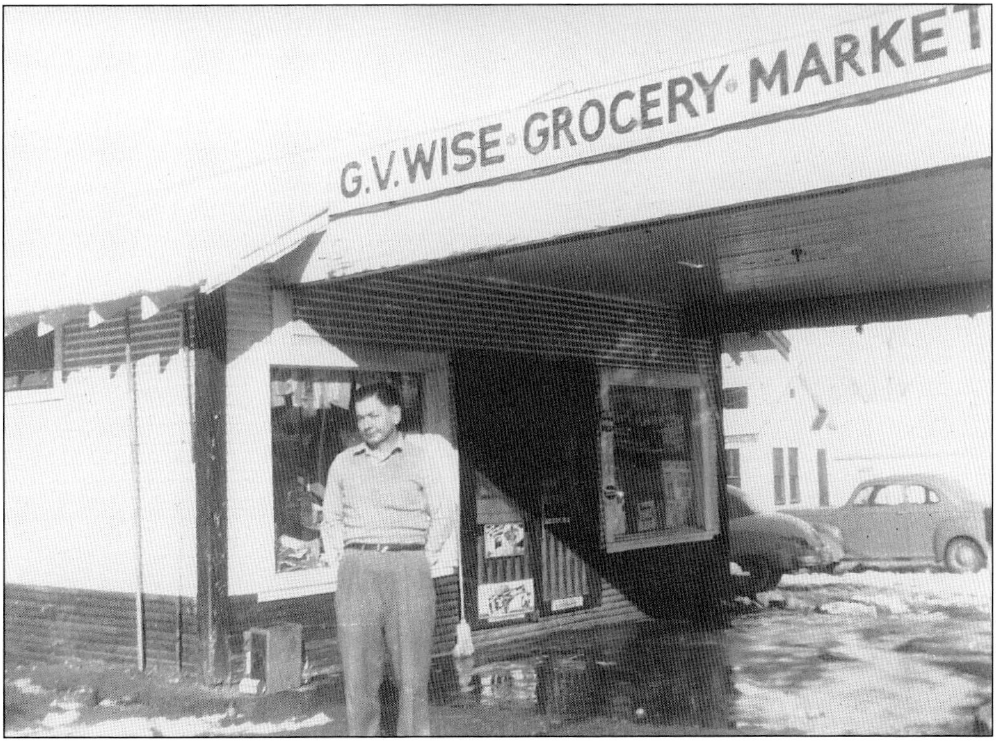

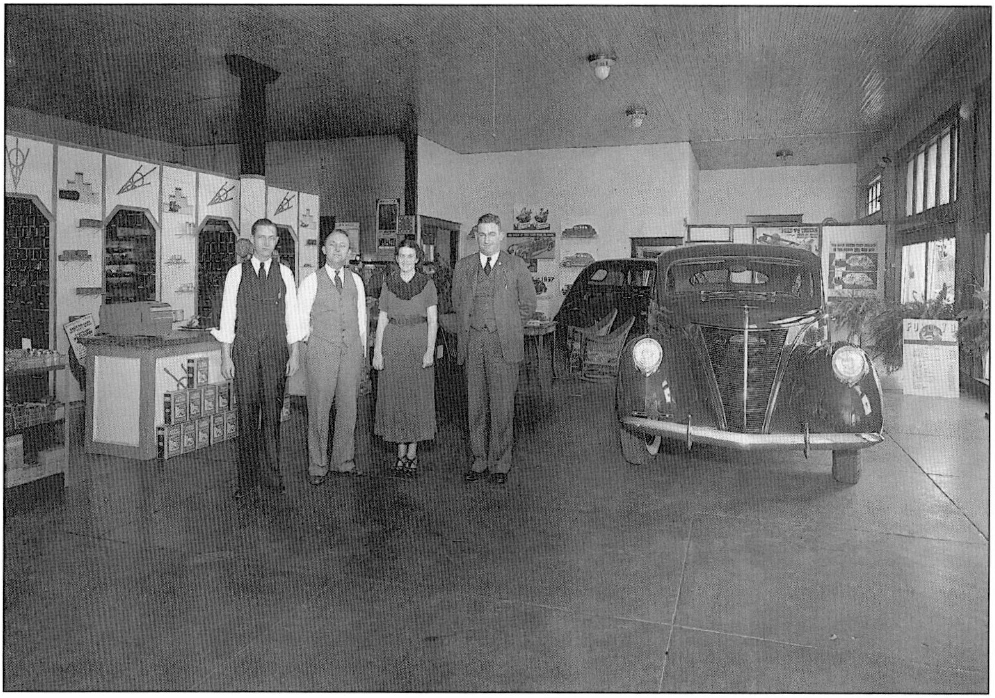

Management of Andress Motors Company is shown on the occasion of the 1937 new car showing in the fall of 1936. Pictured from left to right are Conrad Adkins, parts manager; Leon Adkins, business manager; Elsie Mae Turner, bookkeeper; and Harry C. Andress, owner and general manager. (Courtesy of Thad Andress.)

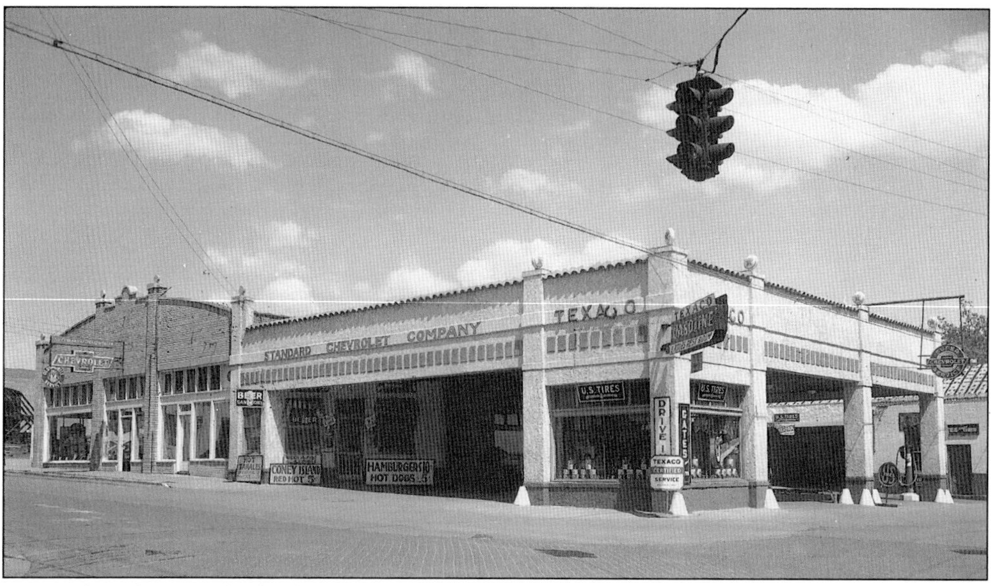

Pictured is the Standard Chevrolet Dealership on the corner of South Broadway and East Union in Minden. Notice the other businesses housed in the structure, including the small restaurant and the Texaco service station. The offerings of the diner, which include hot tamales, hamburgers, Coney Island Red Hot hot dogs, and beer, help date the picture. Beer sales were only legal between 1933 and 1938 in Minden, so the picture falls in that time frame.

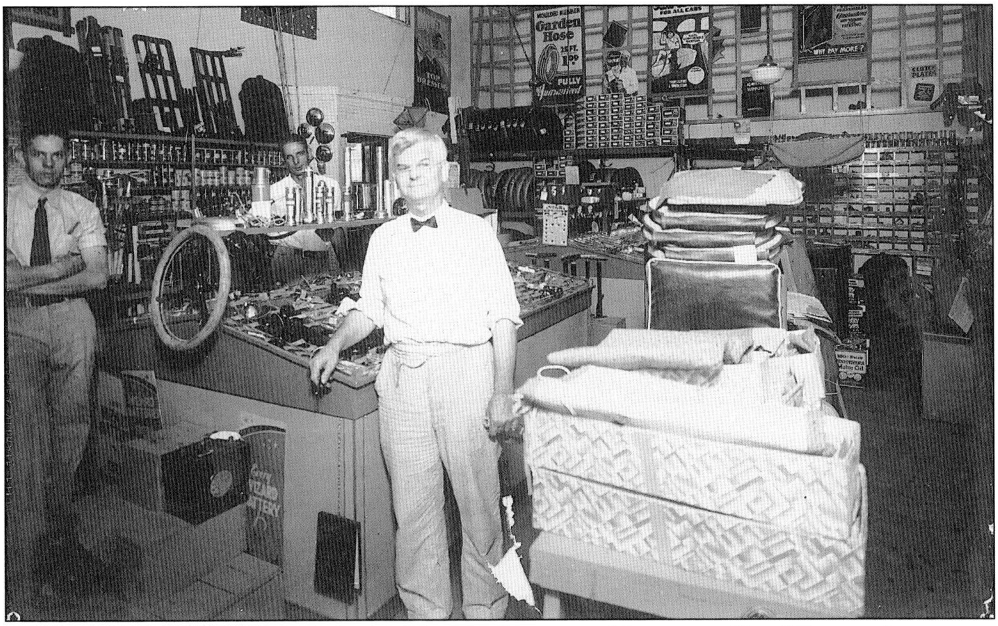

Mr. A.J. Price is pictured in 1936, standing in the original location of his Western Auto store. The store was located on the corner of Fogle and North Broadway, where the Trust Company of Louisiana is located today. (Courtesy of John Collins.)

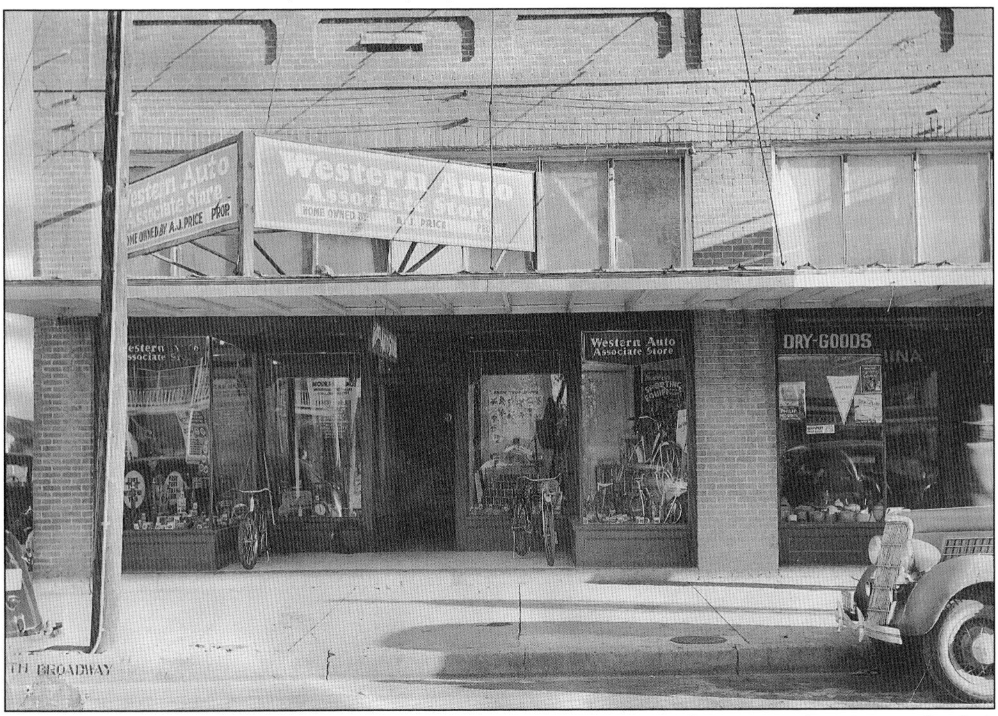

This exterior view of the first location of Western Auto was taken around 1936. In the left foreground, notice the stenciled lettering designating the street as North Broadway. Later, residents of Minden will be surprised to see the two-way traffic on North Broadway, which was changed to a one-way street in the mid-1950s. (Courtesy of John Collins.)

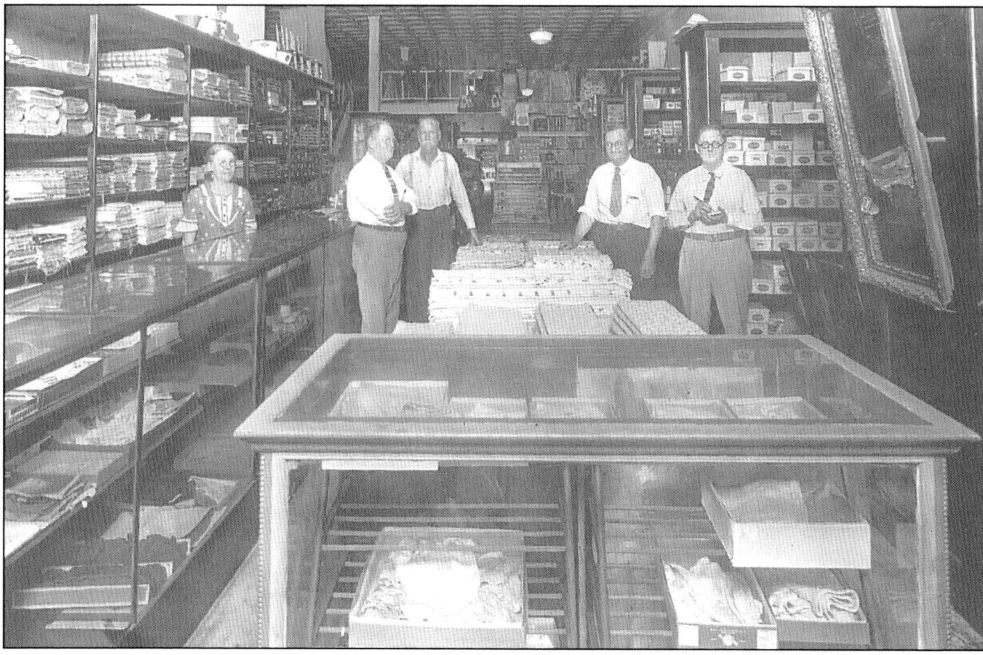

Minden Mercantile, Inc. is shown during the early 1920s. Pictured are Mrs. Pierce, Mr. Bobby Turner, Mr. Penn Turner, Mr. Pevy, and Mr. Sidney Turner. This was one of the many business operations owned by the Turner family, whose family picture from the 1890s was in the first chapter of this book. (Courtesy of Ruth Turner Stinnett.)

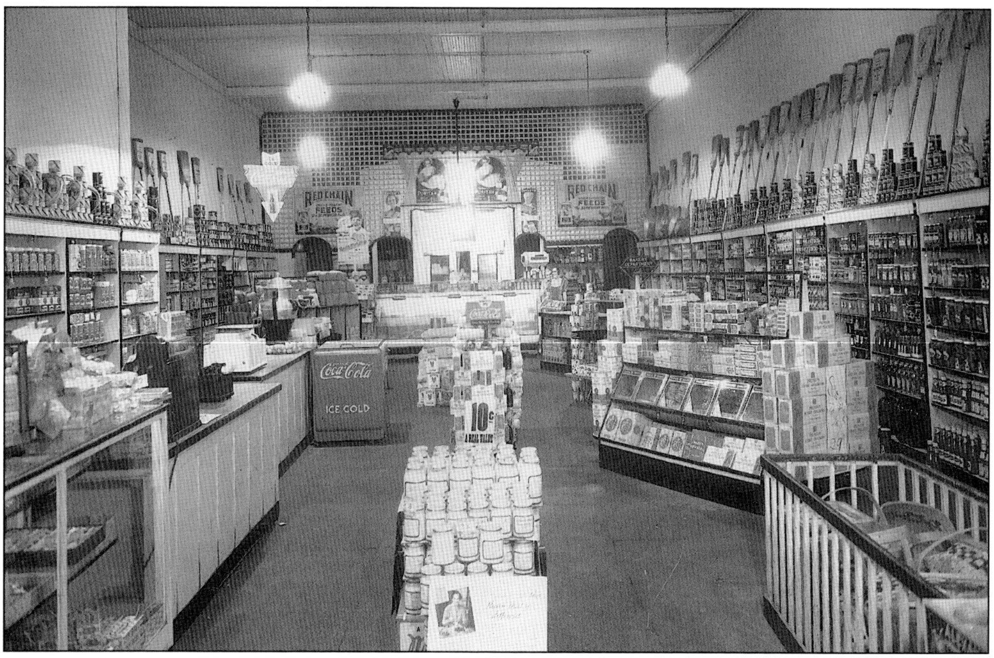

Service Grocery, operated by Mr. Walter McCoy, was located in the Gladney Building on North Broadway in Minden. Earlier, this building had housed Minden's first chain store, Piggly Wiggly, which closed when it could not match the competition provided by the many local stores.

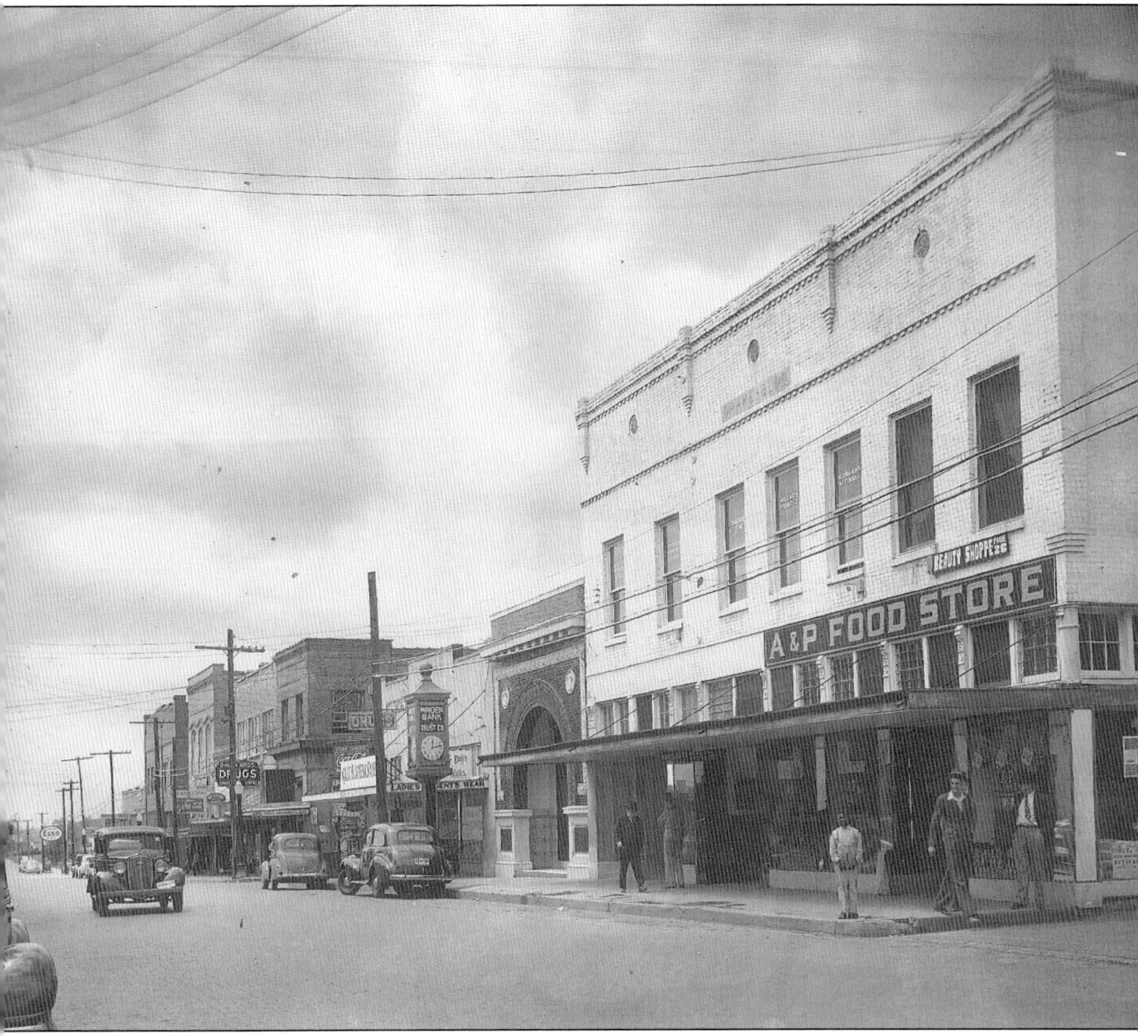

North Broadway is shown in the early 1940s, in a picture taken from in front of the Minden Post Office. Pictured is the second chain grocery store to come to Minden, A&P, housed in the Drake Building. A&P was more successful and remained in business until the 1970s in several locations. Down the street is the Minden Bank and Trust Company, with its distinctive green tile front and the clock erected in May 1939. David Drug was located at this time in the former First National Bank Building. If you notice the windows above the A&P store, you can see advertisements for the attorney offices and beauty shop located in the upper floor of the Drake Building. (Courtesy of Mrs. O.H. Haynes Jr.)

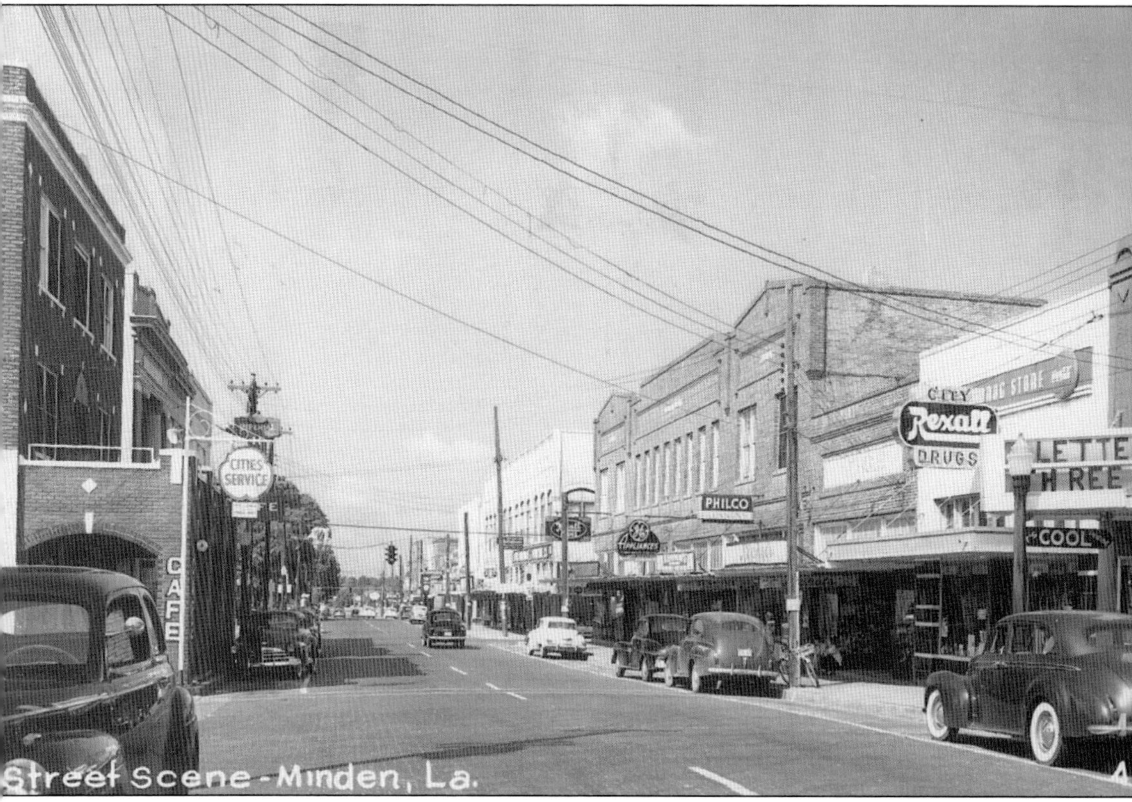

Another view of North Broadway during the 1940s was taken in the block between Fogle and East Union Streets. You will notice the marquee of the Tower Theater, which is showing *A Letter to Three Wives*. Next door to the Tower is the City Drug Store, which opened in 1903, buying out the pharmacy from the Goodwill Store; it did not close until 1999. For many years, it was operated by the Williams family, Rollin Williams Sr., David Williams, and Rollin "Froggy" Williams Jr. In the left foreground is the Imperial Hotel, which also operated a Cities Service gasoline station in the ally next to its building. At the intersection of North Broadway and East Union, you can see a traffic light. The traffic lights were added to downtown Minden in the early 1930s. (Courtesy of George Calvit.)

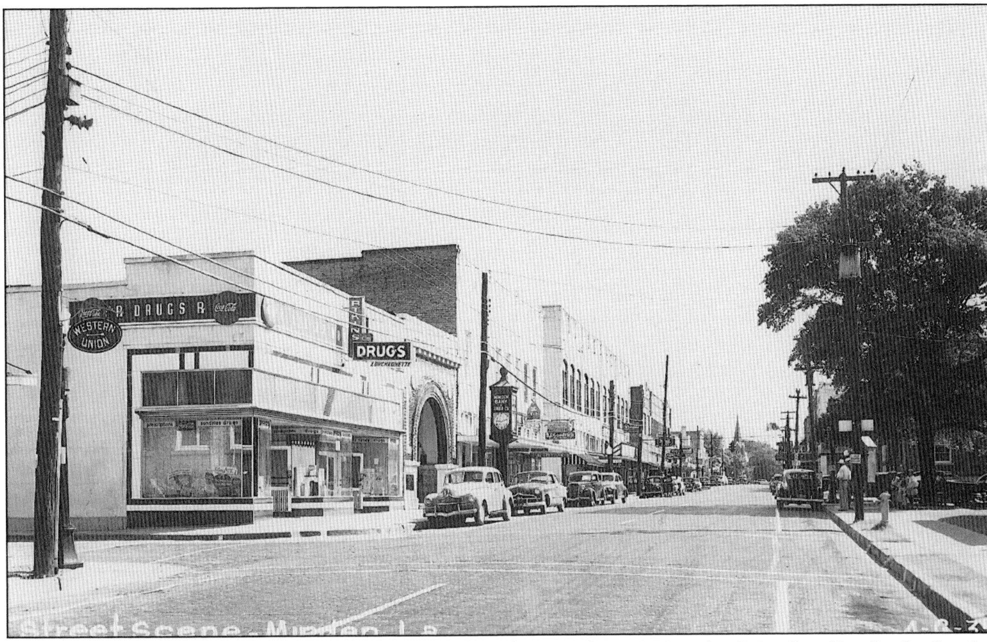

Looking north on North Broadway in Minden during the 1940s, the Minden Bank clock, the Methodist Church steeple in the background, and the two-way automobile traffic are visible. On the left side of the picture, you can again see the "Tree of Knowledge" on the courthouse grounds. (Courtesy of George Calvit.)

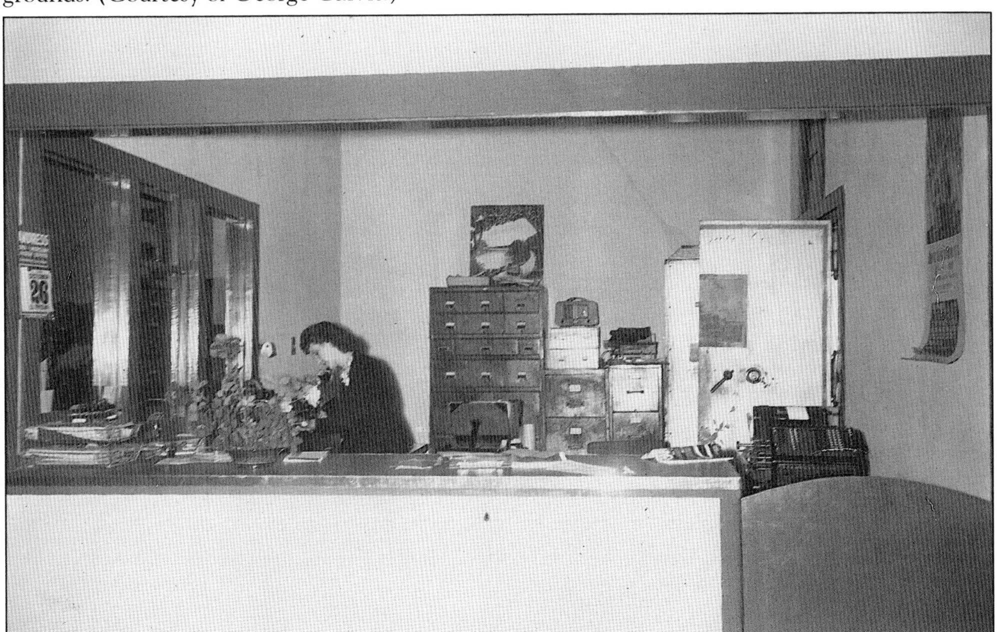

Shown is the business office of Andress Motors Company on October 26, 1945, with bookkeeper Juanita Murphy (today Mrs. J.C. Agan) working in the office. The safe pictured on the right had been purchased from a brewery in Kentucky and often proved very troublesome to open. On at least one occasion, the employees had to stop a passer-by on the street and get his assistance to open the safe.

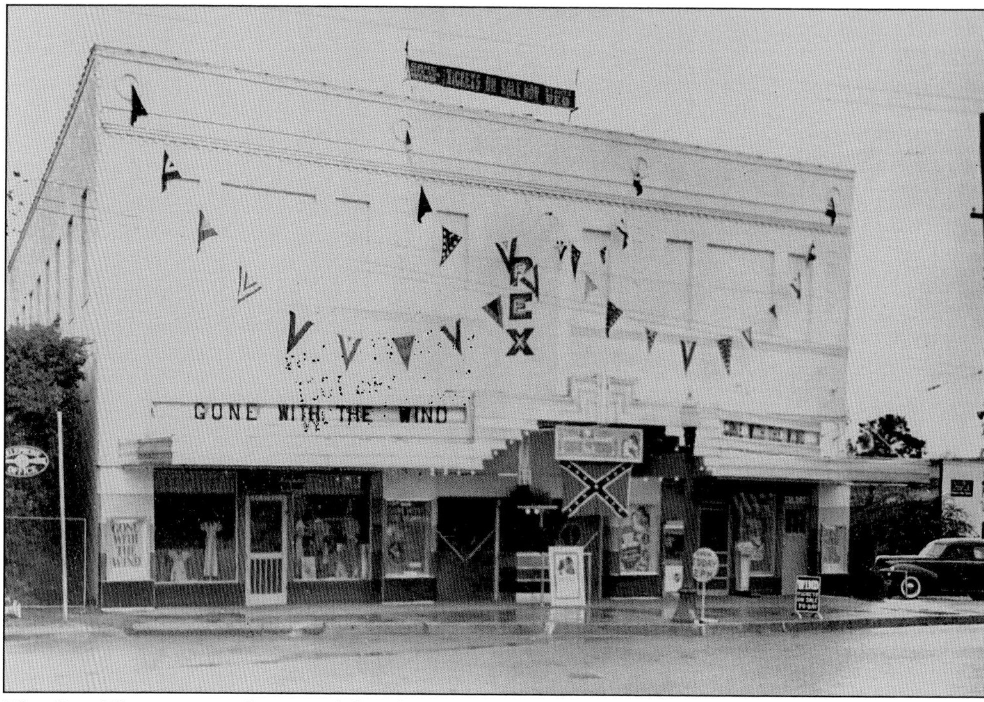

The Rex Theater was decorated for the opening of the epic *Gone With the Wind*. Notice the Confederate battle flag displayed over the ticket booth and the two businesses located in the front of the theater. The store on the left was Mrs. Sullivan's Dress Shop, and on the right was, at various times, a sandwich shop and concession stand. The door on the far right front is the "colored entrance," since in those days, black residents were limited to balcony seating.

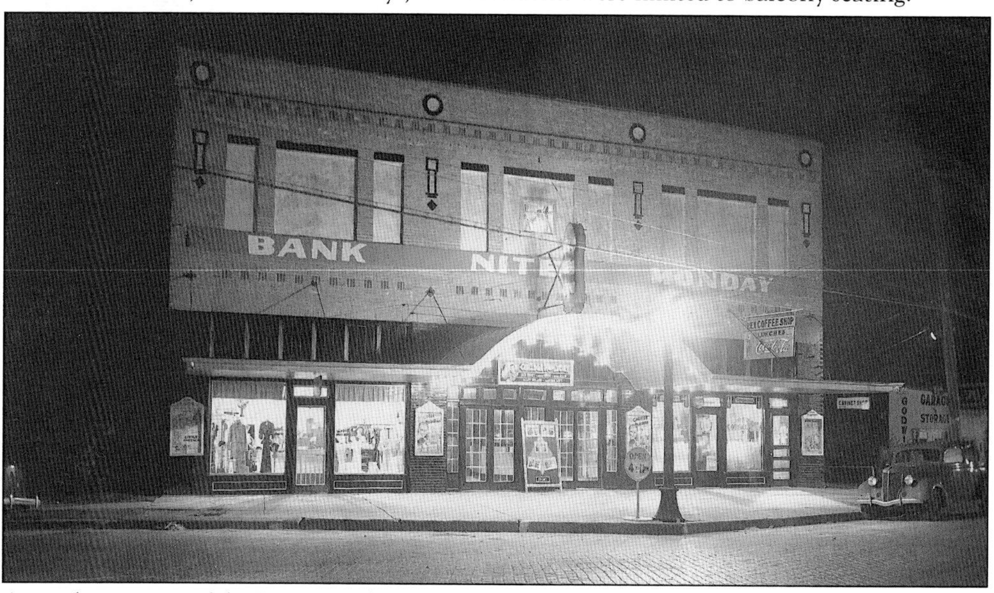

An earlier picture of the Rex was taken on "Bank Nite" during the 1930s. The Rex was built by converting the First Baptist Church building left by the church in 1925. It was first known as the Brownie, while the theater further down North Broadway, which became the Tower, had the name Rex. (Courtesy of Mrs. O.H. Haynes Jr.)

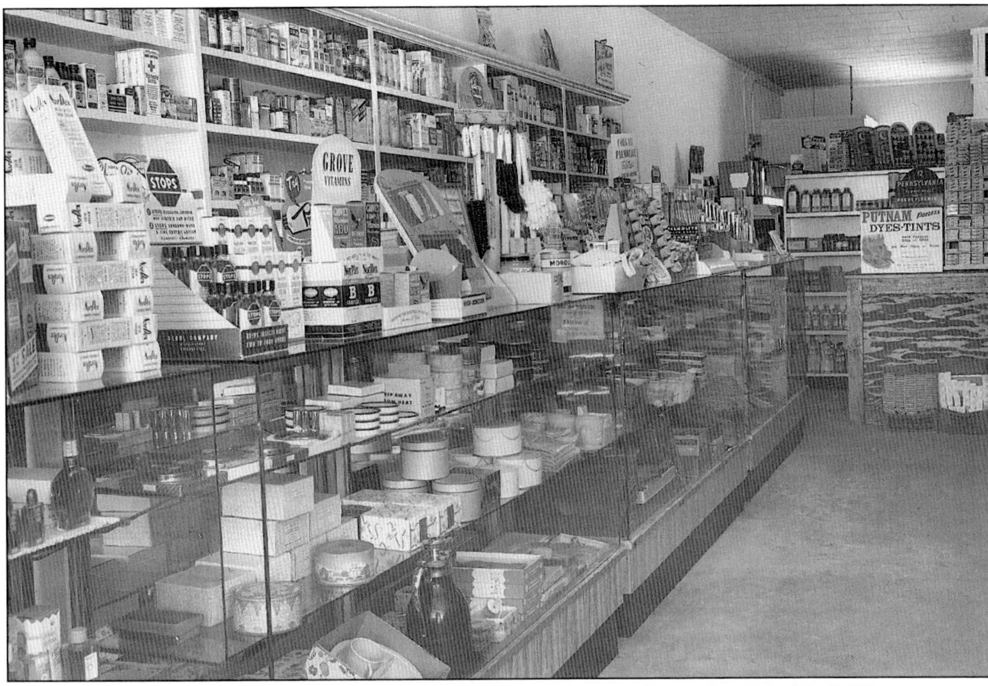

An interior picture of Maddry's Pharmacy was taken during the 1950s. Maddry's Pharmacy was located in a section of stores on South Broadway that were torn down in the late 1960s for the construction of the Minden Civic Center. (Courtesy of Lonnie Maddry.)

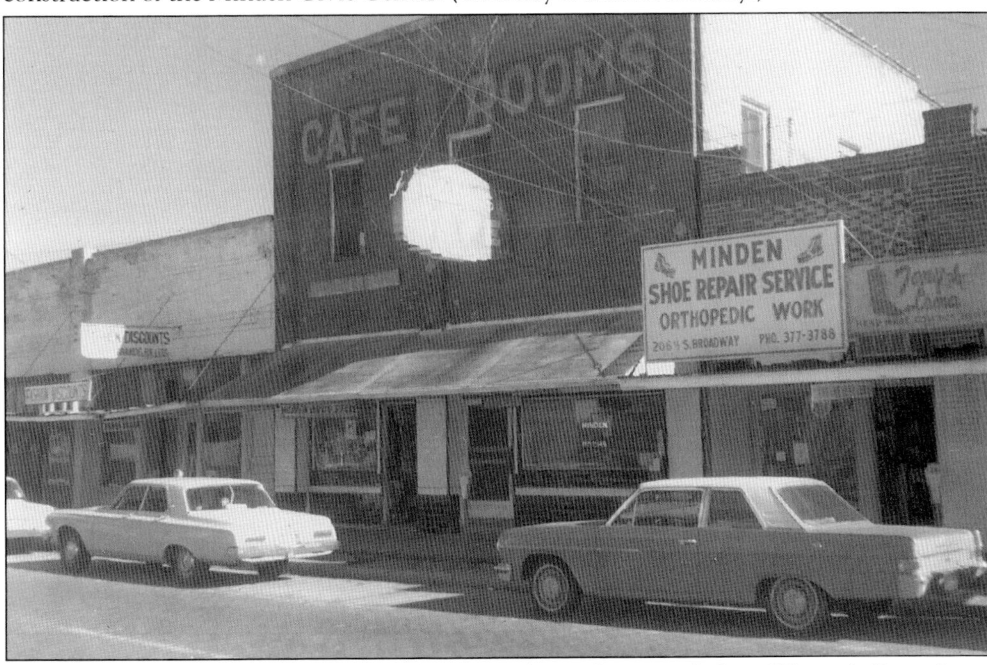

A group of the stores on South Broadway are shown here, including Warren's Drug Store, Kirkikis Cafe, and Minden Shoe Repair. In addition, a hotel was located upstairs over the first-floor businesses. These businesses were also torn down to make room for the civic center and city hall. (Courtesy of B.T. Warren Family.)

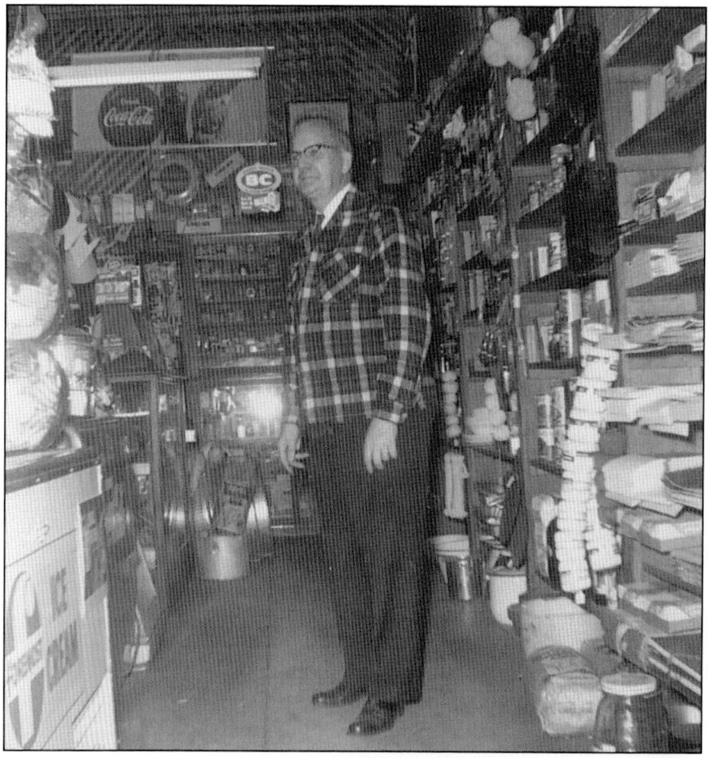

Mr. B.T. Warren is pictured in his drug store in 1959. In addition to filling prescriptions, the store offered a lot of other types of merchandise, including Foremost Ice Cream, as indicated by the cooler in the left foreground. (Courtesy of B.T. Warren Family.)

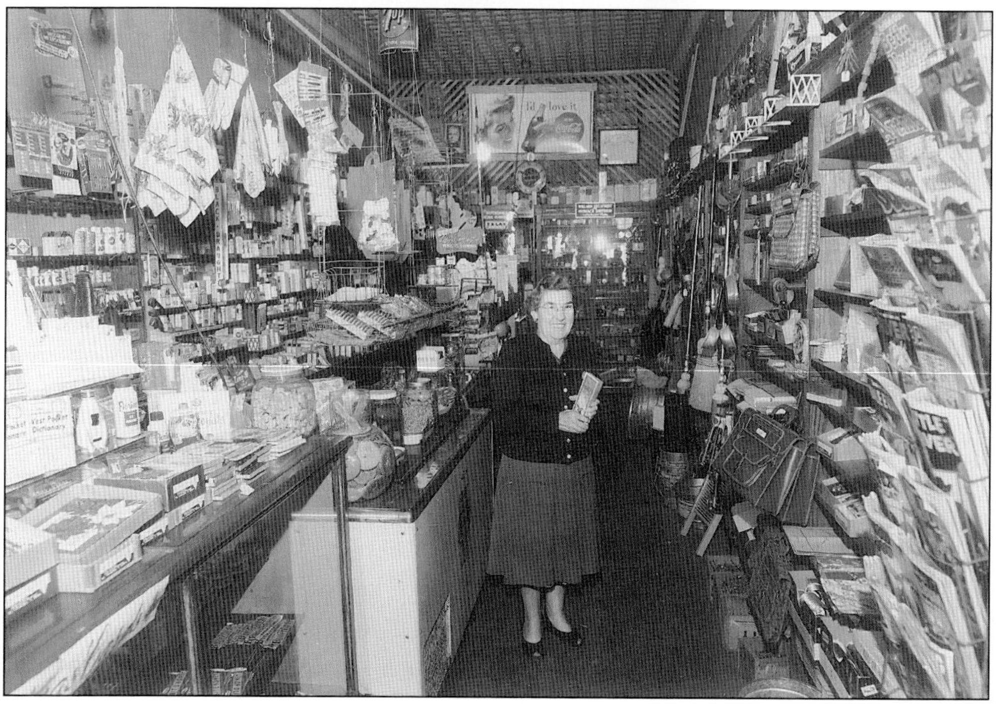

Mrs. B.T. Warren is pictured in another area of the store, showing more of the many types of merchandise available in Warren's Drug Store. The store was affectionately called the "big, little store." (Courtesy of B.T. Warren Family.)

Four

GOVERNMENT

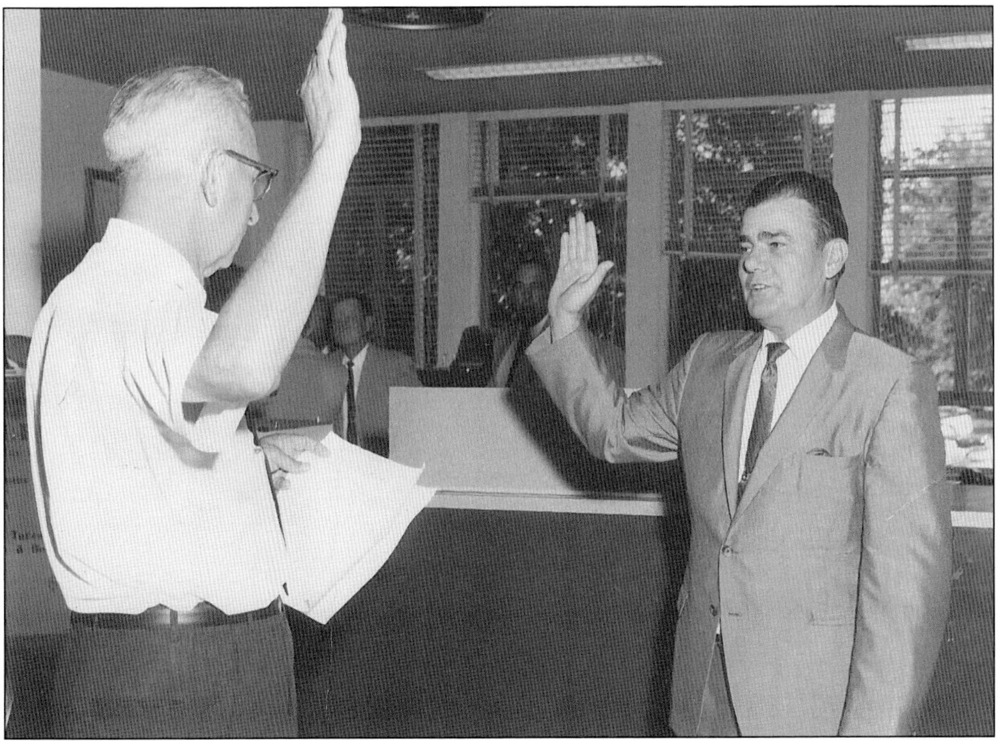

O.H. Haynes Jr. was sworn into office by Webster Parish clerk of court Clarence D. Wiley in June 1964. Haynes, who would hold the office until 1980, was filling the same office occupied by his father, O.H. Haynes Sr., from 1933 until 1952. (Courtesy of Mrs. O.H. Haynes Jr.)

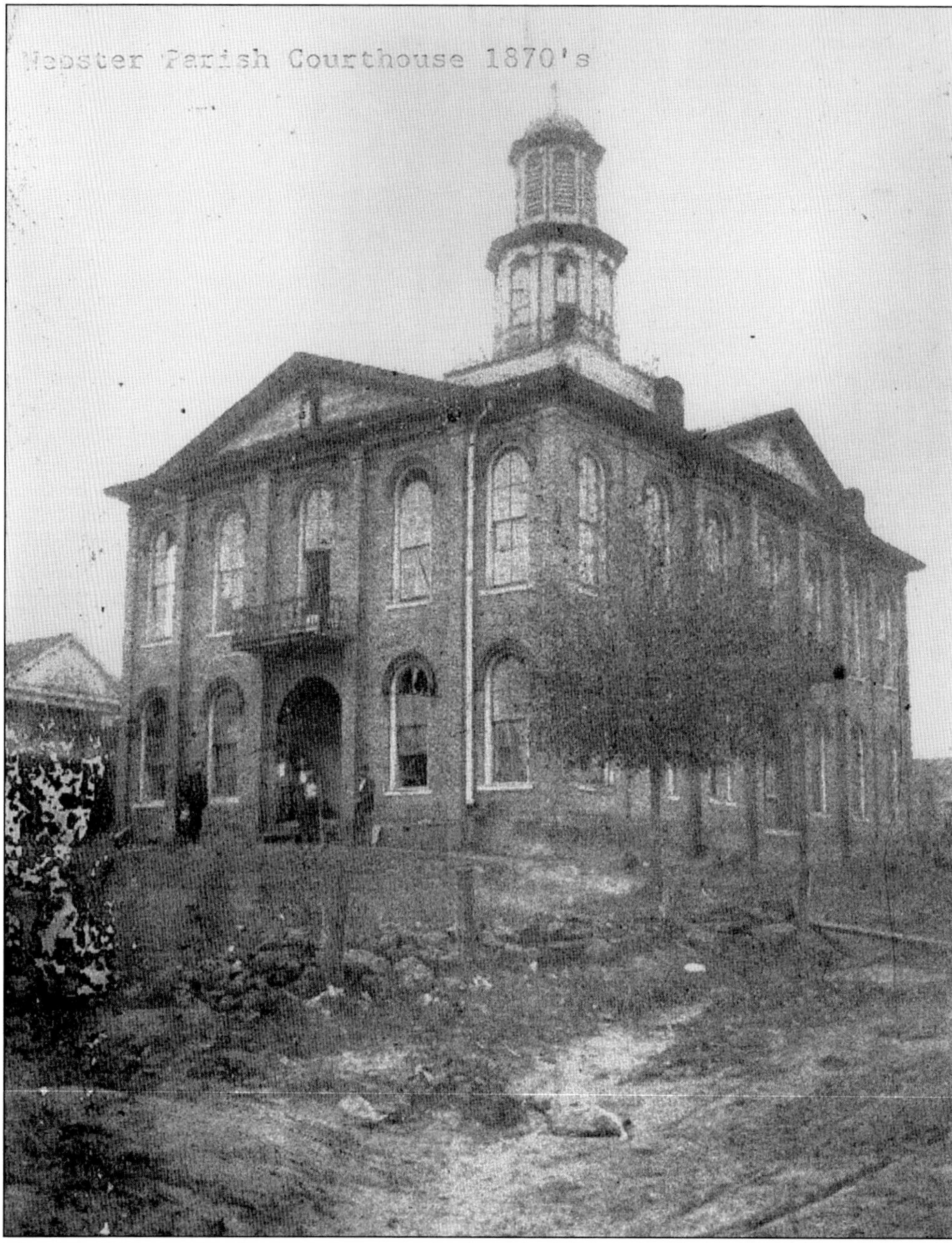

The first Webster Parish Courthouse was constructed in 1872 at a cost of $2,400. Webster Parish was created in February 1871, and until the courthouse could be completed, the parish shared the Minden Town Hall with the city. When the town hall burned in 1874, some of the parish records left in that building were destroyed in the fire. This courthouse was located on the site occupied today by Hibernia National Bank, on the corner of Union and North Broadway. This first courthouse was used until 1905, when it was torn down and replaced. The Minden Post Office was constructed on the site in 1916 and remained in the location until it was torn down to allow for the construction of the bank in 1962. A new post office was built in 1959. (Courtesy of Wanda Pittman.)

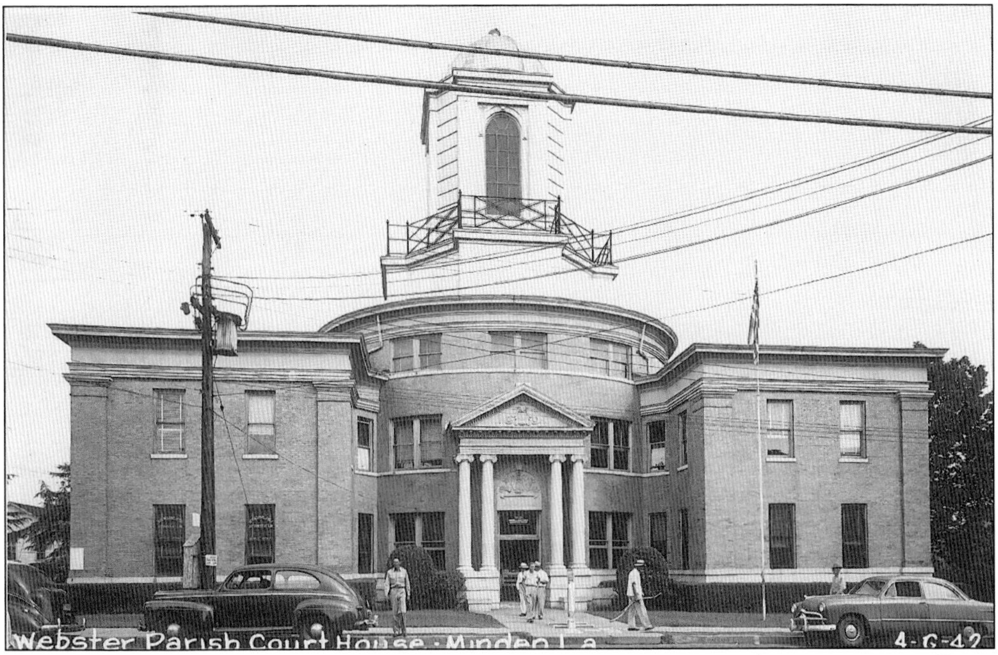

Constructed in 1905, the second Webster Parish Courthouse cost $52,000. Originally, it included a clock in its dome (a feature than can be seen in some of the earlier street scenes), but the clock stopped working in the early 1920s and was removed when the courthouse was remodeled in the 1930s. Eventually replaced in the early 1950s, the building was used as Minden City Hall until 1970. (Courtesy of George Calvit.)

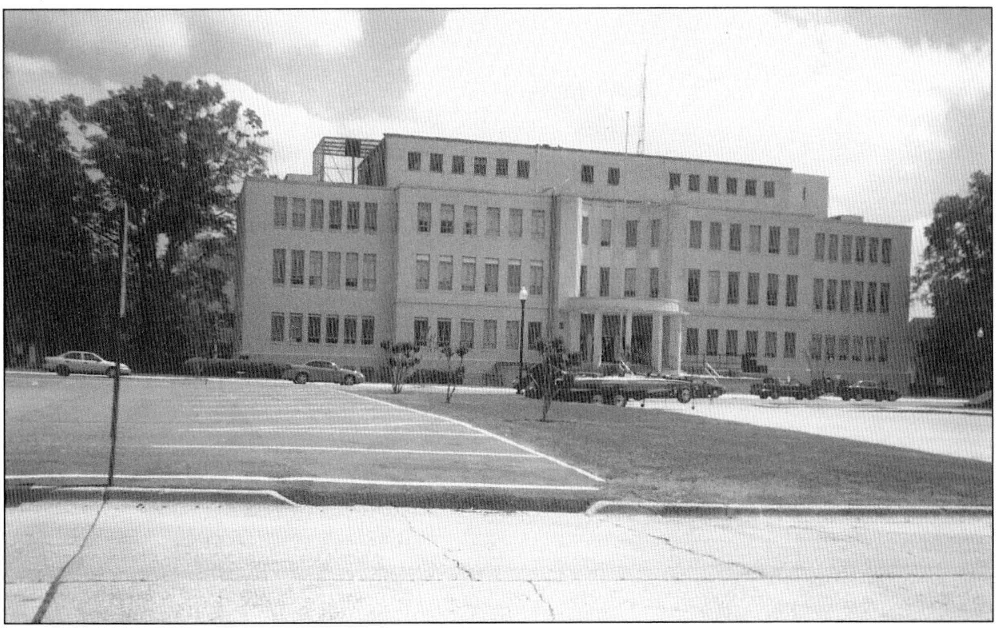

The current Webster Parish Courthouse, built in 1952, is the third in parish history. It was constructed on the site of the Minden City Park, shown in several images earlier in this book. This building has undergone renovations on several occasions in order to keep up with the growth and expanding needs of the citizens of Webster Parish.

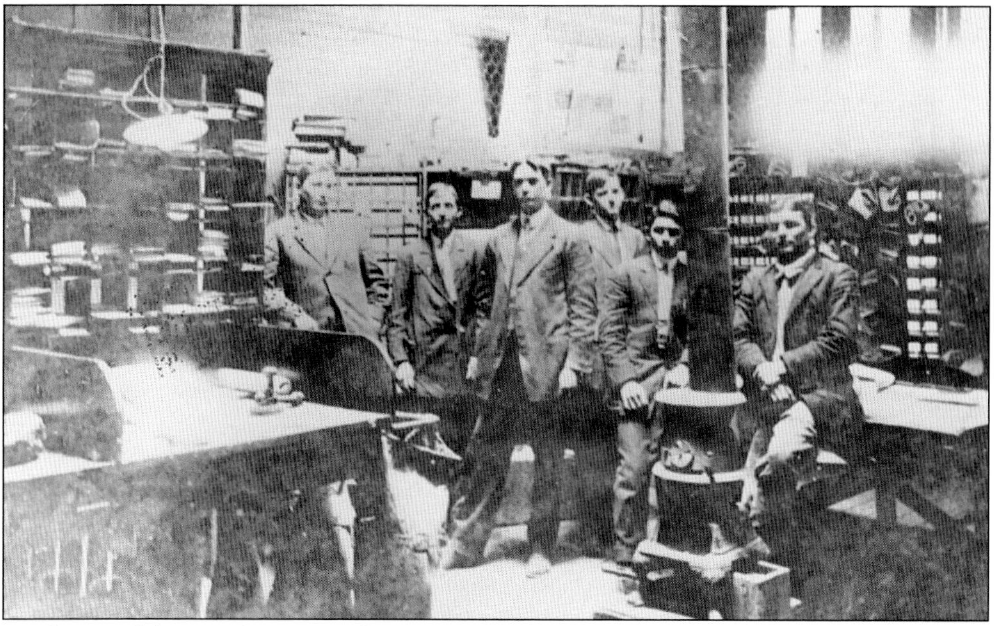

Employees of the Minden Post Office are pictured before 1916. This may be from the period when the post office was housed in the Chaffe Drug Store. From its establishment in around 1840 until 1916, the Minden Post Office had no permanent home, renting space in various buildings in town.

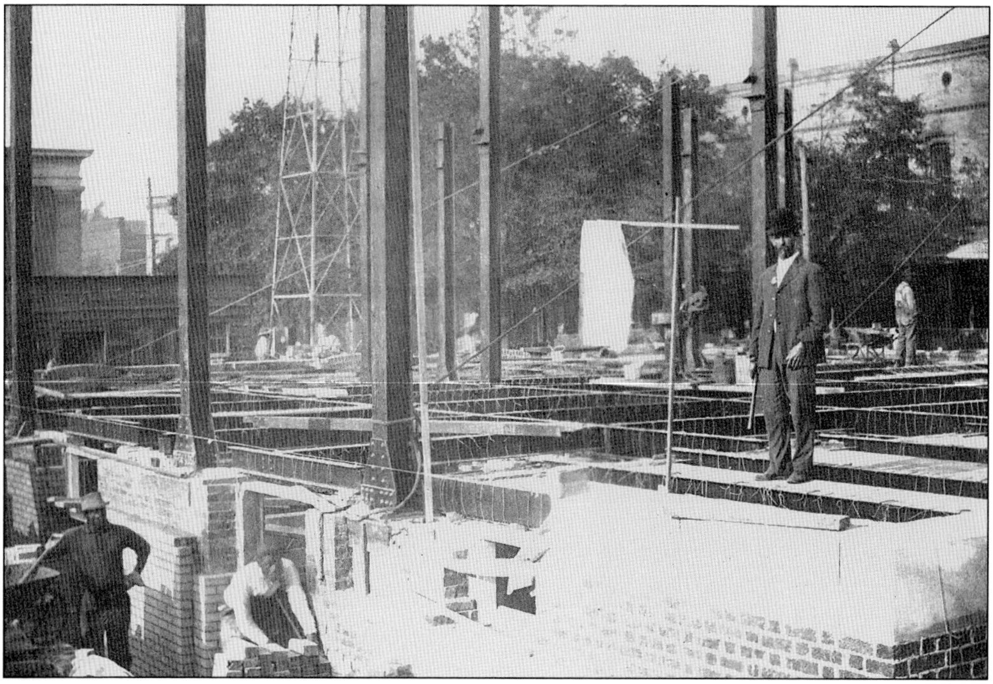

The Minden Post Office was under construction in 1915. The man pictured in the right foreground is city marshall J.G. Maddry. The 1905 Webster Parish Courthouse can be seen in the left side of the picture, and the Drake Building is in the center background. (Courtesy of Lonnie Maddry.)

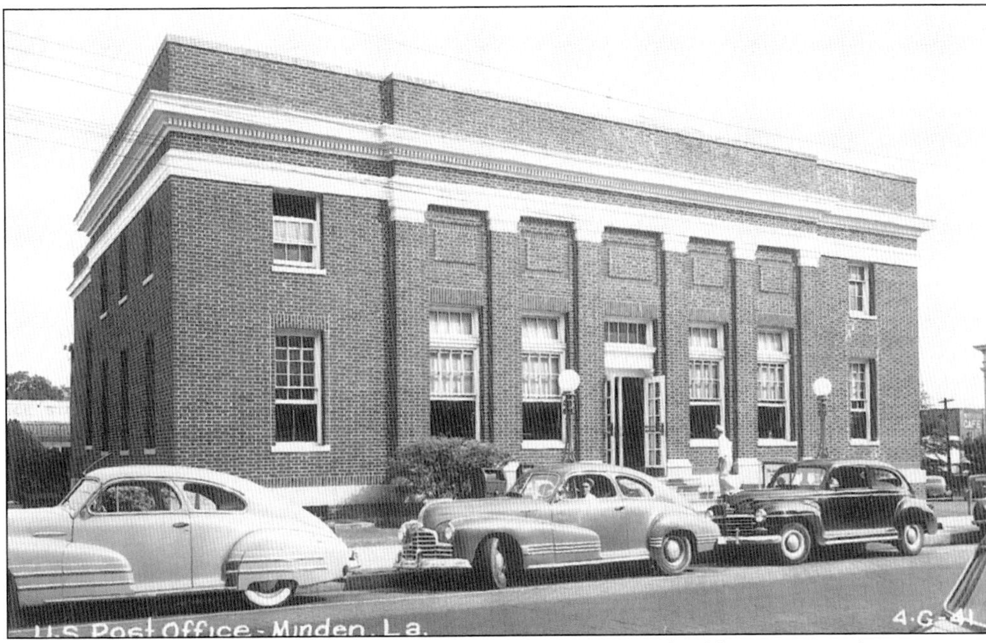

The 1916 post office is shown in use during the 1940s. The building remained in use until 1959, although it had been deemed unsuitable for use for many years before it was replaced. The foundation of the building could not support the weight of the structure, and attempts to replace the building had begun by the late 1940s. (Courtesy of George Calvit.)

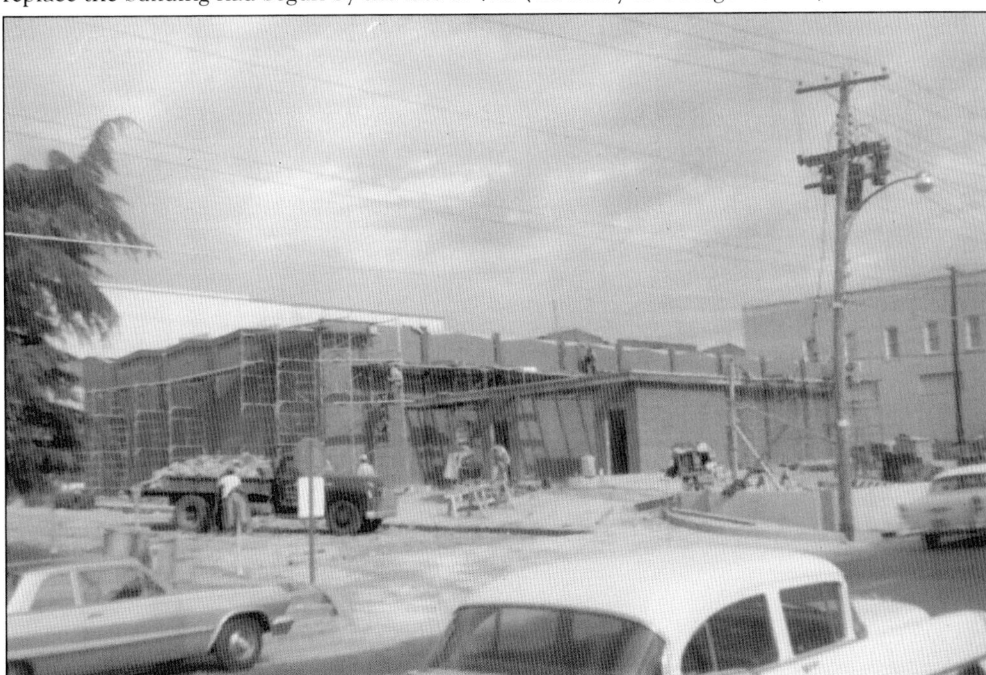
The Peoples Bank and Trust Company is shown under construction in 1962, on the site occupied by the post office from 1916 until 1959. Peoples Bank later sold to Hibernia National Bank, which still occupies the site today. (Courtesy Lonnie Maddry.)

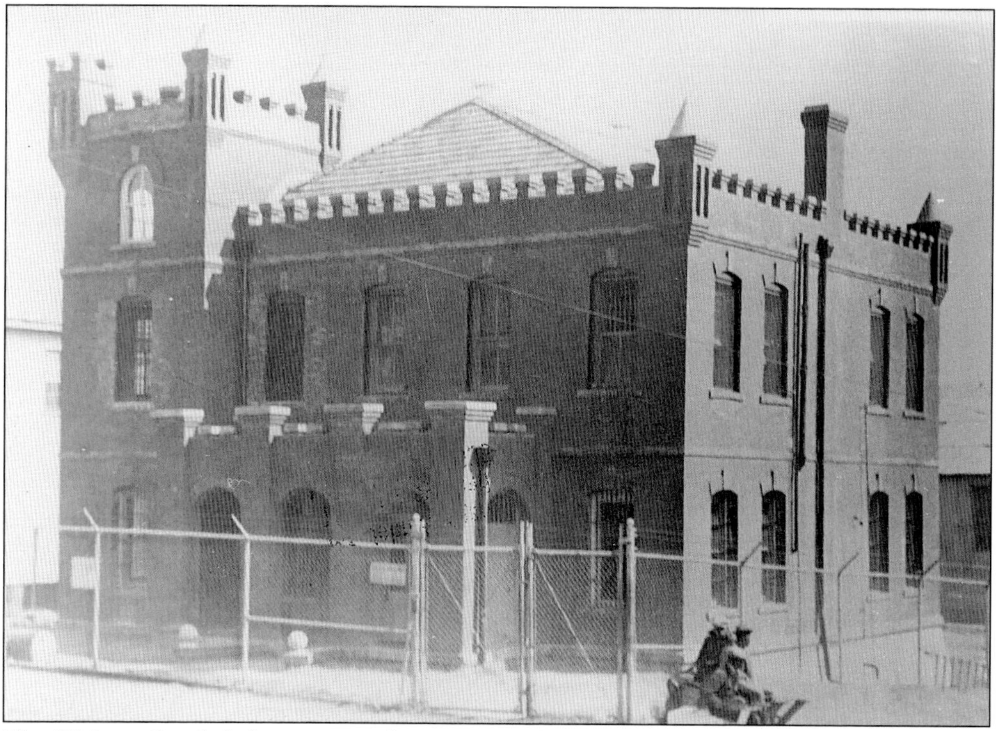

The Webster Parish Jail, constructed in 1909, replaced an older structure that was damaged when a lynch mob blew a hole in the building in 1894. This jail was located on South Broadway behind the post office.

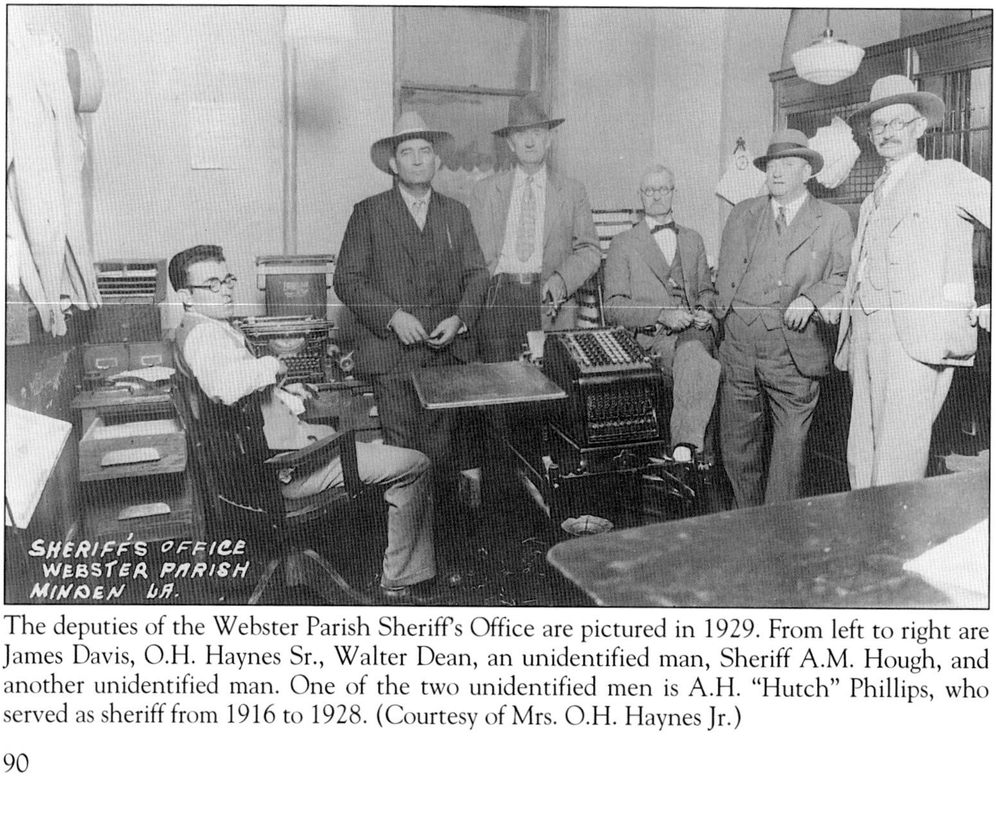

The deputies of the Webster Parish Sheriff's Office are pictured in 1929. From left to right are James Davis, O.H. Haynes Sr., Walter Dean, an unidentified man, Sheriff A.M. Hough, and another unidentified man. One of the two unidentified men is A.H. "Hutch" Phillips, who served as sheriff from 1916 to 1928. (Courtesy of Mrs. O.H. Haynes Jr.)

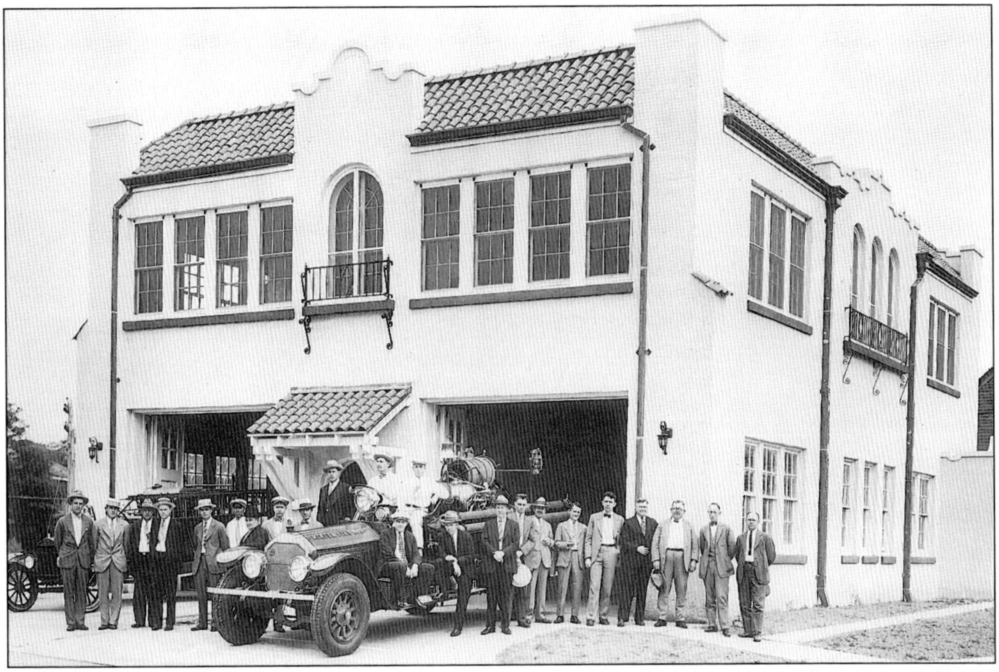

City officials are shown on the occasion of the dedication of the new Minden City Hall and Fire Station in 1926. Before this time, the city rented office space in the Webster Parish Courthouse, and the fire department had no official home. (Courtesy of John S. and Lillian Life Willis.)

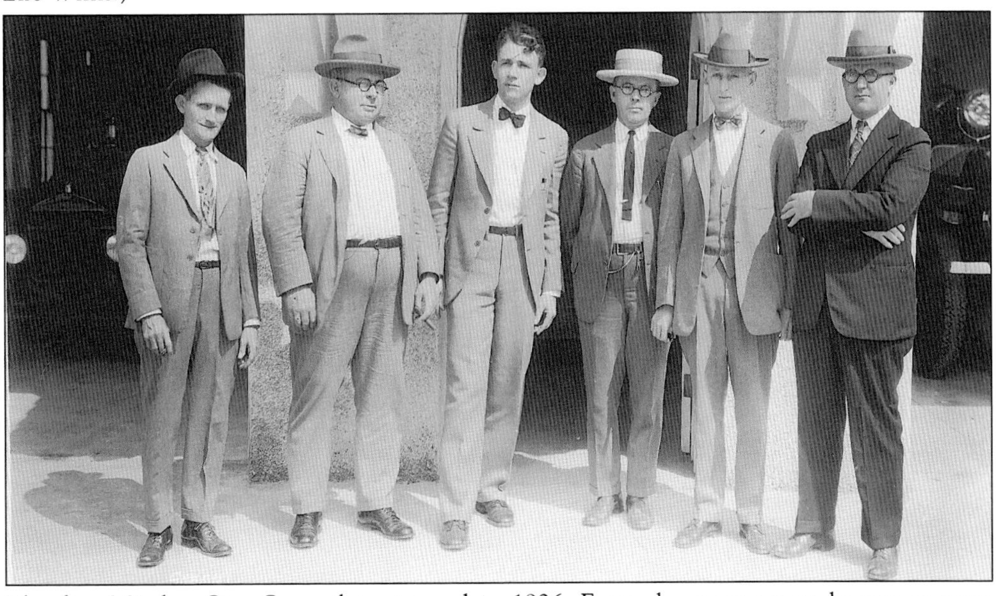

The first Minden City Council is pictured in 1926. Formerly, groups were known as town councils. Minden gained designation as a city in April 1926. Pictured are, from left to right, Councilman J. Ronald Murph; Councilman Will Burnett; Mayor Robert Floyd Kennon, then 23 years old, who would serve as governor of Louisiana from 1952 to 1956; Councilman Richard Garrison Sr.; Councilman Will Life; and Councilman S.H. McCrary Sr. (Courtesy of John S. and Lillian Life Willis.)

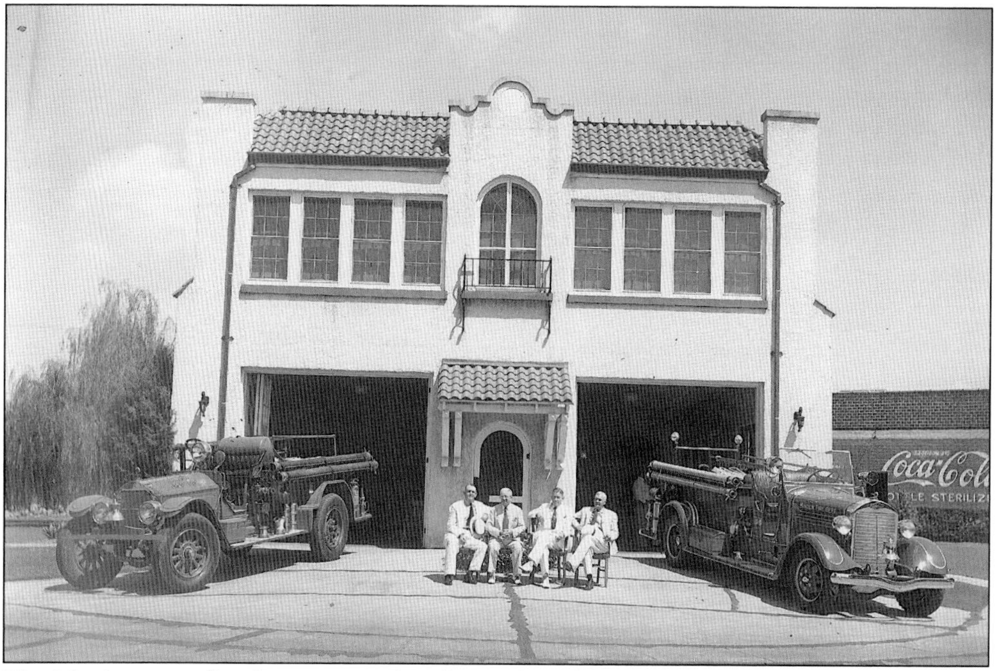

The Minden city officials are pictured in front of city hall around 1936. Second from the left is Mayor David Thomas, a native of Wales who had a fascinating career as a attorney, college professor, newspaper editor, and amateur poet. (Courtesy of Mrs. O.H. Haynes Jr.)

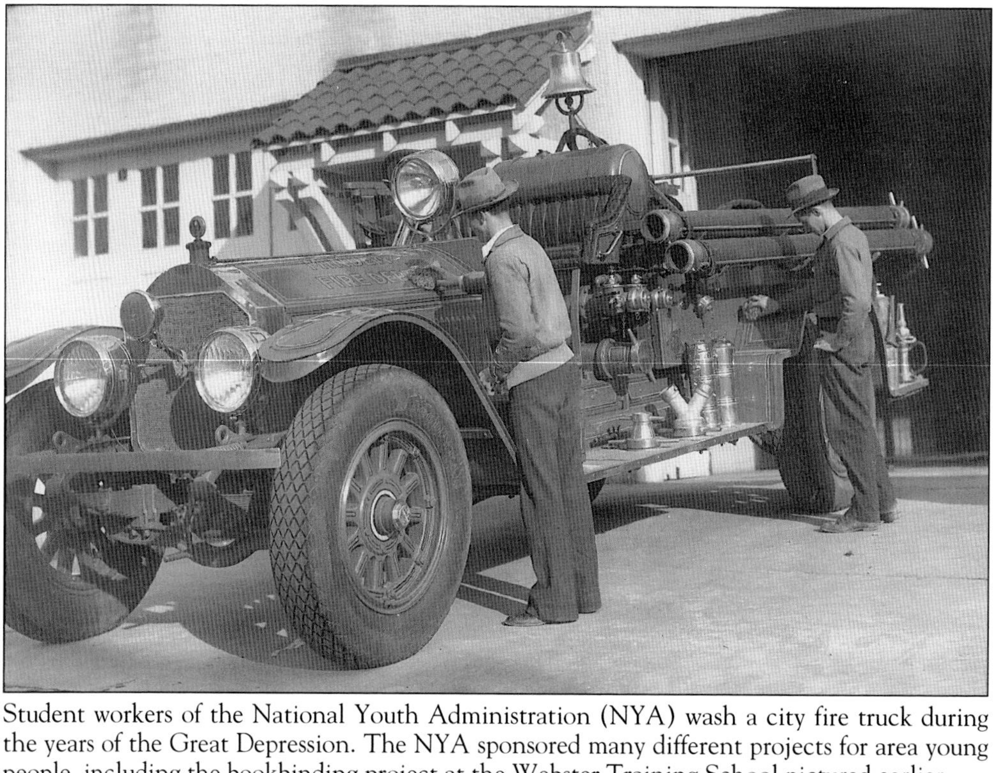

Student workers of the National Youth Administration (NYA) wash a city fire truck during the years of the Great Depression. The NYA sponsored many different projects for area young people, including the bookbinding project at the Webster Training School pictured earlier.

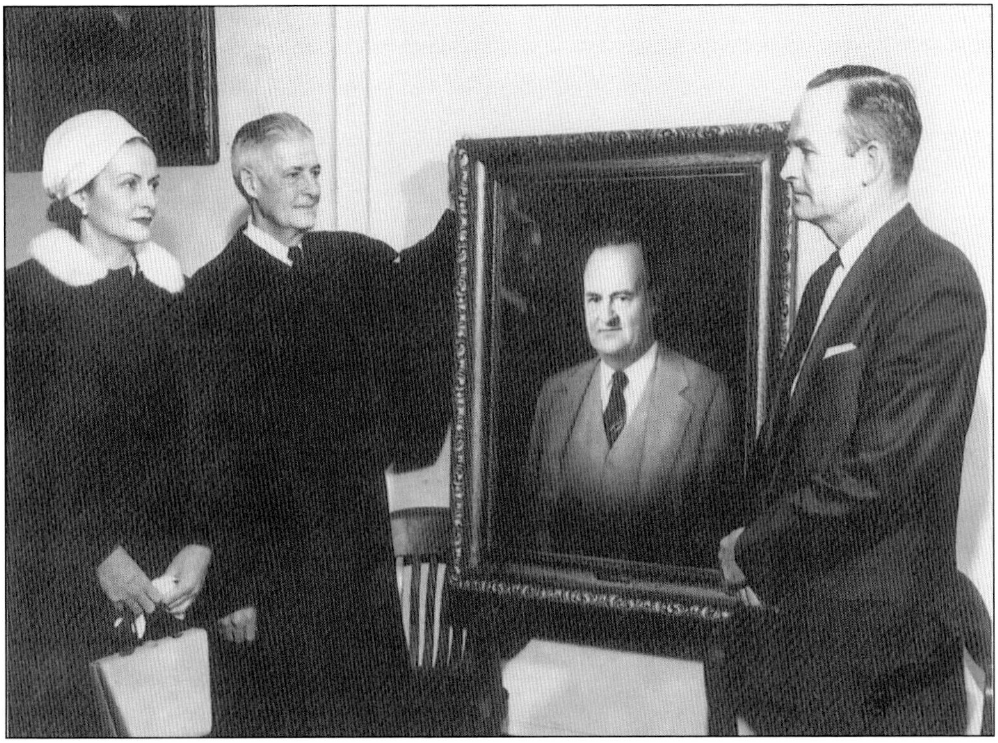

Katie Drew Carey and Judge Richard Harmon Drew Sr. are shown with Judge George Hardy at the unveiling of a portrait of their father, Judge Harmon C. Drew. The picture was displayed in honor of Harmon C. Drew's distinguished service on the Second Circuit of the Louisiana Court of Appeals. (Courtesy of R. Harmon Drew Jr.)

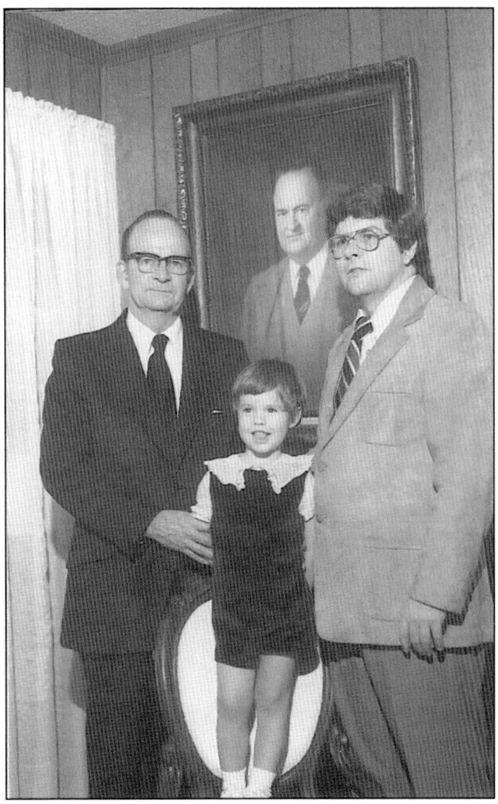

Shown with a picture of Judge Harmon C. Drew are his son, Judge R. Harmon Drew Sr; his great-grandson, R. Harmon Drew III; and his grandson, Judge R. Harmon Drew Jr., in about 1976. Judge R. Harmon Drew Jr. has since been elected to the Second Circuit of the Louisiana Court of Appeals, following in the foot steps of his grandfather, Judge Harmon C. Drew, and his great-grandfather, Judge Richard Cleveland Drew. The Drews are the first family to have three members elected to this court. (Courtesy of R. Harmon Drew Jr.)

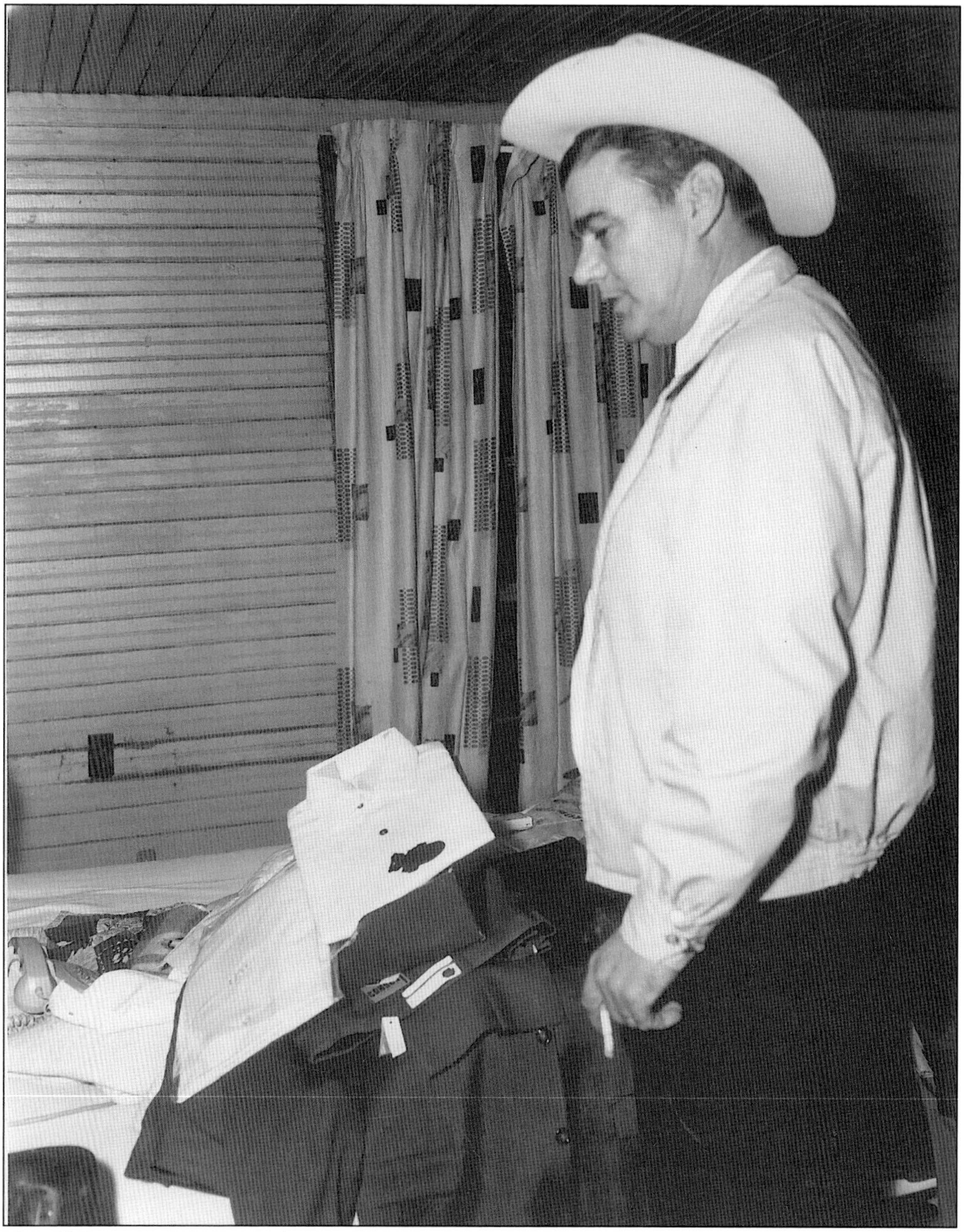

Sheriff O.H. Haynes Jr. is shown examining stolen goods recovered by his department in the late 1960s. Sheriff Haynes worked under his father, Sheriff O.H. Haynes Sr., as a deputy for about eight years before J.D. Batton defeated the senior Haynes in 1952. During the intervening years, O.H. Haynes Jr. was supervisor of the Drivers License offices for all of North Louisiana. In the fall elections of 1963, he avenged his father's defeat by winning in a runoff election over the incumbent Batton. Haynes Jr. held the office for four terms before retiring from office in 1980. (Courtesy of Mrs. O.H. Haynes Jr.)

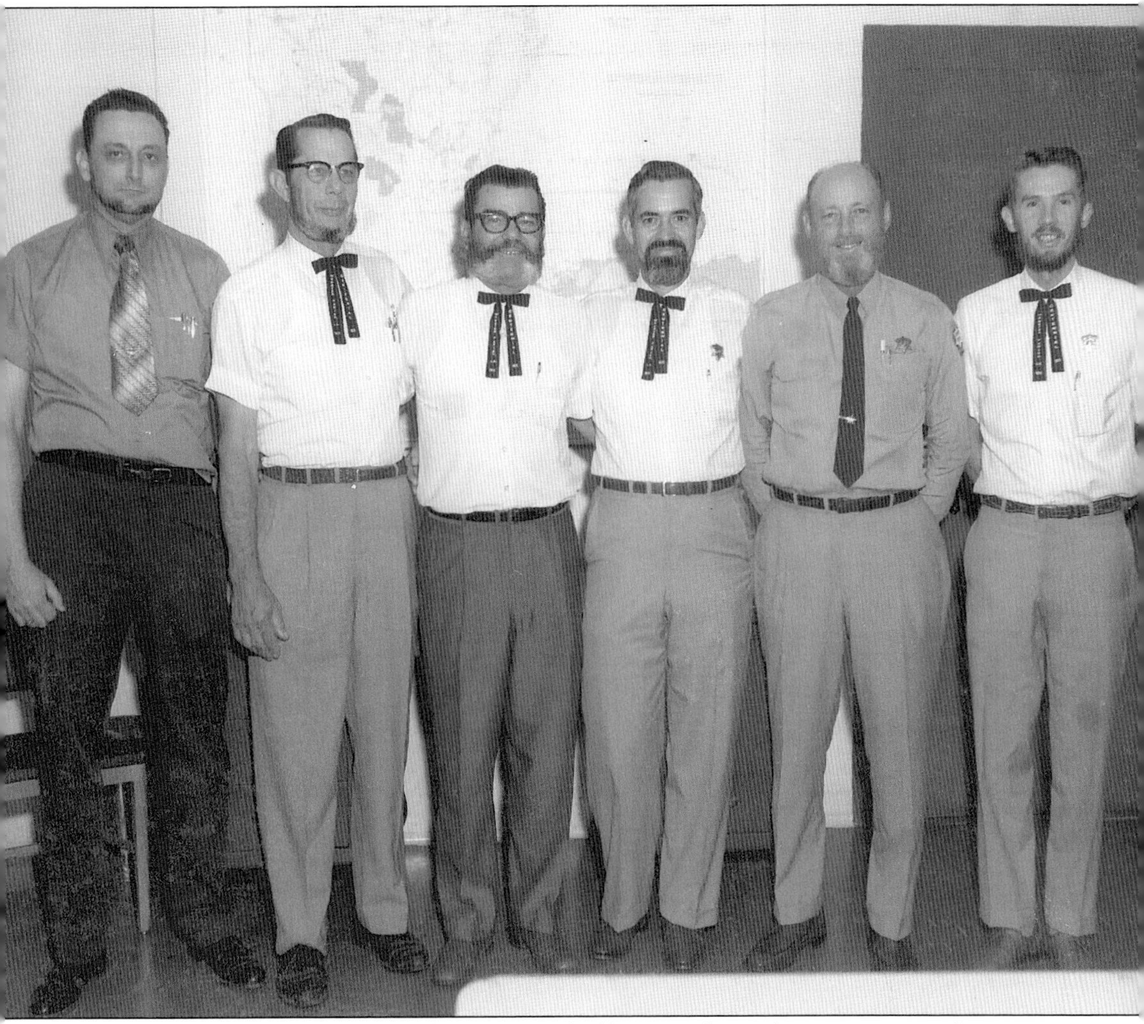

In honor of the 1971 Webster Parish Centennial, all area male residents were invited to grow beards in the style of 1871. Those participating were considered "Brothers of the Brush," and local businesses competed to see who could have the best chapter of the "Brothers of the Brush." Shown above are the Minden deputies of the Webster Parish Sheriff's Office, sporting their centennial celebration beards. Pictured from left to right are Chief Criminal Deputy T.C. Bloxom, today chief of police of Minden; Deputy Albert Simolke; Sheriff O.H. Haynes Jr; Deputy Roy Reagan; Deputy Otis Minter Jr., whose father, Otis Minter Sr., had been Minden police chief; and Deputy J.W. Johnson. (Courtesy of Mrs. O.H. Haynes Jr.)

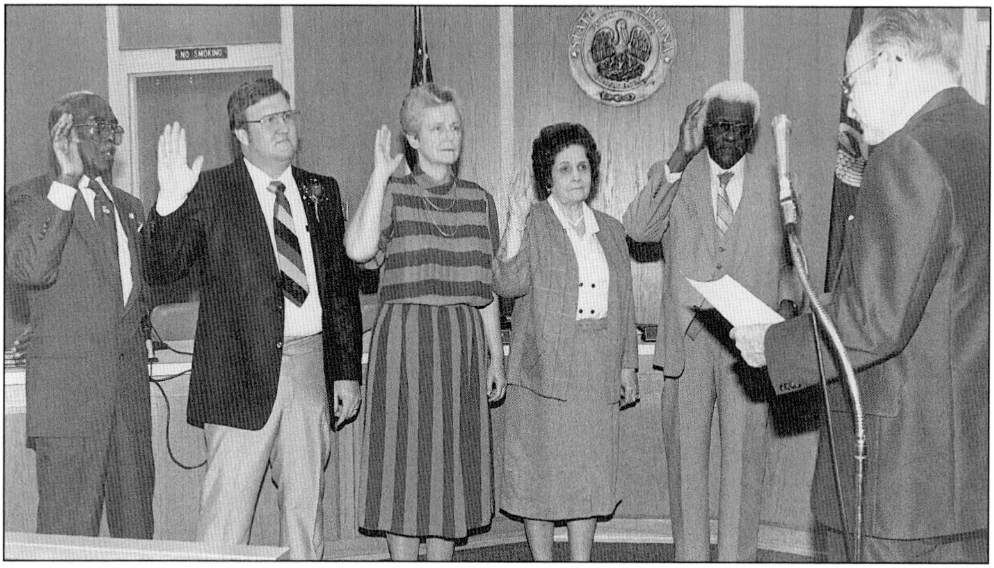

The Minden City Council, elected in 1978, is sworn into office by Judge R. Harmon Drew Sr. Pictured from left to right are councilpersons Robert Tobin, Jim Starkey, Peggy Staples, Rita Brown, and Joe Kirk Sr. Tobin and Kirk were the first blacks elected to the council since the 1880s, and Staples and Brown were the first women ever elected to the council. (Courtesy of the *Minden Press Herald*.)

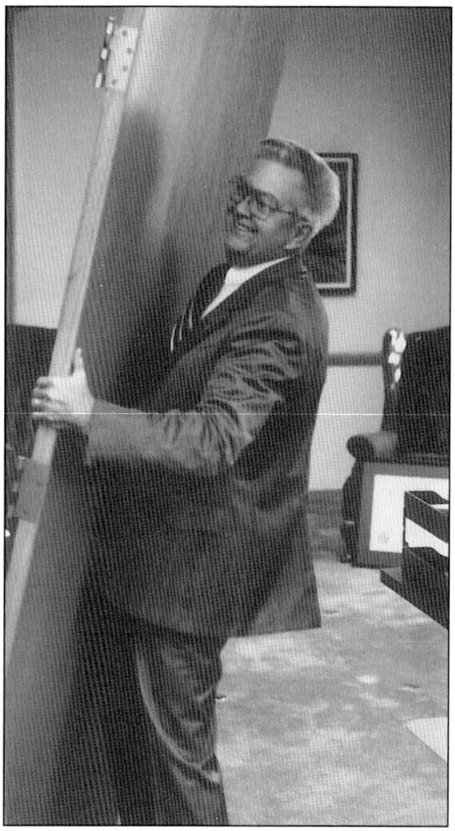

Newly elected Mayor Paul Brown symbolically demonstrates his open-door policy by removing the door to his office after his election in 1986. Brown brought many changes to the city after taking office; he followed a problem-plagued administration that resulted in the previously elected mayor being recalled. (Courtesy of *Minden Press Herald*.)

Five

Education

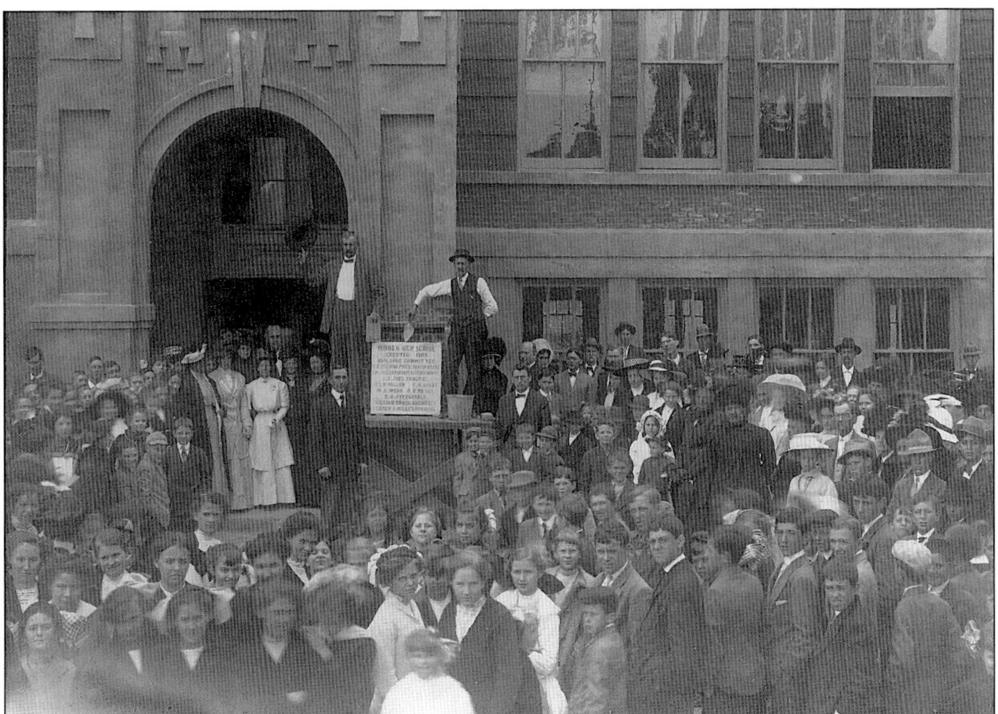

The cornerstone-laying ceremony for the 1910 Minden High School building culminated two years of efforts by Principal C.A. Ives to modernize the Minden schools. He had already earned accreditation for the local high school. Standing in the doorway of the building, directly behind the lady in white, is state superintendent of education J.B. Aswell.

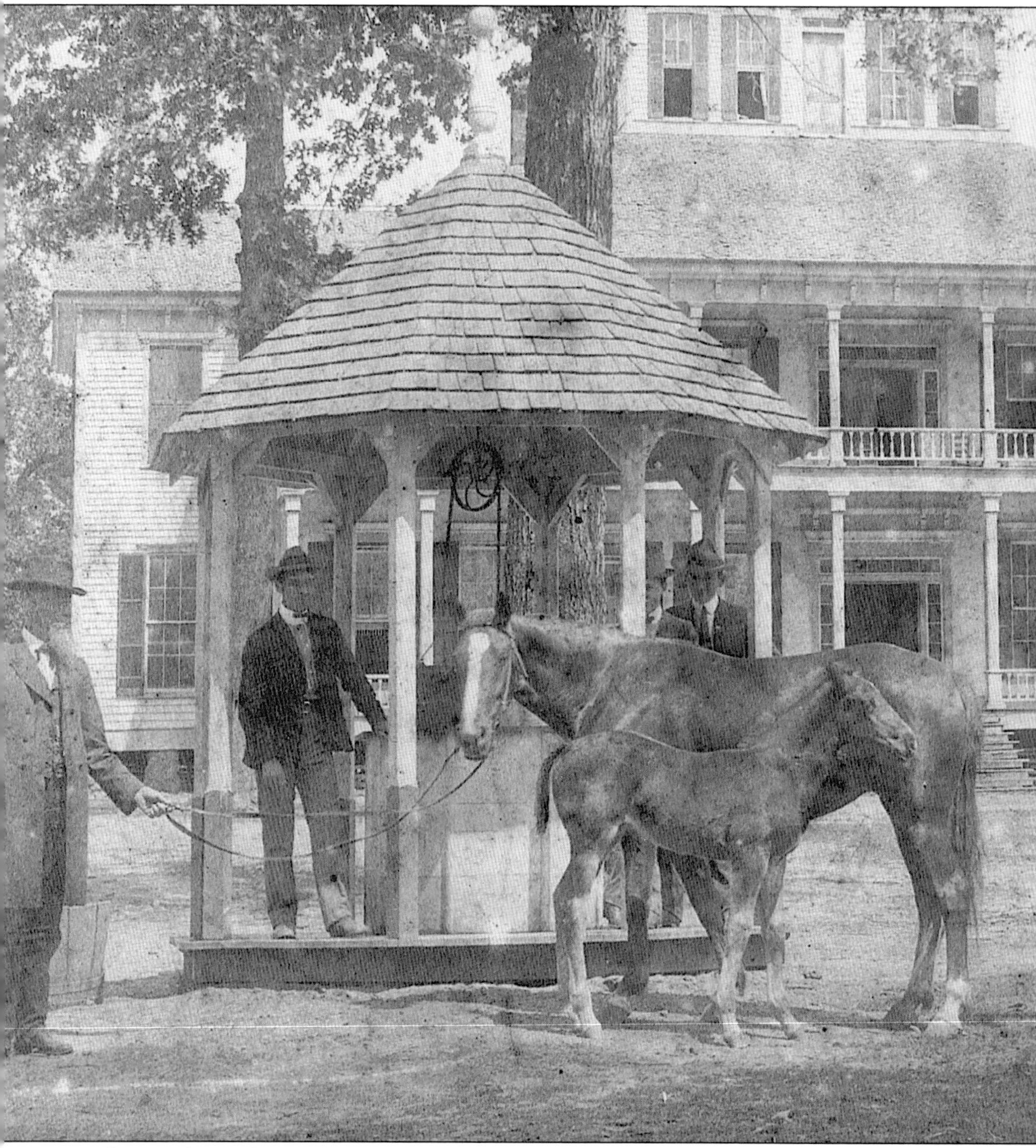

The Minden Male Academy is pictured in the 1880s, with several men watering their horses at the school's well. The academy was founded in 1850 on land donated by W.A. Drake that is today Academy Park in Minden. Many distinguished civic and political leaders attended this school, including two U.S. congressmen, John T. Watkins and John N. Sandlin. Congressman Watkins's father, Judge John D. Watkins, was one of the first principals of the school. Other faculty members who went on to distinguished careers included Judge A.B. George and Henry W. Spofford, a prominent political figure in Louisiana during Reconstruction. The academy operated until about 1898, when the Minden Public School opened in the old Minden Female College buildings. Interestingly enough, today a small gazebo that resembles the well covering sits on nearly the same site in Academy Park. (Courtesy of George Turner.)

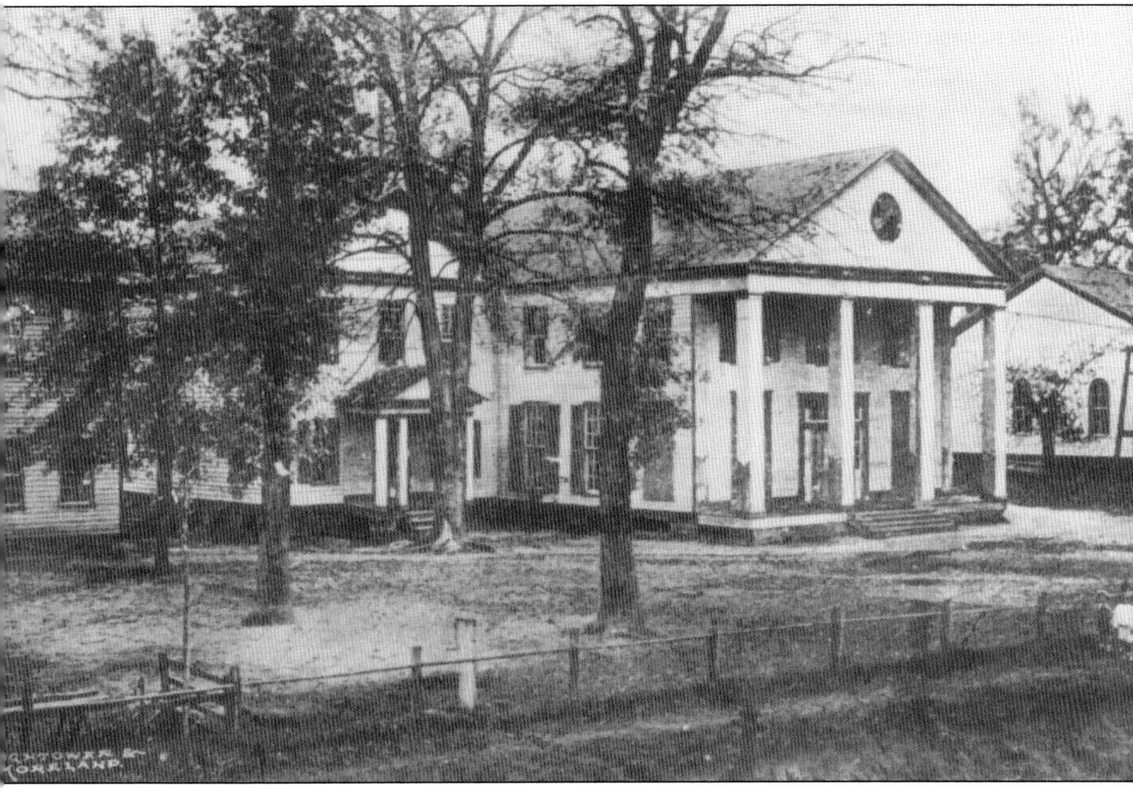

The Minden Female College was founded in 1850 as the Minden Female Academy and upgraded in status to a college in 1854. It was located on the site of the original Minden Academy, opened in 1838. Young ladies from across the South received a quality education at this institution from 1854 until the school closed in the early 1890s. In addition, the cultural life of Minden was greatly enhanced by the well-qualified faculty members that came to teach at the school. The building in the right background was the Concert Hall, which was the scene of numerous musical and theatrical presentations over the years, including some joint efforts during the Civil War years by the students and the young Confederate officers who wintered in Minden during 1864 and 1865. The school is pictured after the college had closed and had become the Minden High School or, in reality, the Minden Public School. The building was used until 1909, finally being moved across College Street to allow for the erection of the 1910 Minden High School. Today's Minden High School is still located on this site. (Courtesy of John S. and Lillian Life Willis.)

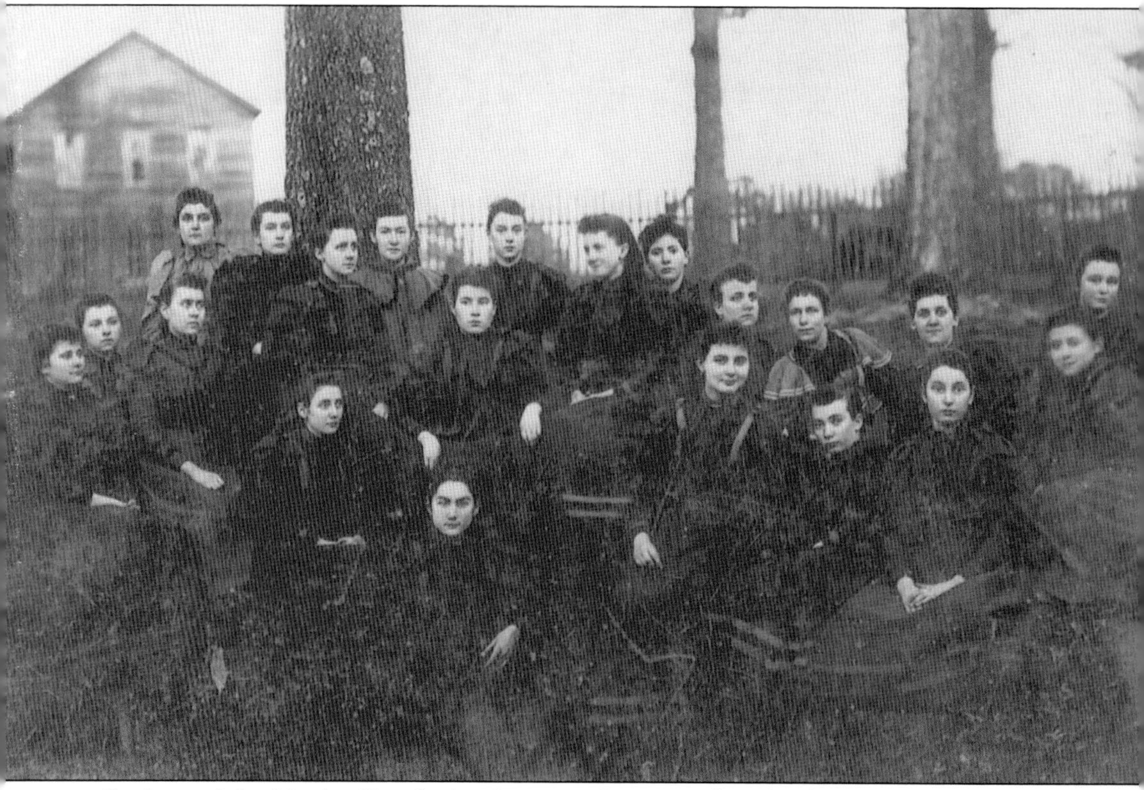

Students of the Minden Female Academy are shown on the school grounds during the latter years of the schools operation, probably in the 1880s. Most graduates of the college were destined for life as upper-class housewives, even though their education included a standard college curriculum, including math and science, along with the more traditional studies for young ladies of music and literature. One exception to this rule was the valedictorian of the Class of 1857, Miss Mildred Boyle. She returned to teach at the college, and in the mid-1870s, when the school was unable to find a president, she headed the school for two years. Because she was female and also lacked a degree from another college, she was not called president, but instead was known as the principal. Miss Boyle later married Dr. S.Y. Webb. (Courtesy of George Turner.)

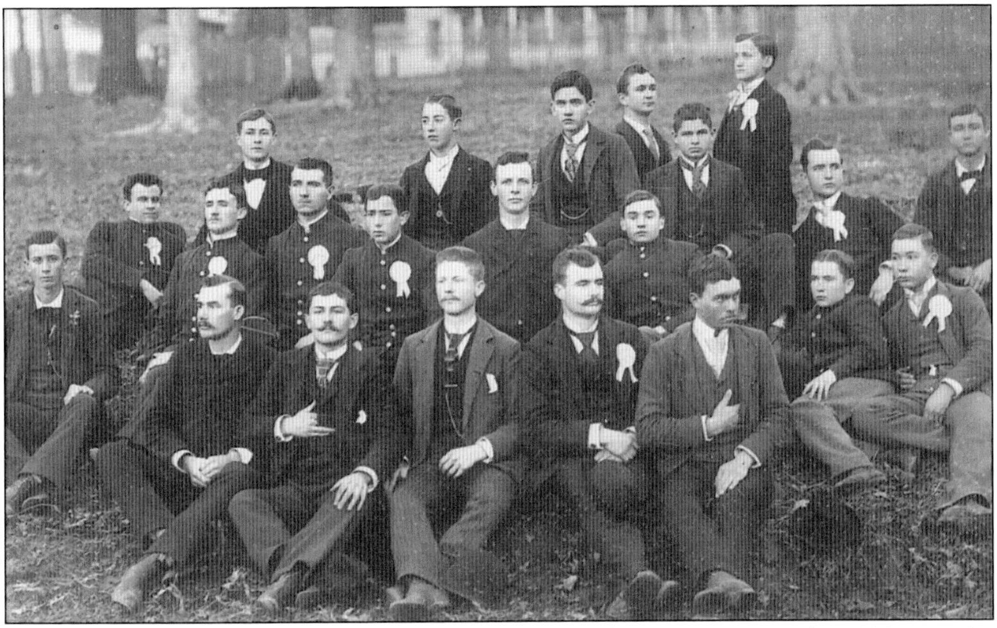

Minden Male Academy students are shown in the late 1870s or early 1880s on the grounds of the campus. Since the school taught boys of all ages, this is probably the high school level or equivalent. The type of uniform being worn by several of the students is unknown; perhaps the school offered some instructions in the military sciences. (Courtesy of George Turner.)

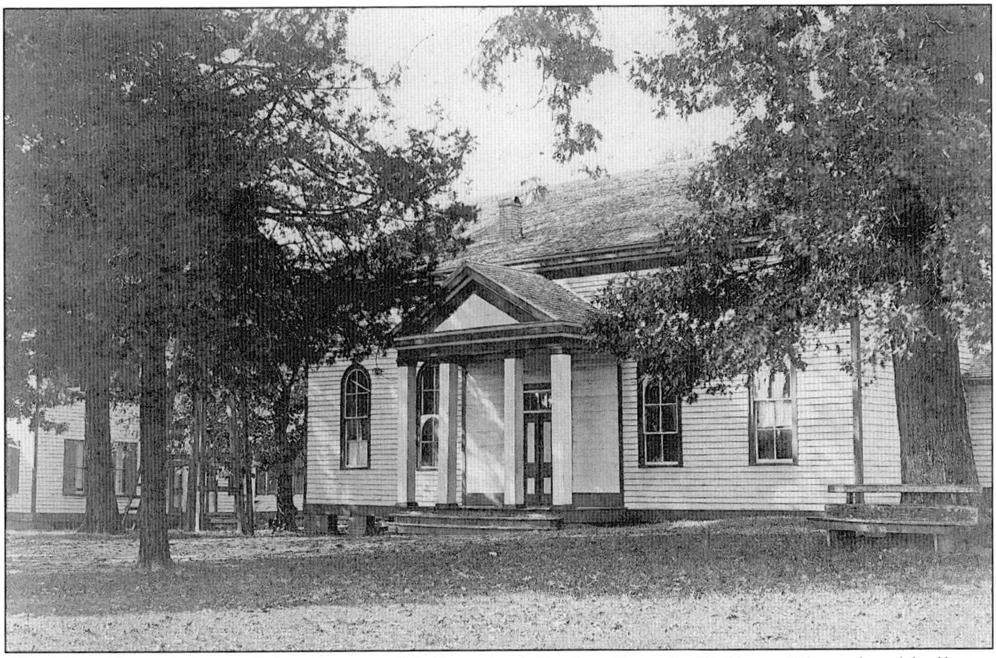

Here is a closer image of the Concert Hall at the Minden Female College. The school bell was on the scaffold just to the left of the building. It was lost for many years and finally recovered through the efforts of Richard Campbell and the MHS student council in 1964. Today it hangs outside Minden High School as the Victory Bell.

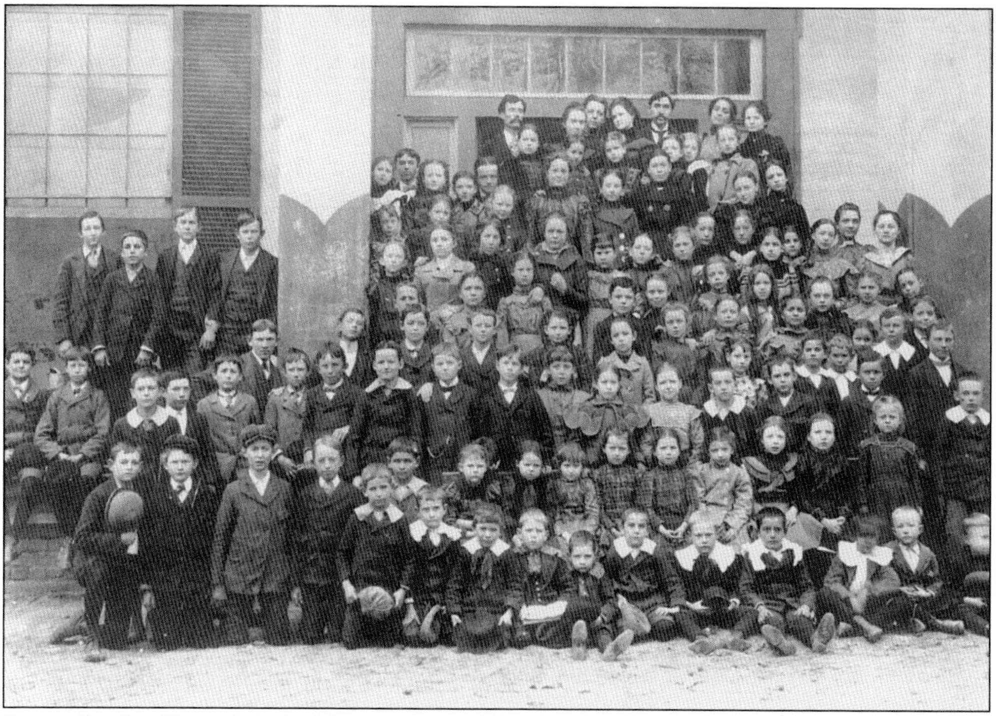

Pictured is the Class of 1898 of the Minden Public School, which met in the old Female College Building. Among those pictured is longtime Minden businessman and city council member Will Life, who is fourth from the left in the front row. (Courtesy of John S. and Lillian Life Willis.)

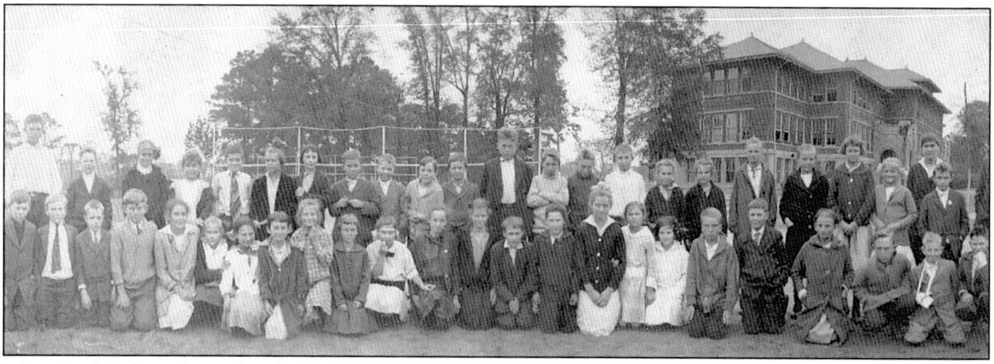

Miss Seals's fourth grade class of the Minden Public School is shown in about 1910. They are pictured on the school playground, later the site of the 1924 Minden High School building, which is still located there today. (Courtesy of Charles Alden and Mary Rathbun.)

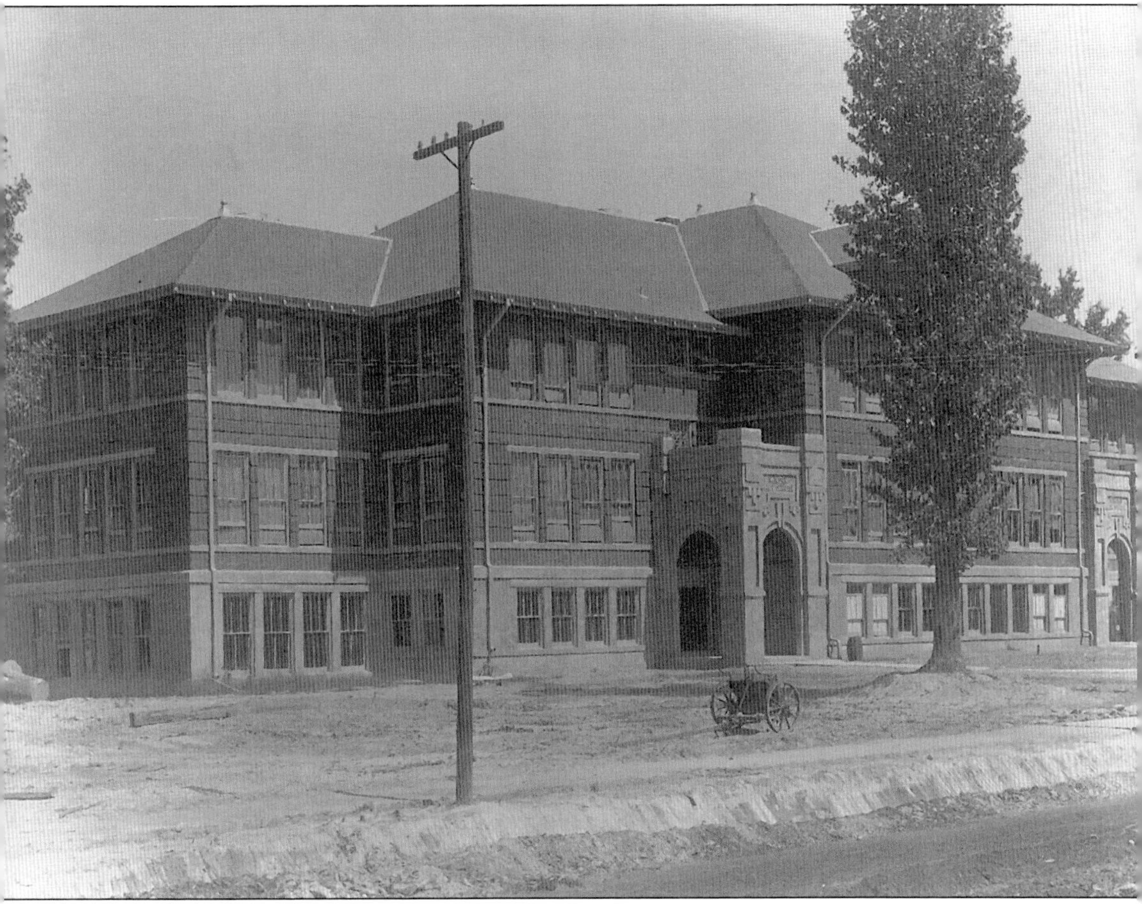

The 1910 Minden High School building is shown as it neared completion. This building was the first public school building erected in Minden and originally housed grades one through eleven. (Louisiana would not add twelve grades to the curriculum until the late 1940s.) This building was used in various capacities for the next 42 years before being torn down in 1953. The three-story structure was considered as state of the art for its time, but the rapid growth of Minden forced the construction of a new high school building in 1924. At that time, this building was converted to house only grades one through seven. After the construction of separate elementary schools in 1948, it became a junior high and housed the school board offices for a time before finally being razed. Today's Minden High is on this site, which has been continually used for education since 1838.

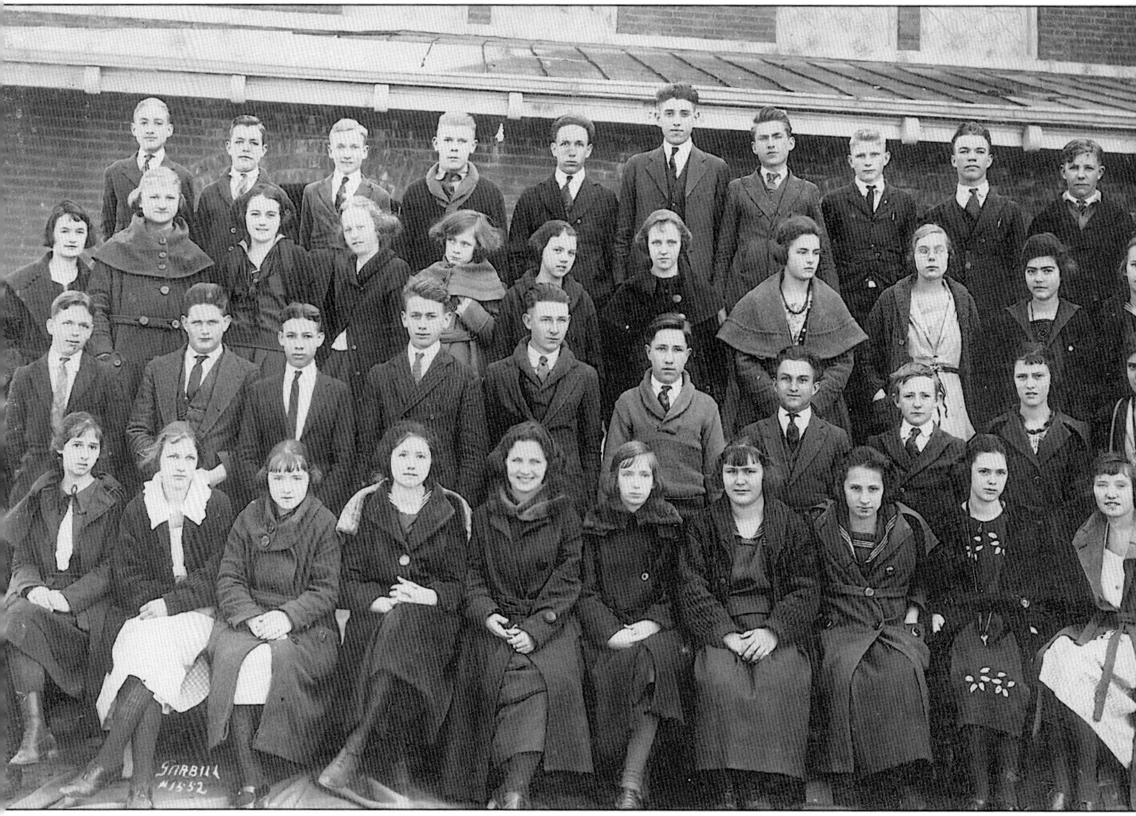

Here is a senior class picture from Minden High School in the early 1920s. Based on the class size of only 41 students, it apparently was before the population boom brought about by the L&A Railroad shops coming to town. After the L&A arrived, class sizes began to exceed 50 and 60 students. The picture must have been taken in winter, as all the students are wearing coats. The background does not correspond to any Minden school, so perhaps the picture was taken on a class outing of some sort. (Courtesy of Charles Alden and Mary Rathbun.)

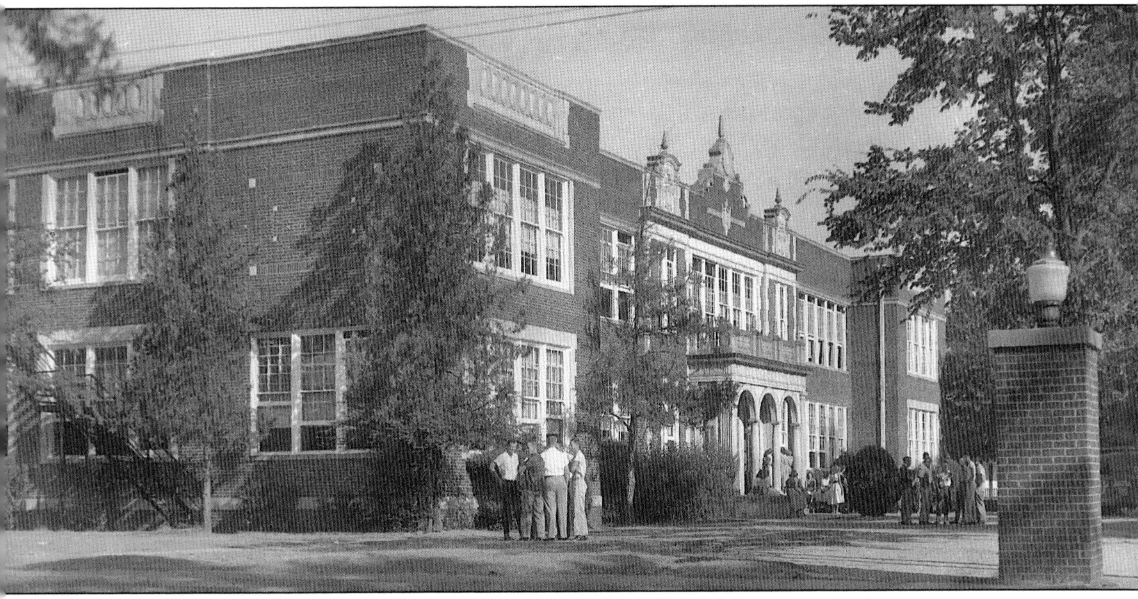

The 1924 Minden High School building is pictured, with students outside during recess or a break period. This photograph apparently dates from the 1940s, as the fire escape was added to the building after 1939. The 1924 building became the Minden Junior High *c.* 1953 when the new Minden High School was completed. It served that purpose until Lowe Junior High School was built in the late 1950s. At that point, it returned to use as a high school building to handle the overflow from the increased student population at Minden High School. The old school auditorium was converted into the "girl's gym" for physical education classes. The 1924 building was remodeled from 1972 to 1973 and is still being used for classes at Minden High School today. (Courtesy of W.W. Williams Sr.)

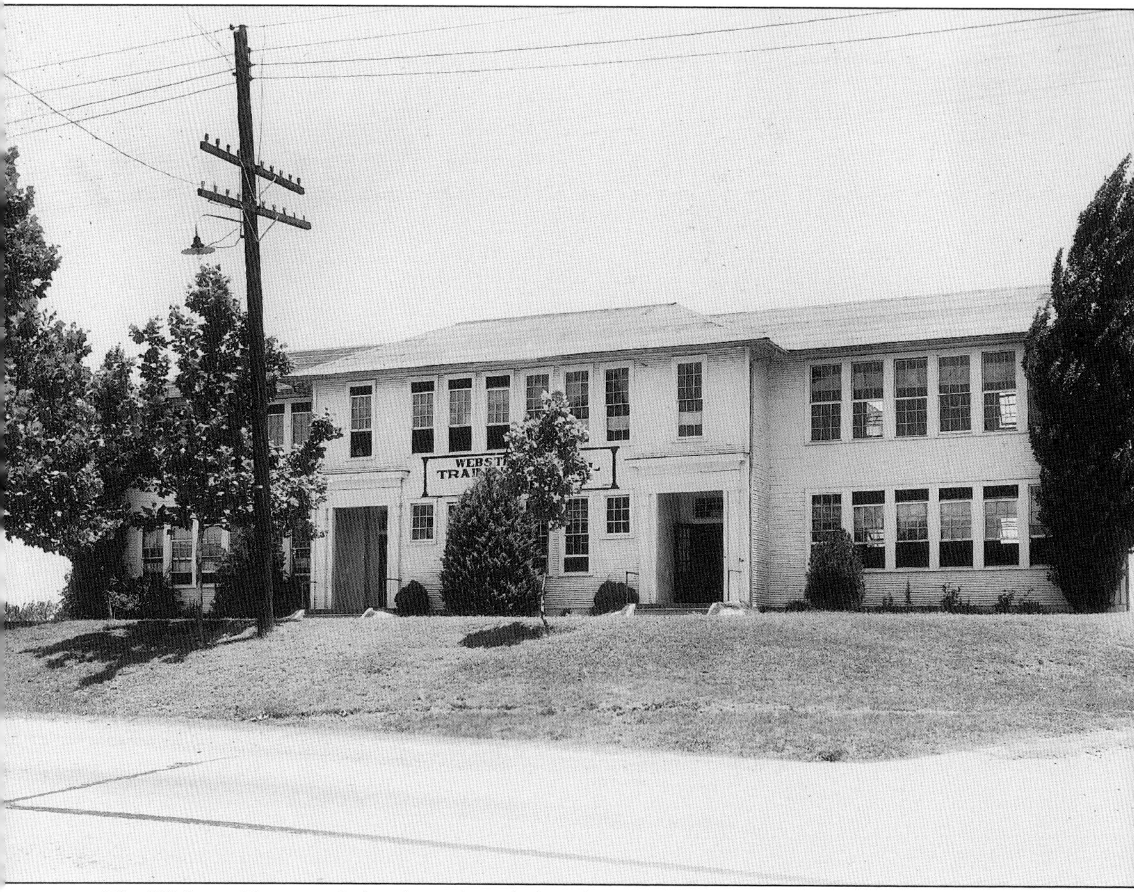

The Webster Training School was founded in the 1920s by E.S. Richardson to provide improved educational opportunities for the black students of Webster Parish. This image dates from the early 1930s. Eventually, the name of this school was changed to Webster High School, and the focus of the school was changed to a more academic approach. The frame building was used until the early 1950s, when a new modern brick building was constructed. Under the leadership of principals such as W. Leon Hayes, Webster High School gained a reputation for academic excellence, despite being underfunded during the years of segregation and "separate but equal facilities." (Courtesy of W.W. Williams Sr.)

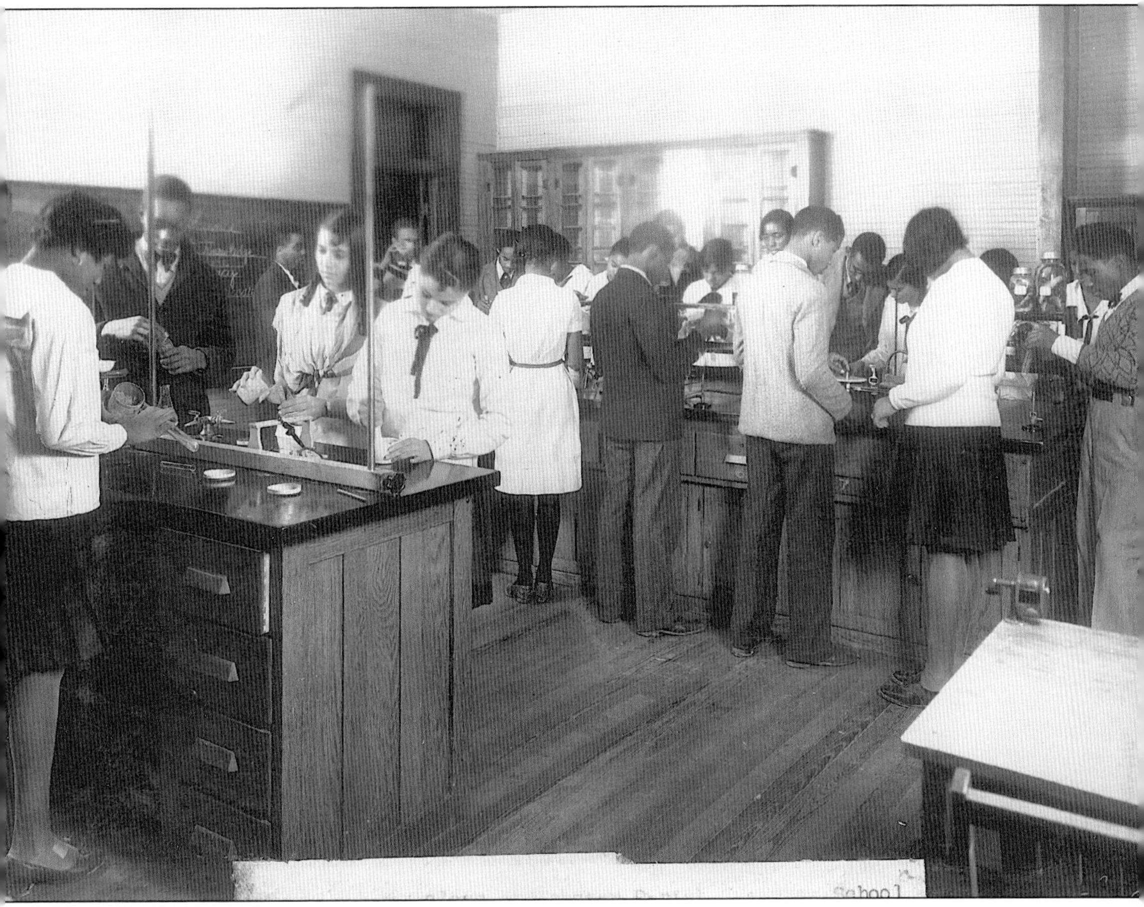

Shown above is a chemistry class in the lab at Webster High School in the mid-1930s. Before the school was renamed, the focus, as the name Webster Training Institute implied, was in training students for immediate employment. After the name change, more academic courses, such as chemistry, were added to the curriculum, along with the necessary facilities, such as this lab. After these changes, many Webster High School students were able to go on to college, and the school produced many outstanding graduates, particularly in the field of education. This was in addition to a strong athletic program that was, at times, dominant in the old LIALO athletic leagues for the black schools.

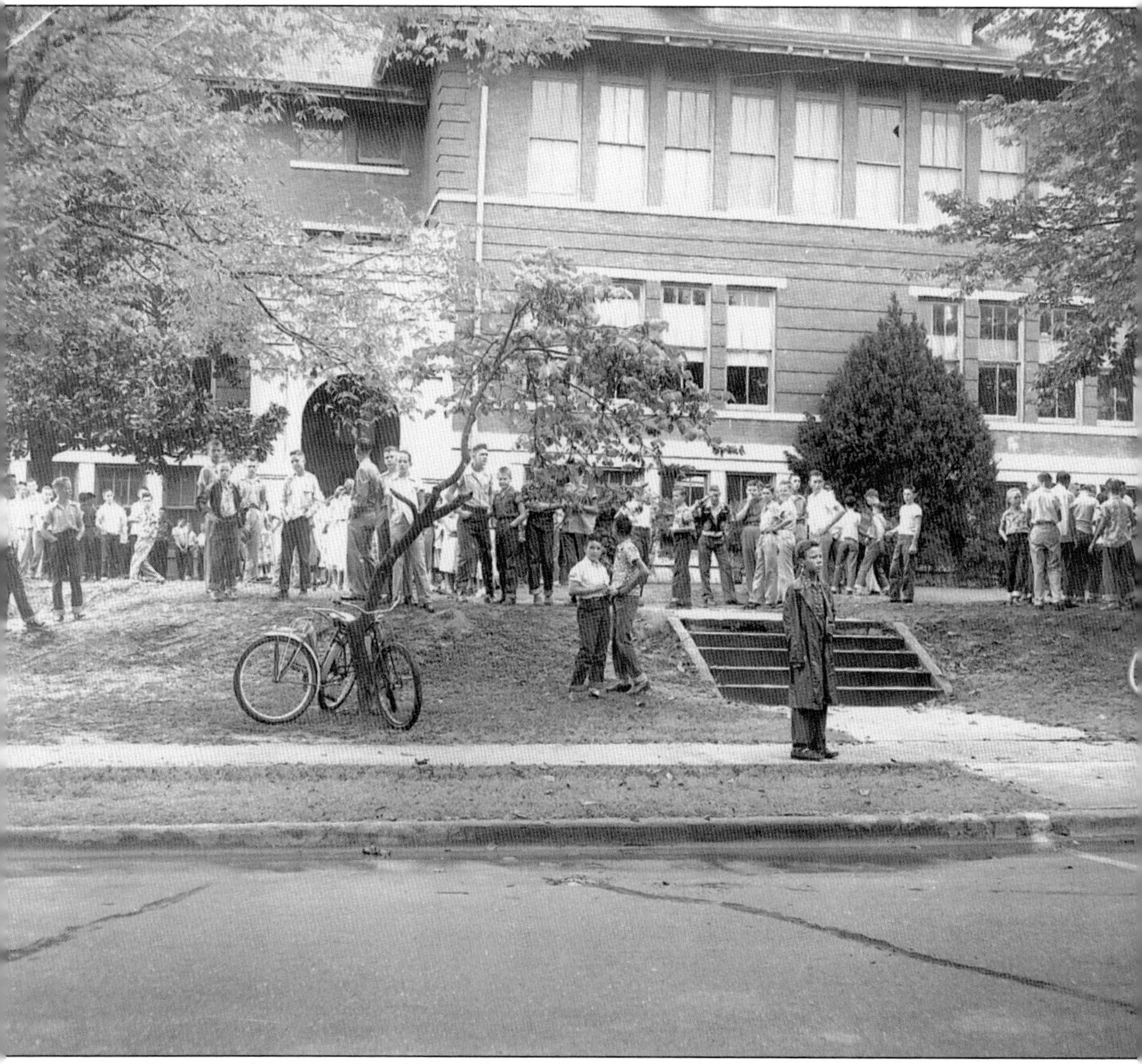

Students are shown at the old Minden High School, by then the Minden Grammar School, in the 1940s. Notice the bicycles resting against the trees, left exposed without fear of theft in those simpler times. The boy on the front sidewalk appears to be waiting for a ride, while the others are enjoying a recess. Several students have obviously focused their attention on the photographer, wondering just exactly why he is taking their picture. Perhaps some examining this book today will find themselves in this photo, which was taken for the school yearbook, *The Grig*. (Courtesy of W.W. Williams Sr.)

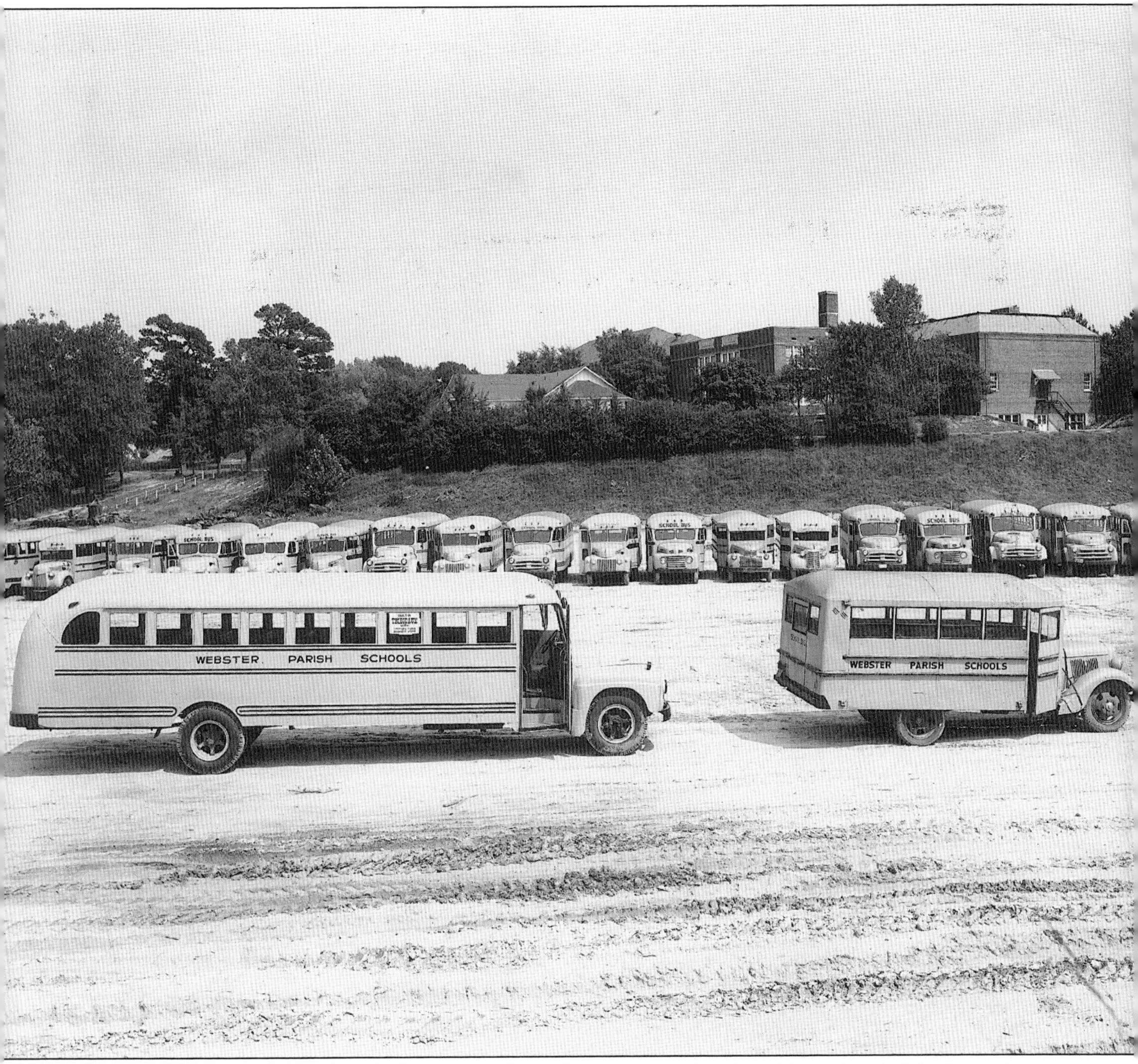

The fleet of school buses for Webster Parish is shown parked behind Minden High School in the late 1940s or early 1950s. Webster Parish pioneered the use of school buses or "trucks" in the 1920s, when the bus bodies were all manufactured in Minden by the W.H. Luck Company. By the time of this picture, school buses were common nationwide, and the parish had begun buying its buses from national companies. These buses are parked on the area that today is the Minden High School track field. The track field was constructed through the efforts of Principal W.W. Williams Sr., athletic director Joe Oliphant, and football coach George Doherty in the early 1950s. (Courtesy of W.W. Williams Sr.)

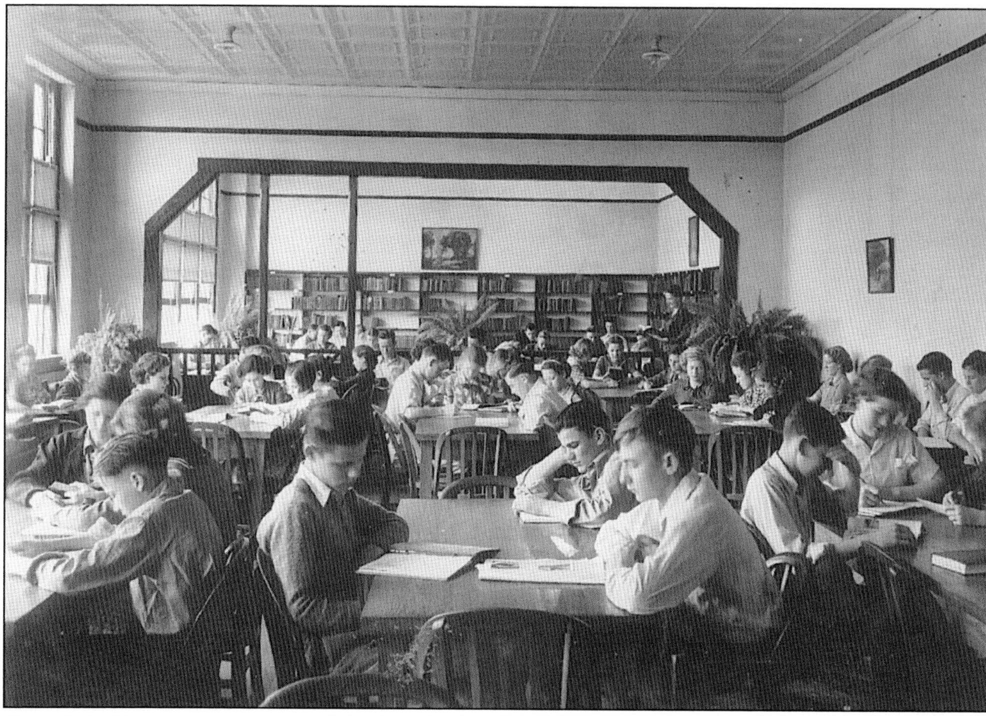

A study hall is in session in the Minden High School library in the 1930s. Standing in the right background is librarian Miss Lillian Phillips. These were Depression years, and funds for books were hard to obtain, so you will notice how few volumes were in the library.

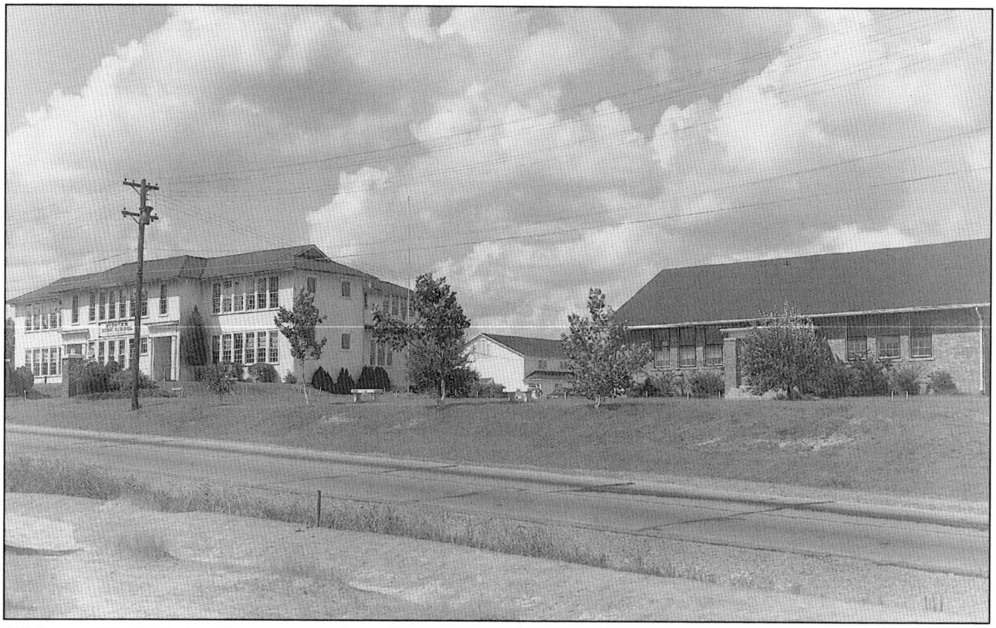

Webster High School is pictured in the 1940s, after it had obtained its new name and status, but before the construction of the 1950s-era brick building. The only remaining building from this campus was later moved to become the J.L. Jones branch of the Webster Parish Library and today houses the Webster High School Alumni Association. (Courtesy of W.W. Williams Sr.)

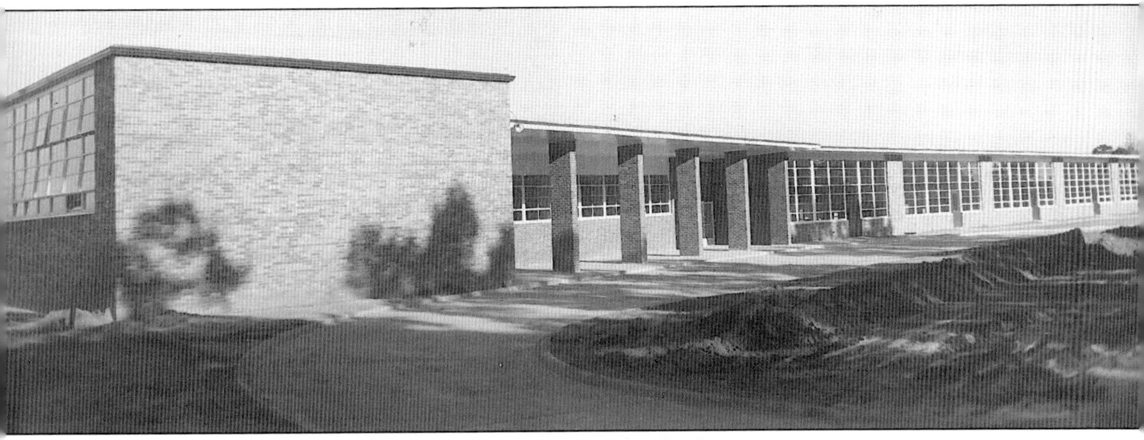

In 1948, Minden Public Schools entered a new era, as for the first time, separate campuses were created for the elementary students in the white schools. Later, in the early 1950s, a separate elementary school for black students would also be built. The two schools built in 1948 were Westside Elementary, shown above, and Eastside Elementary. Westside was eventually renamed W.G. Stewart Elementary, in memory of a longtime school board president. Eastside became E.S. Richardson Elementary in memory of the superintendent of Webster Parish schools from 1919 to 1936. Both Stewart and Richardson Elementary Schools are still in use today, although both have been expanded and, in some cases, forced to use portable buildings. Today, Minden has four elementary schools, housing students in grades one through five; one sixth grade campus; one junior high school for grades seven through eight; and one high school in its public school system. (Courtesy of W.W. Williams Sr.)

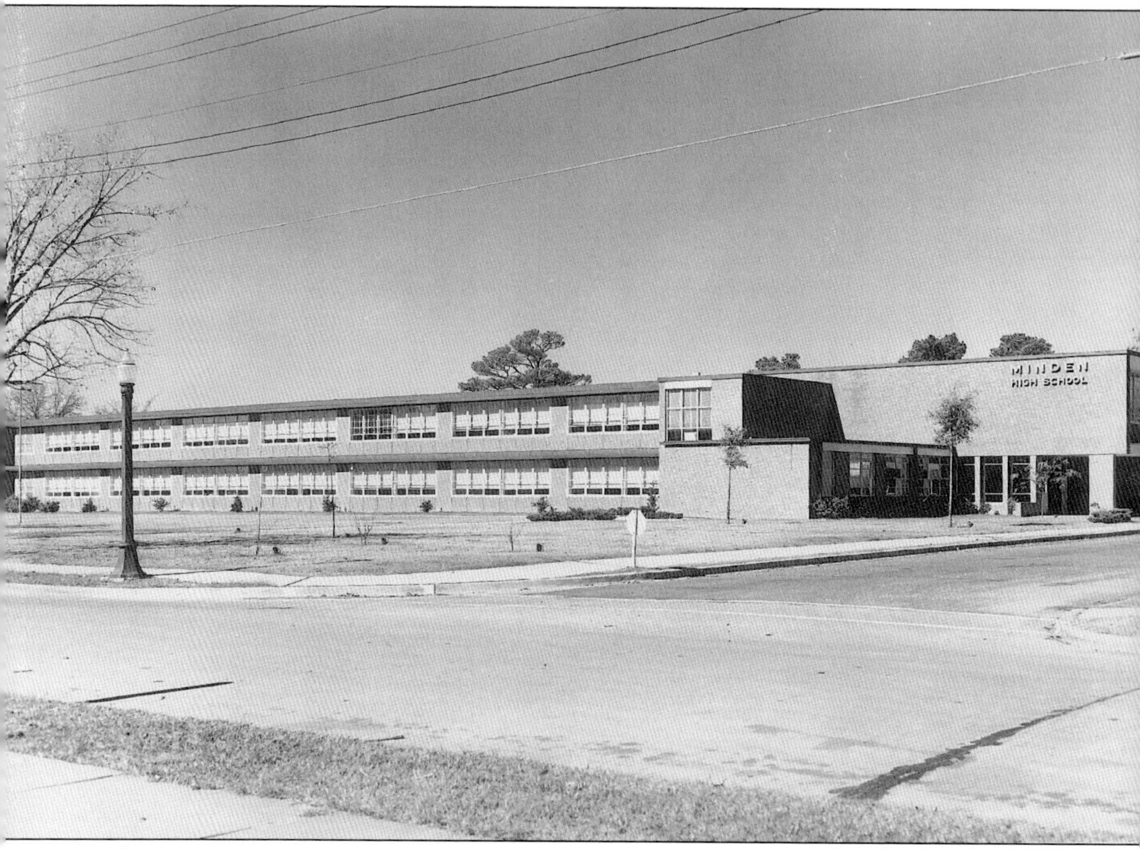

The most recent Minden High School building was constructed from 1953 to 1954. The first class graduated from this school in 1955. At the time of this school's construction, the principal was W.W. Williams Sr., who eventually became parish superintendent of schools. It was during this era that Minden High School gained national recognition for both academic excellence and athletic prowess. Student test scores were consistently in the highest percentages of any schools in the country. The athletic teams earned the nickname "Home of the Champions" for the school. In fact, it was in this period that the school motto became the Latin phrase, "domus victorium." Minden High won state football championships in 1954 and 1956; a basketball championship in 1955; a state baseball championship in 1956; and a state girl's swimming championship in 1955. The Class of 1955 won three of these championships in football, basketball, and swimming their senior year. This building is still in use today. (Courtesy of W.W. Williams Sr.)

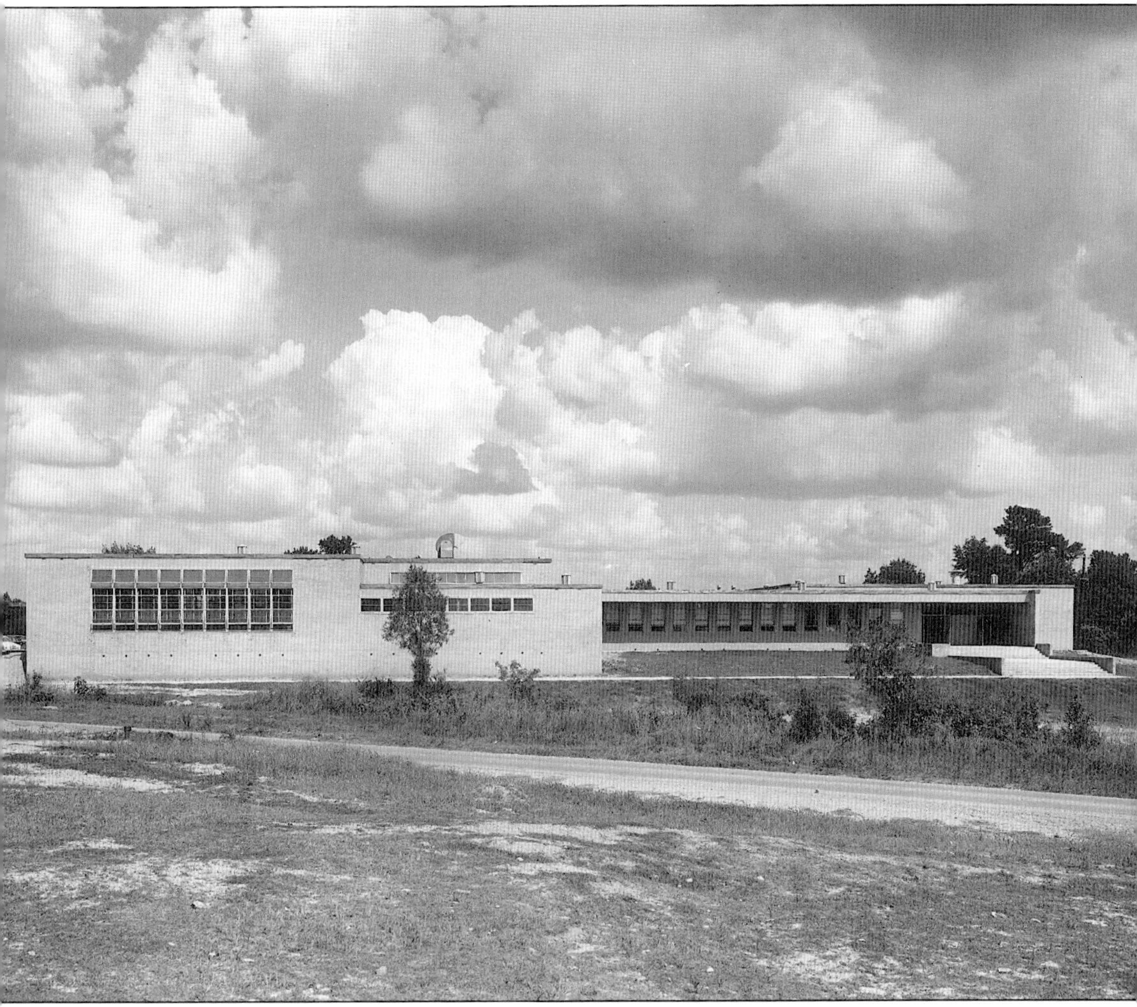

Constructed at the same time as the new Minden High School was the brick Webster High School. The modern building replaced the frame structure that had begun its existence as the Webster Training School. Webster High School was still forced to struggle with the problems of the segregation era, but the upgrade in facilities did make it possible to provide a better educational environment for its students. Many of the students of this 1950s Webster High School have gone on to fill important roles in our nation in all the professions. Minden's first black mayor, Robert T. Tobin, was a faculty member of Webster High School for many years. After the complete integration of Webster Parish Schools in 1974, Webster became a junior high school and is still used in that capacity today. (Courtesy of W.W. Williams Sr.)

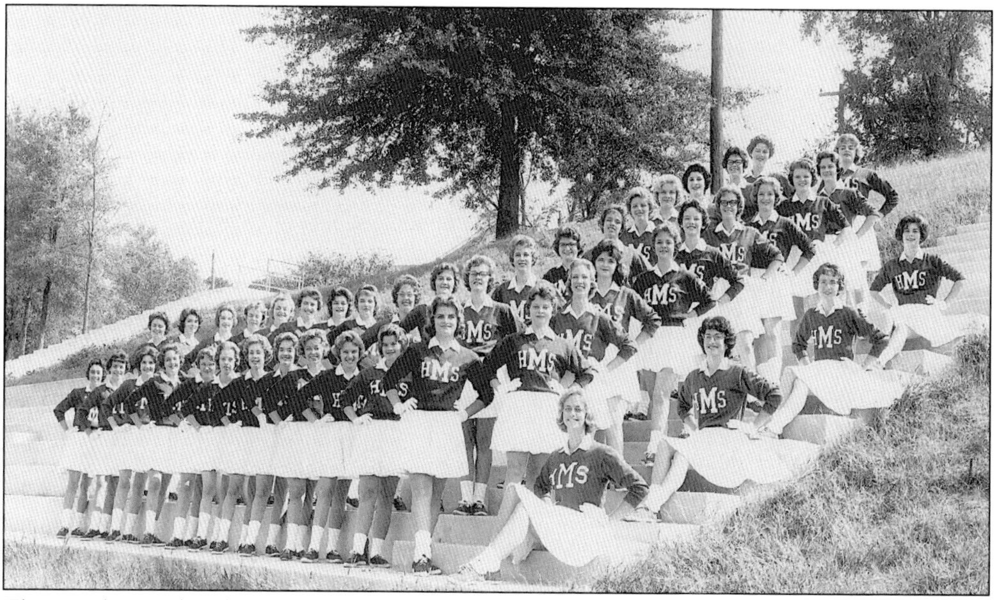

The Minden High School Louisiannes gained recognition throughout the South as a drill team beginning in the 1960s, under the direction of Minden resident Mrs. Nannette Cox. Shown in this picture is one of the early Louisianne groups, posing on the concrete bleachers of the Minden High School track field. (Courtesy of George Calvit.)

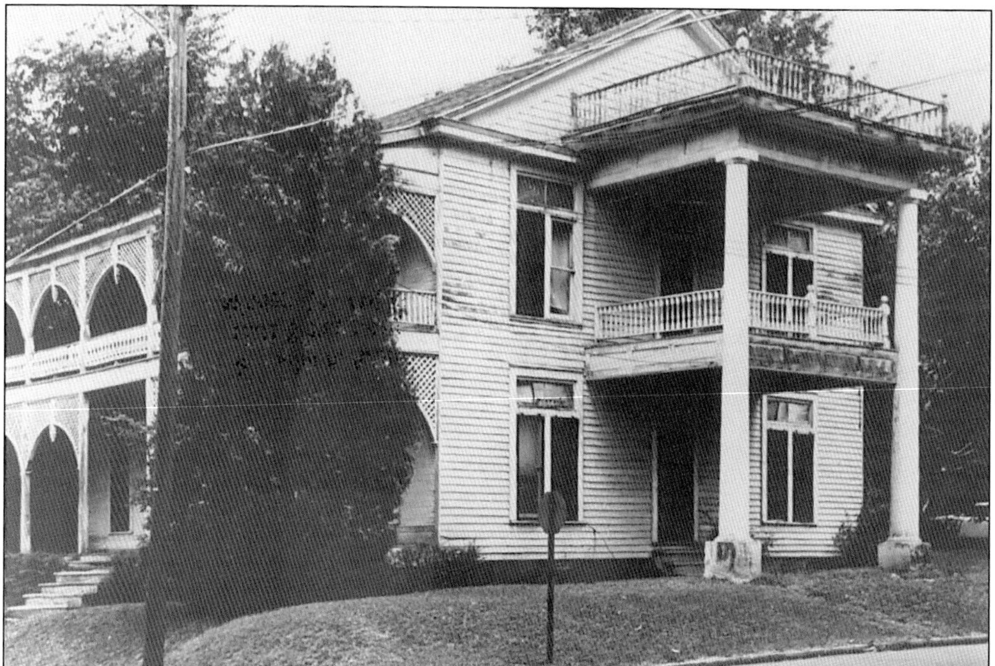

The last remaining building of the Minden Male Academy is pictured shortly before its demolition in the 1970s. The building had been moved a block to the corner of Sullivan and East and West Streets and eventually became an apartment house known locally as the "Honeymoon Hotel," since so many newly married couples began their lives together in the apartments.

Six

Sports and Recreation

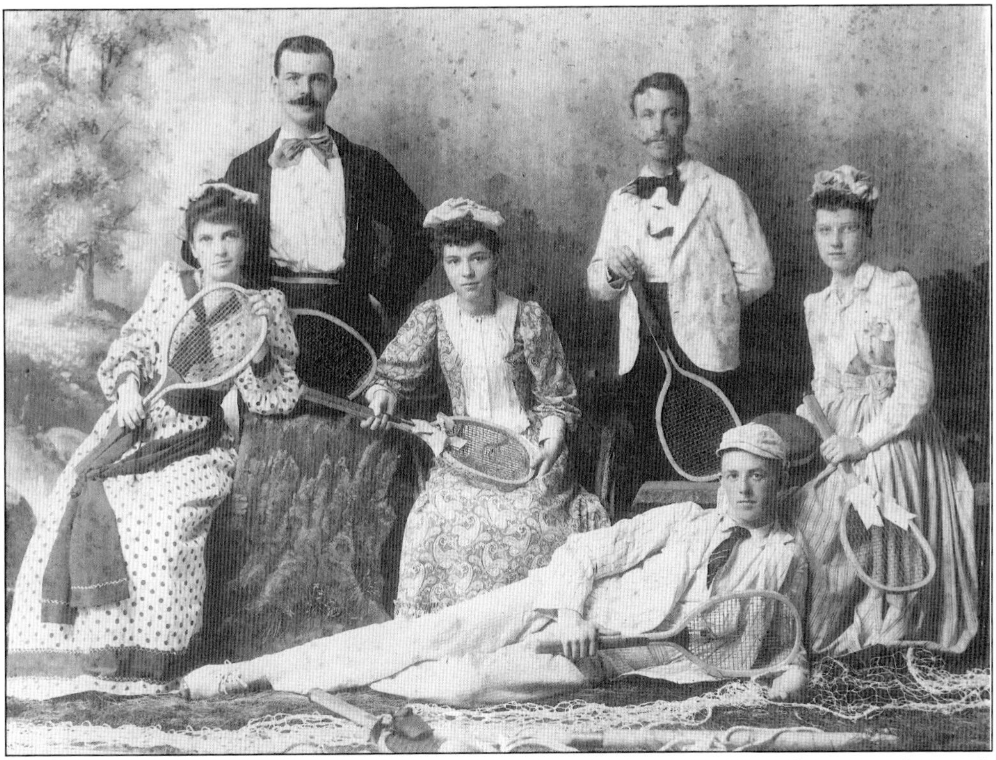

The "Minden Tennis Club" is shown in the 1880s. Actually, this was a posed picture taken with props in a photo studio in Dallas, TX. Seated at the bottom left is Miss Treeby Chaffe, later Mrs. R.H. Miller; standing to her left is her brother, Arthur Chaffe, who would later serve as mayor of Minden. (Courtesy of Thad Andress.)

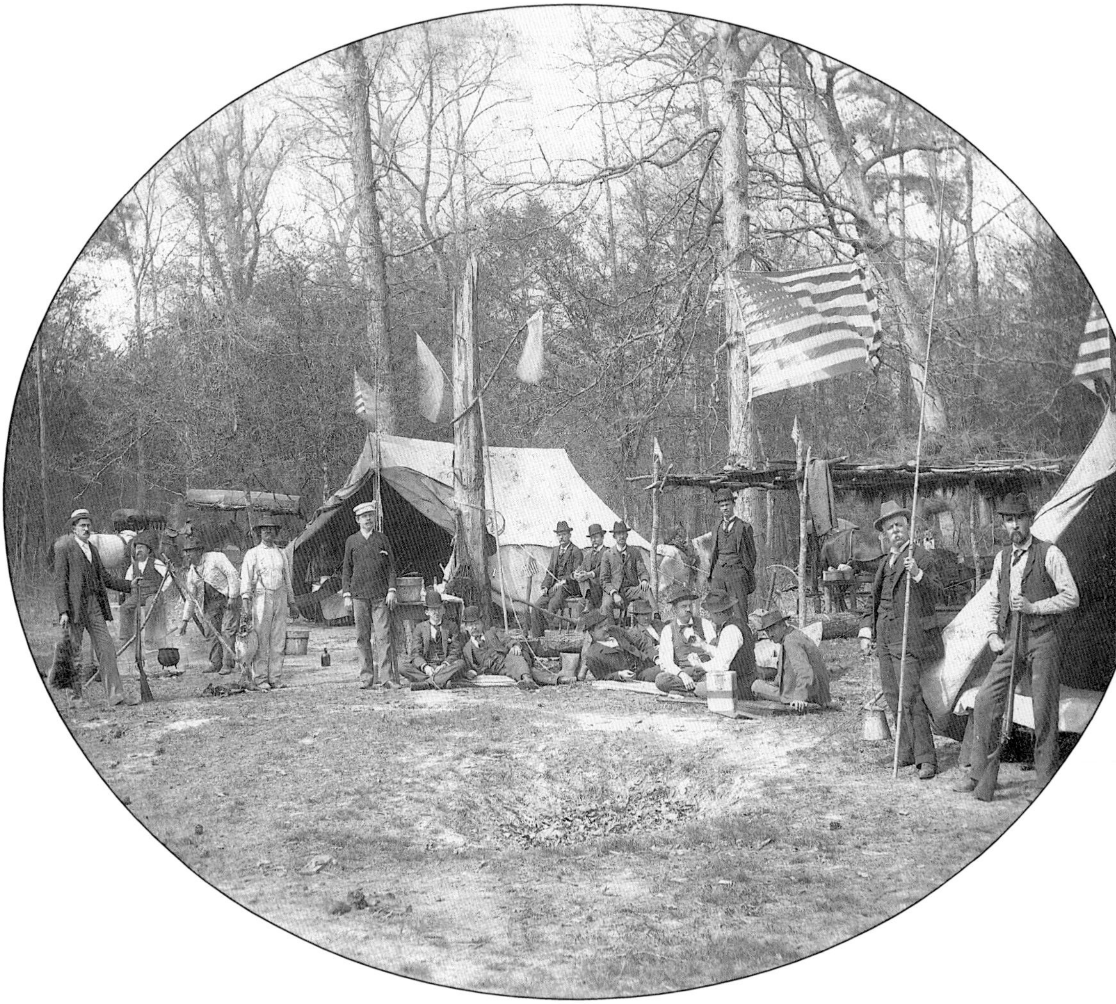

A group of Minden residents is shown on a hunting expedition in the 1890s. Notice the American flags prominently displayed and the trophies of the trip, such as the fish being held by the fourth man from the left and the animal pelt held by the man on the extreme left. It appears that in the main tent, a lady has been brought along, perhaps to cook for the expedition. Among those pictured are ? Hunter, McIntyre Sandlin, Jim Crichton, ? Murrell, Pierce Butler, J.Y. Webb, Arthur Chaffe, Clarence Chaffe, Rhydon Webb, Adam Crichton, Matt Morgan, George English, and ? Goodwill. Based on the attire of the gentlemen in the image, this picture must have been arranged in advance, since the suits hardly seem proper clothing for "roughing it." (Courtesy of Charles Alden and Mary Rathbun.)

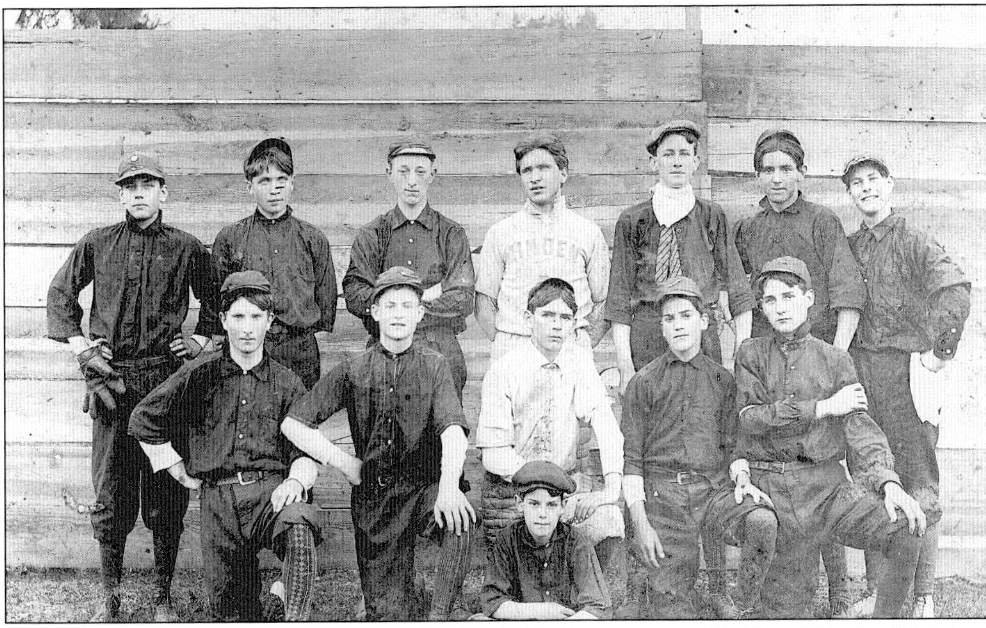

Pictured above is a group of young Minden baseball players around 1905 and 1910. Third from the left in the back row is Will Life, later a successful businessman and city official and a lifelong supporter of local baseball. (Courtesy of John S. and Lillian Life Willis.)

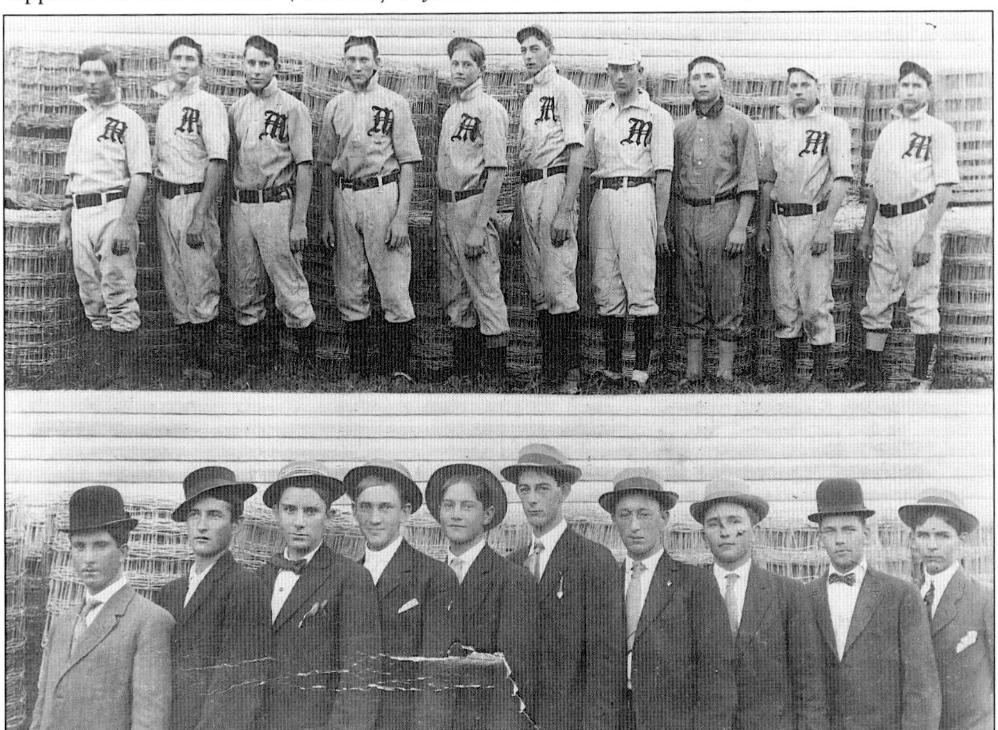

The Minden High baseball team is shown in uniforms and traveling clothes in about 1910. Will Life is again pictured fourth from the right in this picture. (Courtesy of John S. and Lillian Life Willis.)

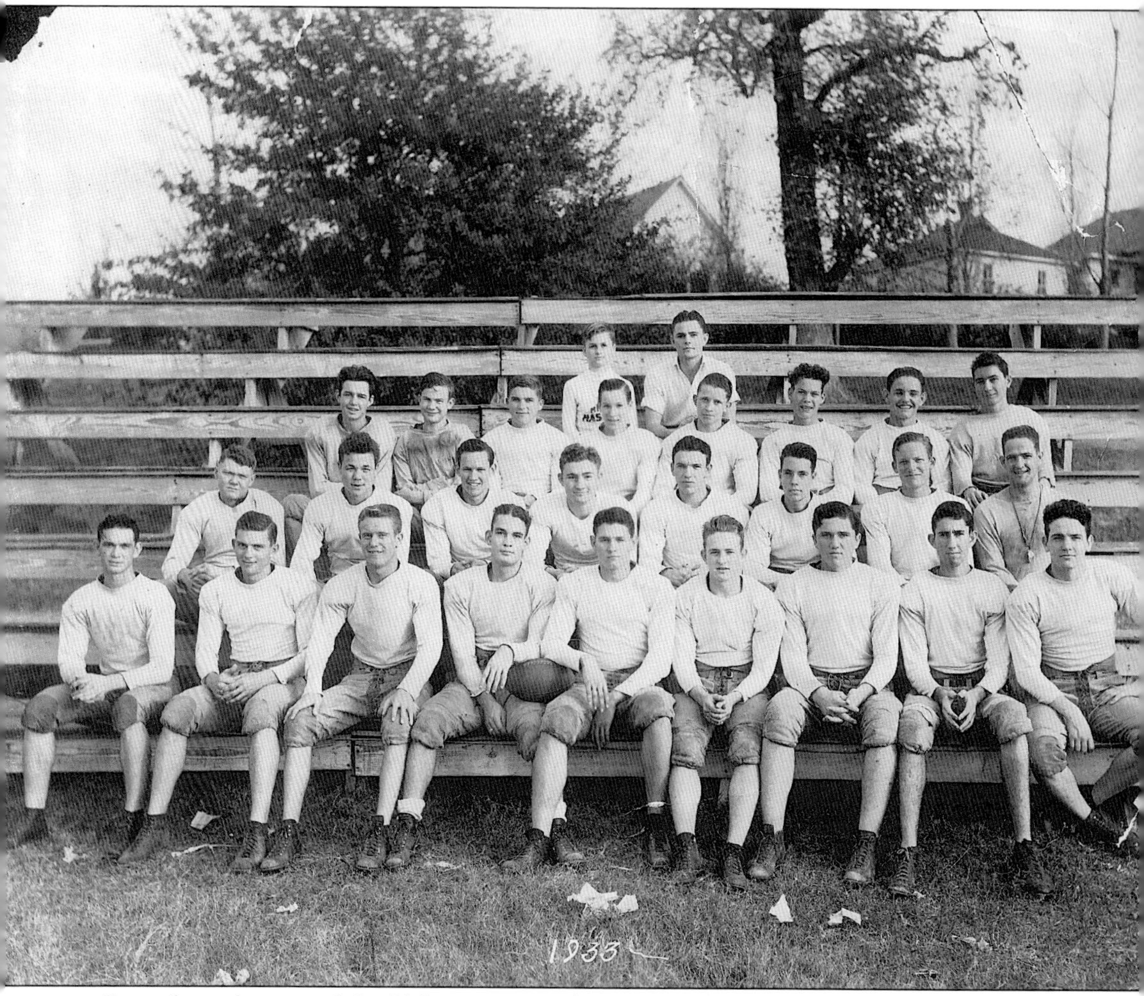

From the early years of the 20th century until 1934, Minden High athletic teams were known as the Greenies or the Greenbacks. This nickname and the school colors of green and white led to the school yearbook being called the *Green Grig*. However, in 1934, inspired by the exploits of the University of Alabama Crimson Tide led by Dixie Howell, Don Hutson, and a young Paul "Bear" Bryant, the coaches decided to change the team's nickname. Perhaps another contributing factor was the disastrous 1933 football season, which included several humiliating defeats by Shreveport schools and a 70-0 loss to El Dorado, AR. For whatever reason, the school athletic nickname was changed, and the school colors changed to red and white. The yearbook name has been retained to this day, although the "green" was dropped. The combination of new colors and the old nickname is an odd one, as "grig" means "grasshopper," and it is doubtful that many red-and-white grasshoppers exist. The team pictured above is the 1933 Minden High School Greenies football team, the last football team to wear the green and white for MHS.

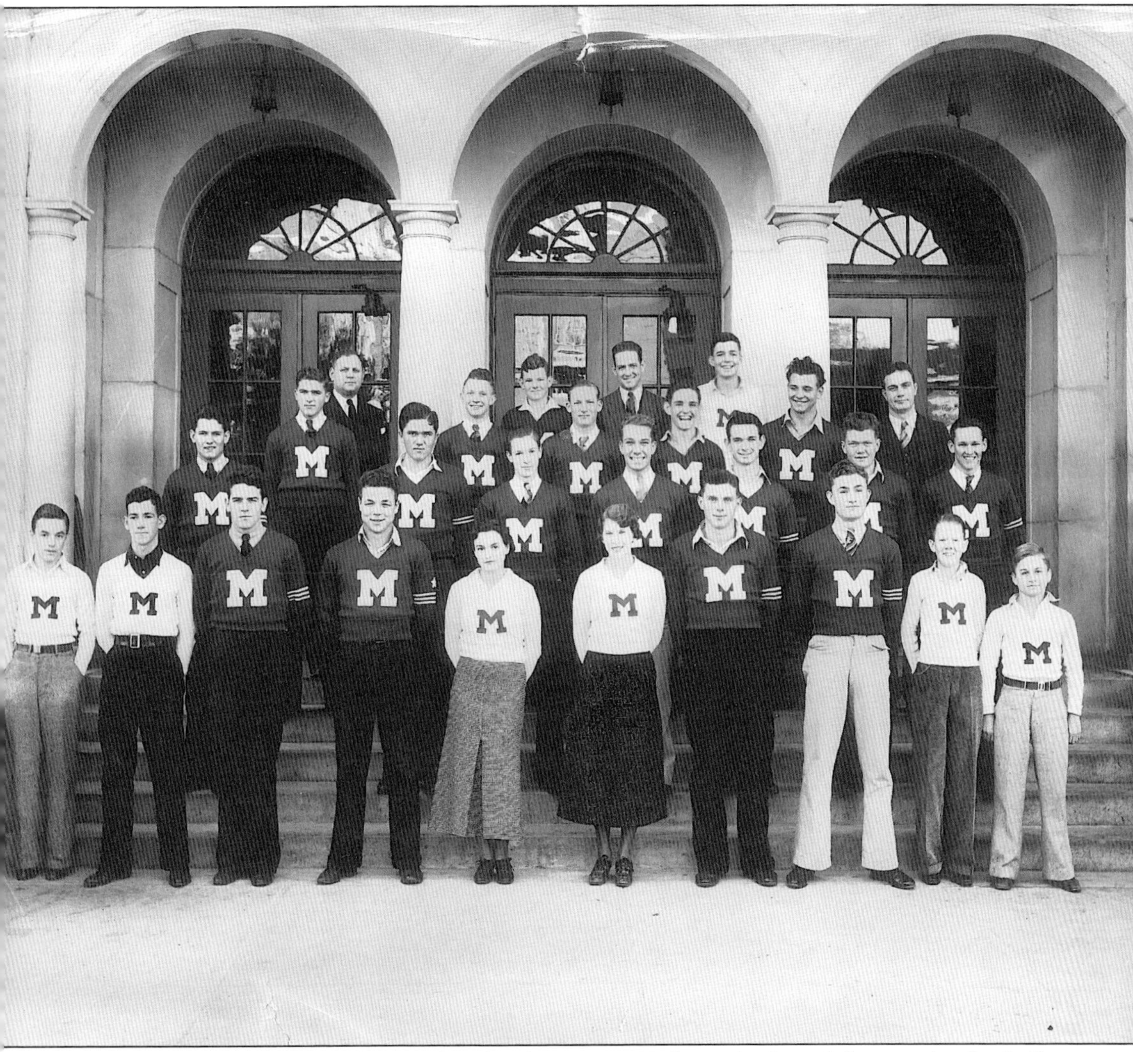

In the fall of 1934, the Minden High School Crimson Tide made their debut on the football field, although the red-and-white uniforms were not available until the second game. Thus in their 1934 debut, the "Crimson Tide" wore green and white. The season was more successful than 1933, and the new nickname stuck. Within a few years, the old moniker of Greenies was nearly forgotten, although local merchants were stuck with a large backlog of MHS merchandise colored green and white. In the fall of 1938, the Crimson Tide won Minden's first state football championship. Pictured above in their newly awarded red letter sweaters are the 1934 MHS Crimson Tide and the cheerleaders.

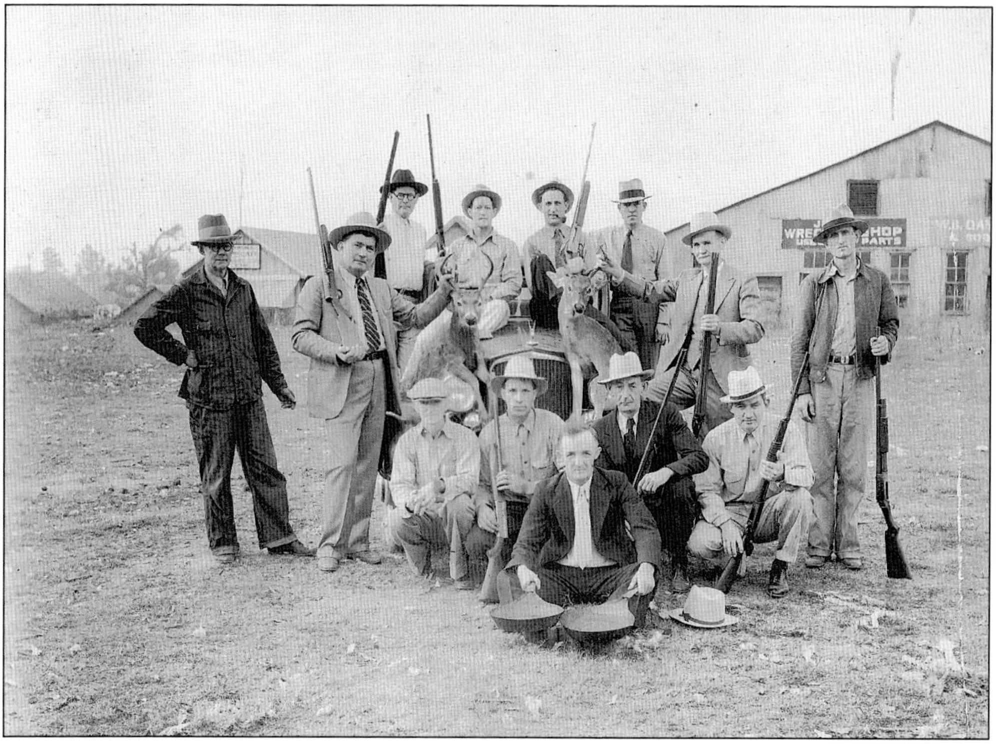

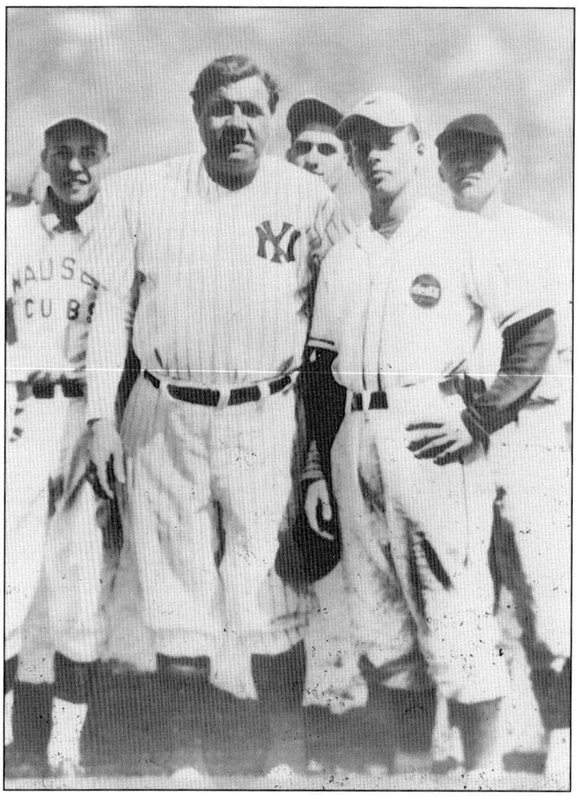

Pictured above are Minden residents showing off the results of a deer hunting expedition in 1934. Like the 1890s trip, the hunters have obviously changed clothes before posing for the picture. Among those pictured are Sheriff O.H. Haynes Sr. (who owned the car), Melvin Jones, Glen Moreland, and Johnny Jeter. The picture was taken along U.S. Highway 80 East in front of Jeter's Garage, just outside downtown Minden. (Courtesy of Mrs. Melba Jones Lowery and Mrs. O.H. Haynes Jr.)

One of the many good deeds performed for local youth by Larry Hunter was providing the opportunity for promising baseball players to receive professional instruction. This picture shows Minden resident Carter Norman with Babe Ruth at a Florida instructional school, which Mr. Hunter had paid for the young man to attend.

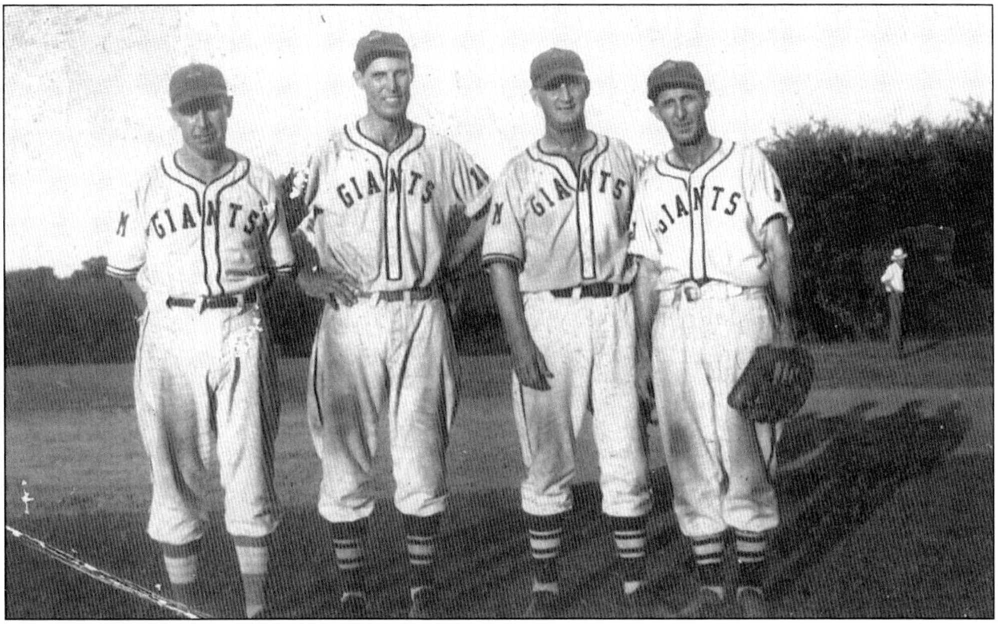

For many years, the Humphrey brothers were mainstays of the Minden town baseball teams. Pictured here in the uniform of the Larry Hunter-sponsored Minden Giants are Gilbert, Newt, Louis, and Bud Humphrey. (Courtesy of Ben Hunter.)

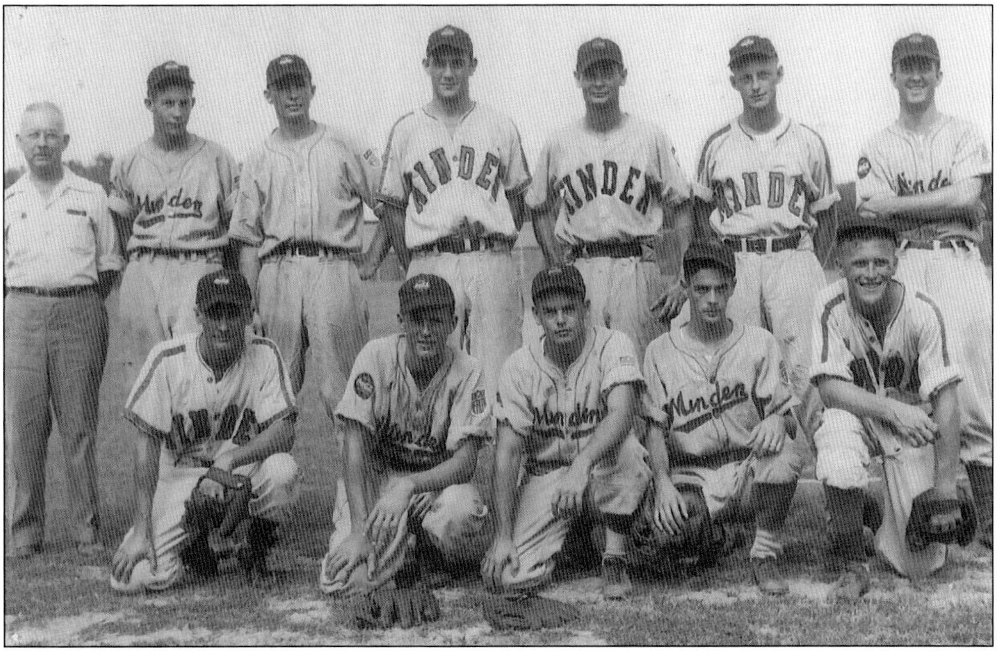

This Minden Redbird team was Larry Hunter's favorite. His 1946 Redbirds were largely local boys who had just returned home after fighting for their country in World War II. Pictured are as follows, from left to right: (front row) Jimmy Rogers, James Logan, Carter Norman, Harrison Castleberry, and Gene Rogers; (back row) Larry Hunter, A.L. Burkhalter, Kenneth Wallace, Rusty Gilbert, Shorty Baugh, Otis Minter, and Budge Dennis. Mr. Hunter wrote each of these players monthly during their tours of duty in the military. (Courtesy of Ben Hunter.)

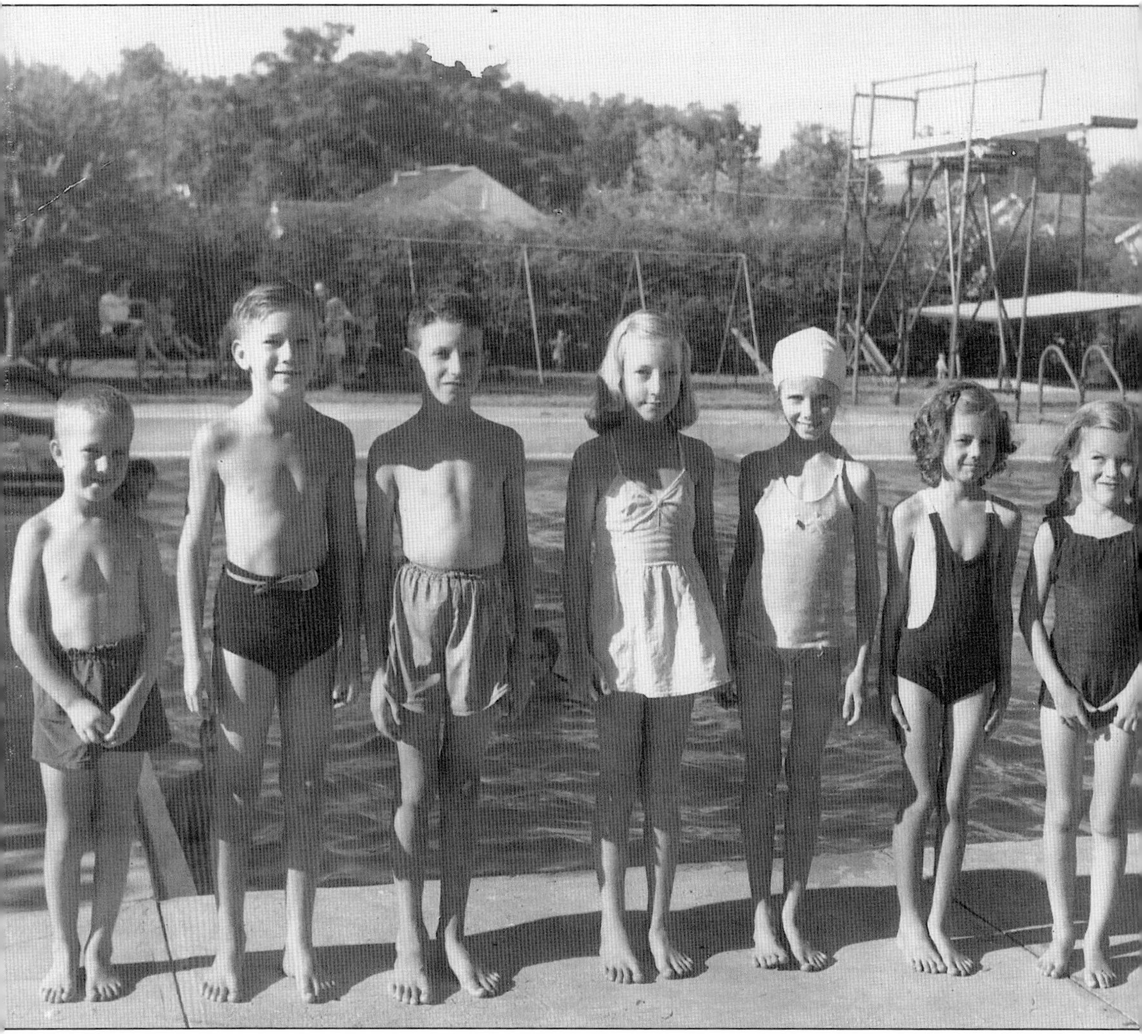

For many years, the only swimming pool available for local kids during the summer was also provided by Larry and Gladys Hunter on their property behind the Coca Cola Bottling Plant. The Hunter's sponsored recreational activities for Minden youth from the 1930s through the 1960s. Hunter's Playhouse, which hosted dances and general social gathering, was the unifying memory of generations of Minden teens. Pictured above are several Minden youth taking advantage of Hunter's Pool during the late 1940s. From left to right are Jimmy Fitzgerald, W.D. Roberts Jr., James Bishop, Marilyn Greer, Suzanne Roberts, Shirley Rowe, and Martha Fitzgerald. Hunter's Pool remained open until the 1960s, continuing to offer a supplement to the city recreation program that Hunter's helped to inspire. (Courtesy of Ben Hunter.)

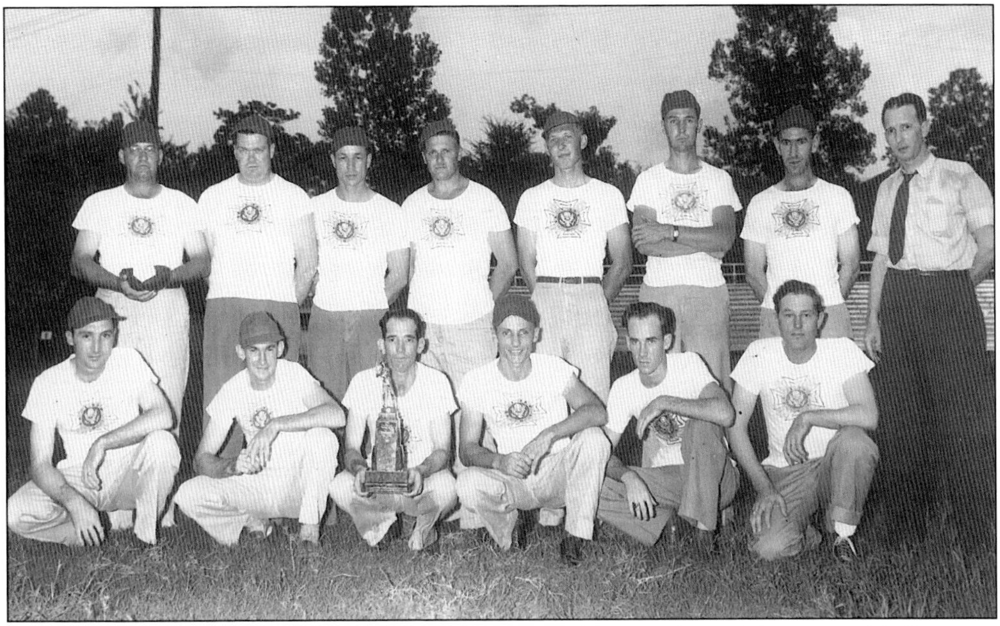

The 1948 Knights of Pythias softball team won the championship of the city softball league. The coach of this team, on the right end of the back row, was Clarence Wiley, who later served 20 years as Webster Parish clerk of court. (Courtesy of George Calvit.)

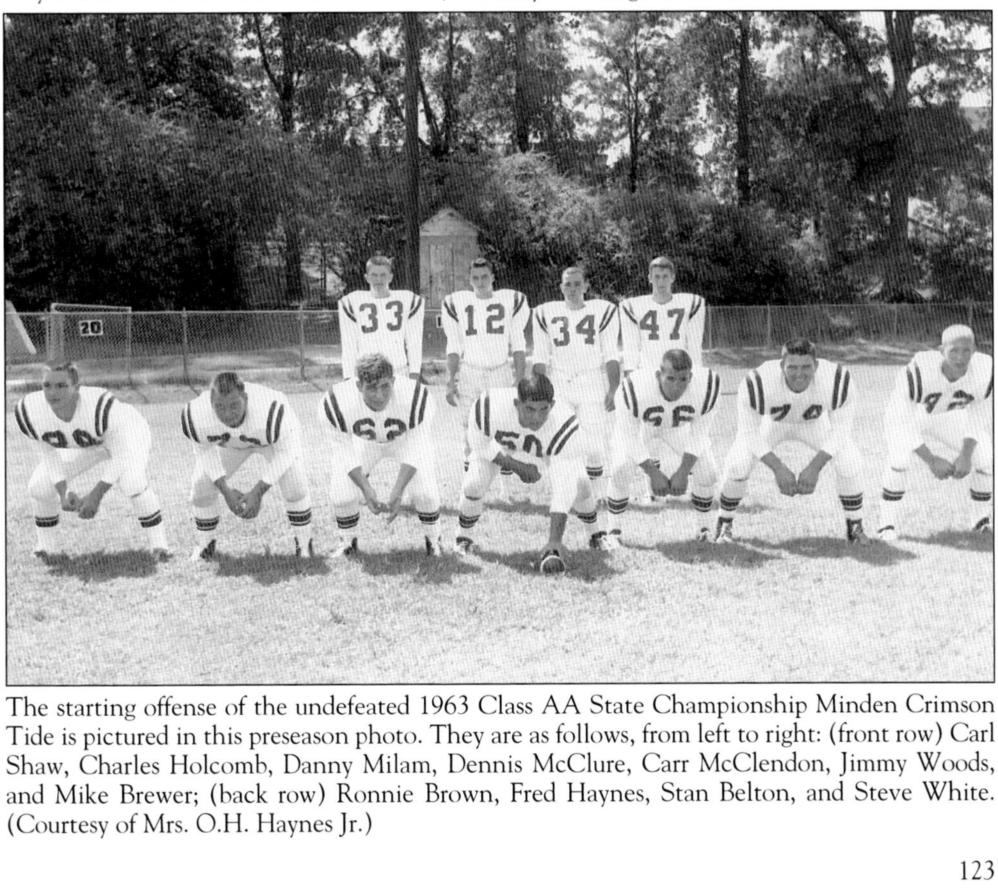

The starting offense of the undefeated 1963 Class AA State Championship Minden Crimson Tide is pictured in this preseason photo. They are as follows, from left to right: (front row) Carl Shaw, Charles Holcomb, Danny Milam, Dennis McClure, Carr McClendon, Jimmy Woods, and Mike Brewer; (back row) Ronnie Brown, Fred Haynes, Stan Belton, and Steve White. (Courtesy of Mrs. O.H. Haynes Jr.)

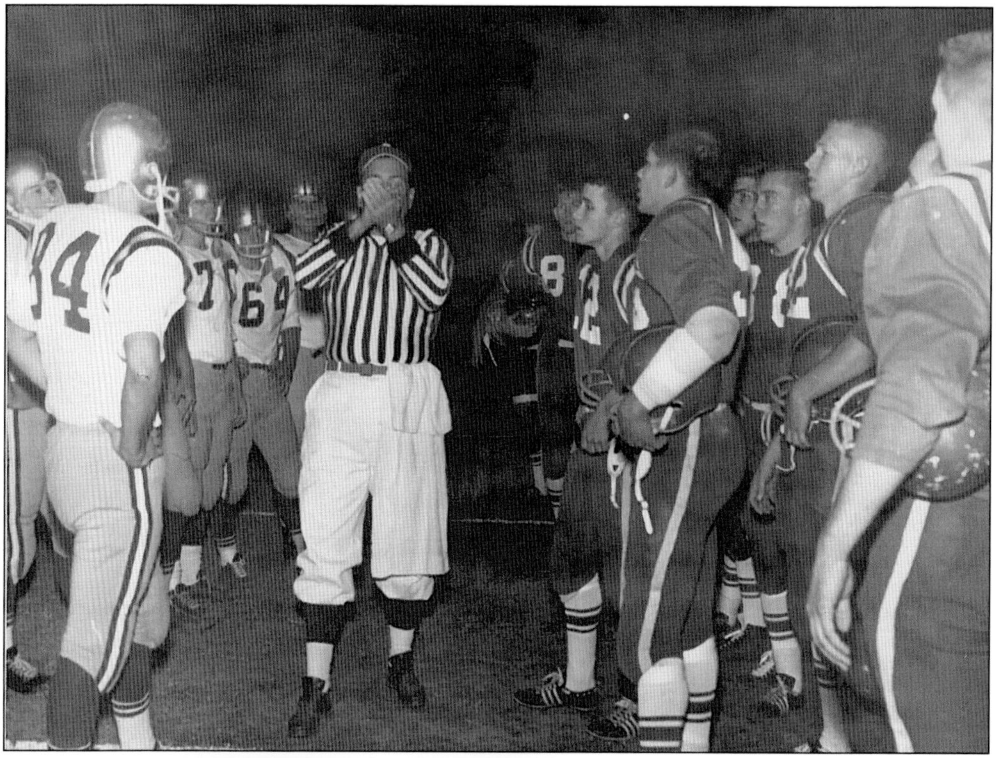

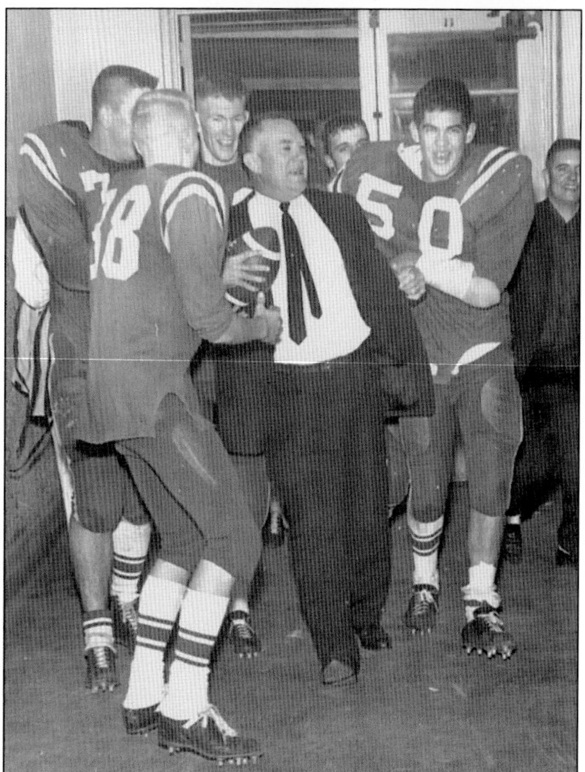

Here is the coin toss before the start of the 1963 state championship game between Minden High School and LaRose-Cutoff High School. (Courtesy of Mrs. O.H. Haynes Jr.)

After winning the state championship with a 28-21 defeat of LaRose-Cutoff, the celebrating Tide players escorted coach Elton Kelly for the traditional dumping in the school gym's swimming pool. (Courtesy of Mrs. O.H. Haynes Jr.)

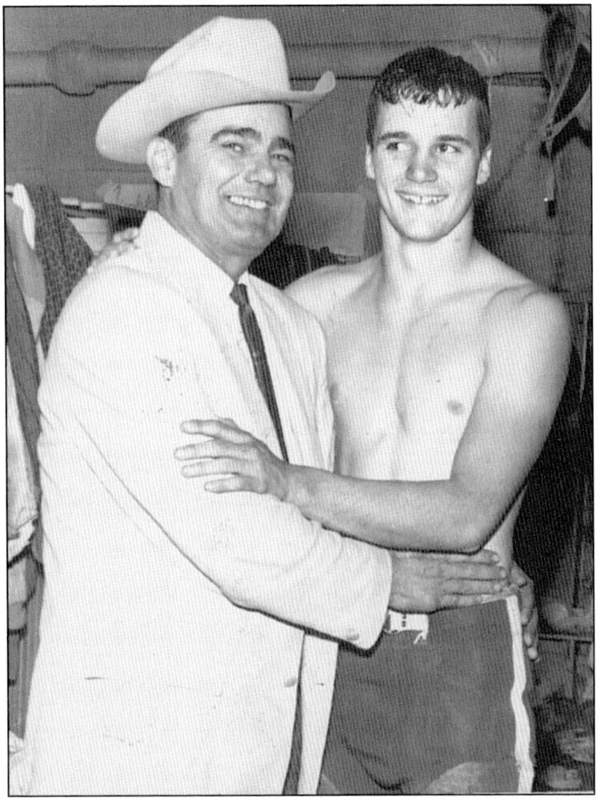

O.H. Haynes Sr., quarterback of the 1938 State Champion Crimson Tide, savors the victory with his son Fred, quarterback of the 1963 State Champion Crimson Tide. The day after the game, the elder Haynes would win election as Webster Parish sheriff. (Courtesy of Mrs. O.H. Haynes Jr.)

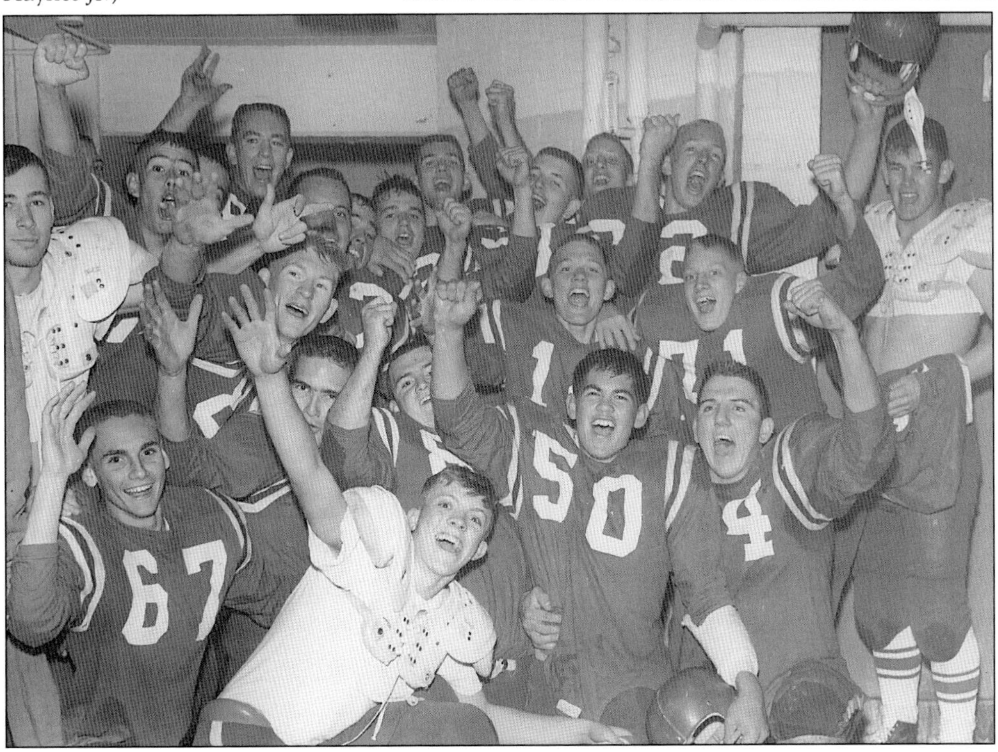

The victorious Tiders celebrate for the camera, led by #50, Dennis McClure, who would be named the outstanding lineman in AA football for 1963. Other Tiders named to the All-State team were quarterback Haynes and end Mike Brewer, seen at the back left holding his helmet in the air with the number "2" visible on his jersey. (Courtesy of Mrs. O.H. Haynes Jr.)

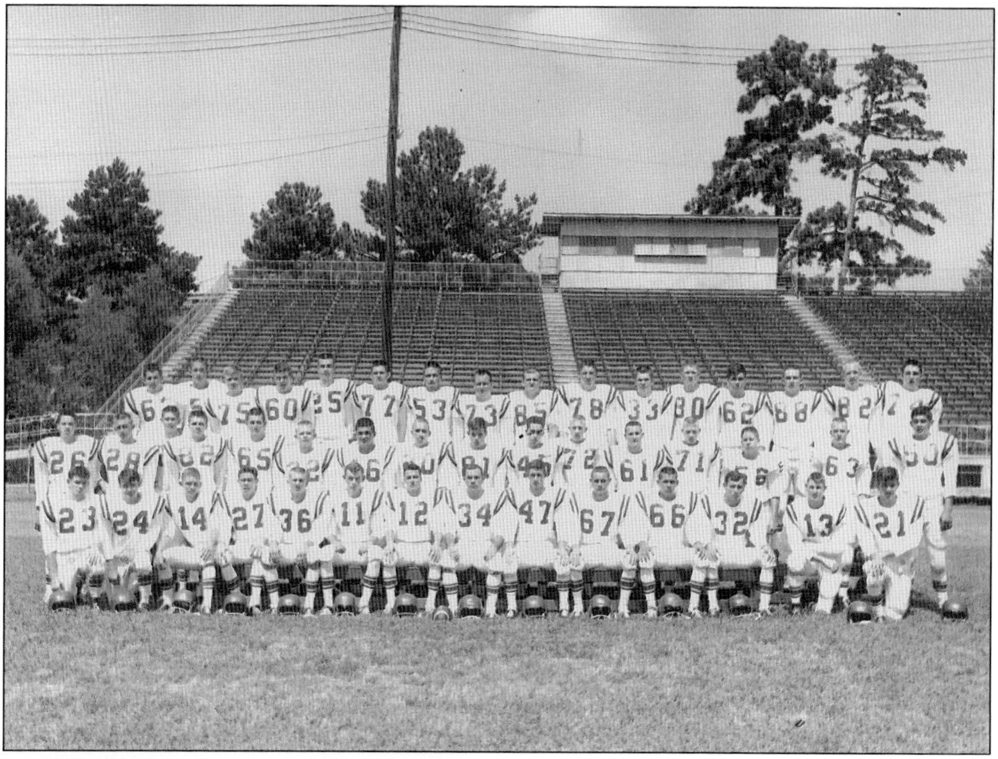

Shown is the team picture of the 1963 Minden Crimson Tide, the only undefeated team in the more than 90-year history of football at the school. Although Minden has won four other state football championships, no other team managed to be undefeated, although the 1921 team was undefeated and unscored upon before losing the state championship game to Warren Easton of New Orleans 7-0. (Courtesy of Mrs. O.H. Haynes Jr.)

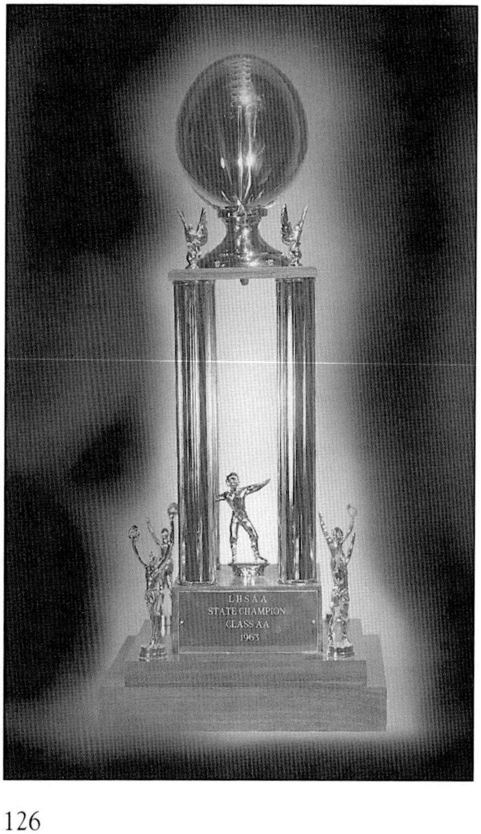

Here is the 1963 State Football Championship trophy. (Courtesy of Mrs. O.H. Haynes Jr.)

Jimmy Upton was probably the most outstanding track athlete in the history of Minden High School. A sprinter and hurdler, he earned high school All-American honors in 1967, while setting all-time Louisiana records in the 180-yard low hurdles. He also starred as Minden won three consecutive state track championships in 1964, 1965, and 1966. Upton went on to earn similar honors as a college athlete at Northeast Louisiana State College. (Courtesy of Mrs. Mary E. Upton.)

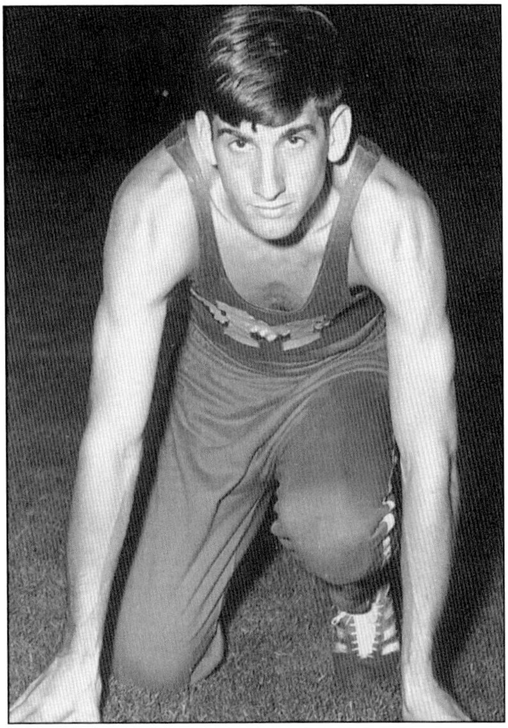

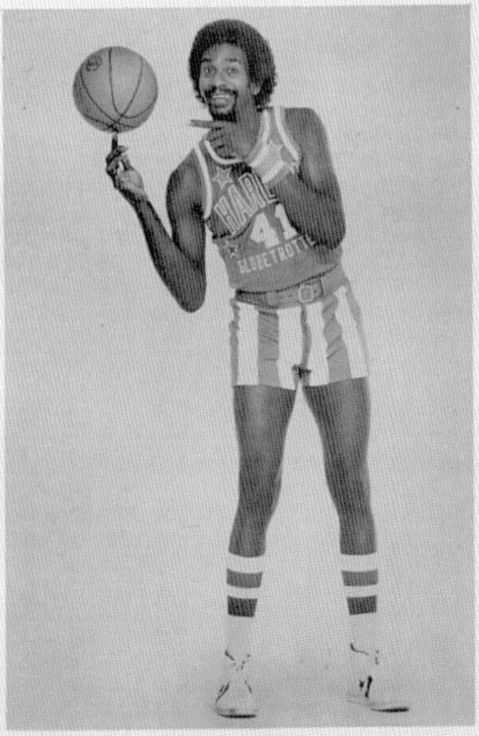

"SWEET LOU" DUNBAR — HARLEM GLOBETROTTERS®

Louis "Sweet Lou" Dunbar of the Harlem Globetrotters is pictured here. An All-American at Webster High School, he led the Webster Wolves to the state championship in their first year of competition in the Louisiana High School Athletic Association in 1971. Dunbar went on to star at the University of Houston and then spent many years as the featured performer with the Globetrotters, filling the role left by Meadowlark Lemon. (Courtesy of *Minden Press Herald*.)

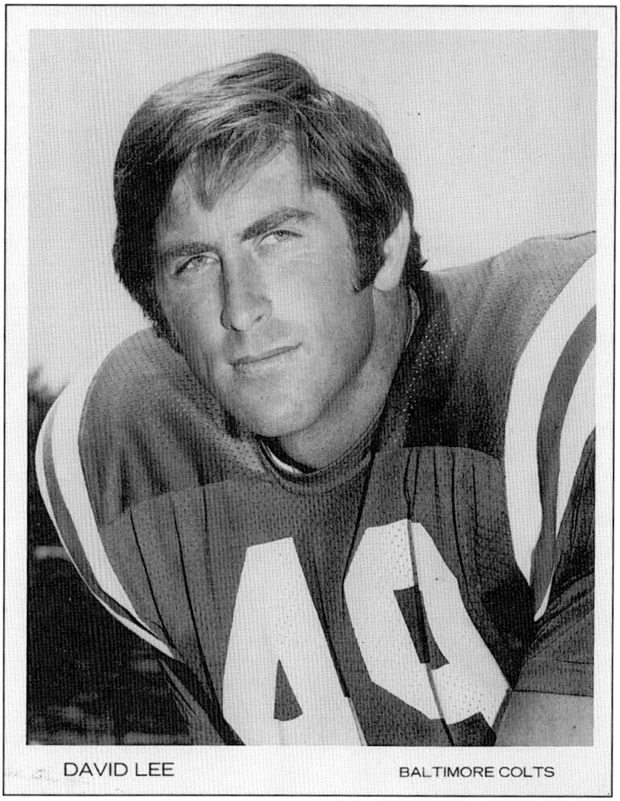

After an all-state career at Minden High School and an all-star career at Louisiana Tech, David Lee played with the Baltimore Colts of the NFL from 1966 to 1978. Lee earned All-Pro honors and participated in Super Bowls III and V with the Colts. (Courtesy of Mrs. Hazel Lee.)

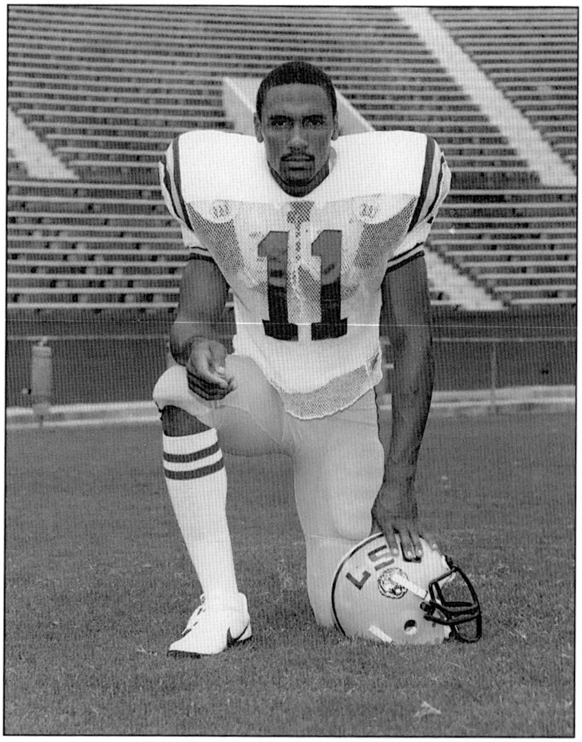

James Britt quarterbacked Minden High School to its first playoff appearance in 12 years in 1977. That same year, he was named the Outstanding Defensive Player in Class AAAA, then the largest classification in Louisiana high school football. Britt went on to LSU, where he earned All-American honors as a defensive back and had a successful career in the NFL with the Atlanta Falcons. (Courtesy of Mrs. Ivory Britt.)